The Holy War
of Sally Ann

with best wishes

Robert Collins

The Holy War
of Sally Ann

The Salvation Army
in Canada

Robert Collins

Western Producer Prairie Books
Saskatoon, Saskatchewan

Printed and bound in Canada
by Modern Press 1
Saskatoon, Saskatchewan

Cover photograph courtesy Canadian Press
Cover design by Warren Clark, GDL

Western Producer Prairie Books publications are produced and manufactured in the middle of western Canada by a unique publishing venture owned by a group of prairie farmers who are members of Saskatchewan Wheat Pool. From the first book published in 1954, a reprint of a serial originally carried in the weekly newspaper, *The Western Producer*, to the book before you now, the tradition of providing enjoyable and informative reading for all Canadians is continued.

Canadian Cataloguing in Publication Data

Collins, Robert, 1924–
    The holy war of Sally Ann

Includes index.
Bibliography: p. 215
ISBN 0-88833-158-4 (bound). — ISBN
    0-88833-120-7 (pbk.)

1. Salvation Army (Canada) — History.   I. Title.
BX9716.C64 1984   267'.15'0971   C84-091500-4

For Lesley and Cathy
who, like the Sally Ann, are always there

Contents

viii   *Contents*

Preface

Like nearly every ex-serviceman alive, I remember them first from World War II—the doughnuts and coffee, the hostels, the writing paper, the willingness to do you any kind of favor—those decent people of the "Sally Ann," so nicknamed from an earlier war.

In after years there were other, fleeting images: a brassy little band blowing notes of cheer under a hospital window on a Sunday morning. A man in blue lifting a drunk from his own vomit. A pair of uniforms in a smoky bar, leaving smiles and the *War Cry* and a few ripples of guilt among the potbellied beer guzzlers in their wake.

Over the years, during the writing of two magazine articles on the Army, my curiosity grew. *Who are these Salvationists?* What do they believe? My daughter spoke of a Salvationist classmate she had known in high school. "You know, I always envied her!" she remembered. Why? "Well . . . because she seemed so *happy.*"

And yes, they do seem happy. Indeed, they seem unassailable. Do they ever laugh or cry or hurt like the rest of us? Why do some Army officers flee the ranks?

Their influence is profound, in proportion to their numbers, but most of us never really know them. "They're good people," we say, and "I always give to them, even if I don't give to anybody else," and leave it at that. Are they as good as we hope and think? What do they do with the money we so willingly give them? What else do they do besides beat the drum?

They seem, at first glance, to be riddled with paradox. Why have they been far ahead of their time in their treatment of drunks, unwed mothers, prostitutes, and down-and-outers yet, unlike some other Christian segments of society today, relatively unyielding on homosexuality? Why do they march and lustily sing but turn thumbs down on dancing? Why do they ban smoking and drinking but accept money from the makers of cigarettes and alcohol?

This is a non-Salvationist's attempt to answer some of these questions; a layman's look at the Sally Ann, its people, its paradoxes, and its everlasting war on sin and despair. It is not a sponsored or official book. It was personally researched, from coast to coast, and written without one cent of public money or financial support from the Salvation Army. Army people, however—from Commissioner Arthur Pitcher and retired Generals Arnold Brown and Clarence Wiseman to the rawest recruit—were unfailingly courteous, and generous with their time.

Some of those mentioned here will have changed posts or rank by the time this reaches print, but their stories are true case histories of the moment. Somewhere, at this moment, they and other officers and soldiers are living out stories like them.

This, then, is how the Salvation Army in Canada works and lives.

Acknowledgments

It is impossible to name all of the several hundred officers, soldiers, and adherents whom I interviewed, but each has my deepest thanks. A few, who were particularly kind and in some cases shared their lives and homes with me, deserve special mention: Commissioner Arthur Pitcher, retired Generals Clarence Wiseman and Arnold Brown, Lieutenant-Colonels Albert and Lydia Browning, Majors Don and Myrna Ritson, Majors Bill and Marion Ratcliffe, Majors David and Margaret Hammond, Lieutenants Ross and Brenda Bungay, Captain Iain Trainor, Captain Ed Pearce, Majors Stuart and Charlotte Booth, Major Gilbert Fowler, Lieutenant-Colonels Edwin and Dorothy Brown, Majors Ken and Miriam Evenden, Majors Max and Patricia Ryan, Lieutenants Henry and Lorraine Legge, Major Carson Janes, Captain George Swaddling, Major Ron Bowles, Majors Travis and Juanita Wagner, Major Bill Merritt, Major Lloyd Eason, Lieutenants Ken and Ellen Whatman, Lieutenants Dave and Gloria Woodland and Envoy Ken Clarke.

Special thanks go to my daughter Lesley, for her research assistance, and to my daughter Catherine, for her sharp editorial eye. I'm grateful to the editors of *Reader's Digest* (Canada) for permission to use a few brief excerpts from my December 1982 article "Hallelujah! Sally Ann Keeps Marching On." I'm indebted to Major Ken Evenden for answering hundreds of questions with speed and good humor, and to Major Don Ritson and Major Max Ryan for reading the manuscript, not in any "official" capacity but as knowledgeable friends.

Every effort has been made to double-check facts but in a work of this magnitude errors are almost inevitable. For these I, of course, bear full responsibility.

1

A Voice
in the Night

Christmas Eve 1981, 11:30 P.M. The shrilling phone catches Captain Ed Ostrom on his way to bed. Tonight he is manning Calgary's suicide prevention line from his home.

"Salvation Army, can I help you?"

"I'm gonna kill myself!" The girl's voice is thick and drowsy. "I've taken these pills. . . ."

Instantly Ostrom is alert but calm. He must keep her talking. This call is a cry for help.

"You don't really want to die, do you? Please tell me what you've taken."

"Sleeping pills . . . had thirty-three 'n' I've taken eighteen. . . ."

Ostrom—thirty-five, thick fair hair and eyes that seem to peer gently into your soul—grabs a pen. His voice is soothing, persuasive. "Tell me your name, please? And your address? And phone number?"

Over the next half hour she gives up only her first name. Then: "Have to go. Maybe call you back. . . ." Click! Ostrom looks helplessly at his wife and finally goes to bed.

An hour later the phone jerks him awake. She is back, still reaching out for help. Carefully, sympathetically, he keeps her on the line, her fragile link with life, and ekes out her story. She is twenty-four. Two years before, she came from Montreal to a new job in Calgary and the loneliness of a city teeming with hundreds of newcomers—all looking for streets paved with gold, all jockeying for position. Her family hasn't been writing. Her mother promised to come for Christmas but has just phoned to cancel. So now, on this loneliest night of the year, she keeps gulping pills.

1

"There goes another . . . there go two more. . . ."

She is becoming incoherent. Over and over Ostrom begs her address and number. About 2:00 A.M. she finally whispers it. Ostrom hangs up and dials the police. While they rush a squad car to her, he phones back.

"Keep talking, keep talking!" he pleads, when she finally answers.

"Gotta sleep," she mumbles. But he keeps her awake until a policeman's voice shouts over the line, "We're here, she's alive!"

At hospital they pump out her stomach and she recovers. And on Christmas morning, as so many other times in the previous twelve years, Ed Ostrom thanks God for calling him from a warehouse job in North Battleford to his life's work in this most remarkable Army on earth.

It was a true "call," for Ostrom was not born to the Army tradition. He grew up in Meadow Lake, Saskatchewan, where his grandparents had homesteaded. The family was not Salvationist but sometimes, in their pioneering days, an itinerant Army officer on horseback paused for prayer meetings at the grandfather's farm.

By the time Ed was six the Army was established in Meadow Lake and the local officer sometimes drove around in his small black Austin, inviting kids with no church affiliation to attend his Sunday school. The boy piled in with a dozen others and immediately learned what few Canadians realize: that the Salvation Army *is* above all a church, each member dedicated to a personal quest for holiness.

Young Ostrom warmed to the fellowship. He became a corps cadet, played bass horn in the band (although he claims he is tone-deaf, and they let him in out of kindness), and at fifteen went to the first-ever corps cadets congress in Toronto.

To that point he'd wanted to be a radio announcer. Now he felt the call, and pledged himself to an Army future. That autumn his family moved to North Battleford. Suddenly his life blossomed. In Meadow Lake he had been too embarrassed to tell friends and classmates about his religion. Now he announced from the outset that he was a Christian.

"I loved my teen years," he remembers. "I took a lot of ridicule and teasing, but sometimes kids came to me with real problems."

Once a classmate was killed in a car accident and the teacher asked him to speak to the class.

"Our friend has died and some of us don't have anything to hang on to," the teacher said. "What can we do? There is a thing called faith and Ed is going to talk to us about it."

Ostrom did, to a respectful silence, followed by a few questions.

On graduation day he skipped the dance and party that followed. He was one of only two who showed up in class the next day. "The rest were sick, some were in jail, two had gotten into a serious car accident."

In North Battleford he worked for a wholesale hardware dealer, until he could get into Army college. He graduated in 1970, an ordained churchman *and* a warrior, ready for an everlasting battle with all the wrongs and sorrows of this world.

By then Ostrom knew that this is an army in nearly every sense, with its uniforms, flag, marching bands and ranks up to general. Prayer is "knee drill," "marching orders" means a new posting, a congregation is a "corps," a choir is a "songster brigade," a "cartridge" is a church money envelope and to die is to be "promoted to Glory." The weekly newspaper is the *War Cry*. There is even provision for court-martial—used in rare cases where an officer is told to resign but prefers to take his case to Army court.

"We are a democracy up to a point," says a senior officer, "but if need be I can give an emphatic order which must and will be obeyed." Consequently, the Army, unlike some businesses and many governments, gets things done fast, which is one reason it has adhered to the military format for more than a century.

The Salvation Army touches the lives of thousands, perhaps millions of Canadians, yet its numbers are relatively small. Around the nucleus of 2,000 officers in Canada is a second tier of some 26,000 "soldiers"—laity who wear uniforms and work part-time in many Army roles. Beyond them is an outer ring of 100,000 civilian adherents who call the Army their church but do not necessarily embrace its strictest rules.

Those rules, though far less stringent than when the Army was founded in England in 1865, are stiff enough by today's standards. Officers and soldiers must never drink, smoke, or use any mind-bending drugs. Officers may marry only other officers, must have Army approval for the marriage, must be formally engaged for at least six months, and must take a marriage counseling course before the nuptials. Living together out of wedlock, or infidelity during marriage are grounds for dismissal.

The Army shuns pornography and profanity. (In two years of associating with Salvationists, the strongest expletive I heard, in one moment of unguarded passion, was "Nuts!") Dancing is officially frowned upon because "modern dances are at times deliberate means of inflaming sexual feelings," although teenage adherents sometimes ignore this rule. All kinds of gambling are out, including card games or the buying of lottery tickets, because gambling leads to dishonesty, broken families, and also depends on an un-Christian belief in luck.

Most Canadians would openly rebel at such constraints. For Ostrom, like most of his fellows, the rules sometimes chafe but the rewards far outweigh the strictures. Since graduation he has worked in many places and ministered to every kind of human misery—but none closer to the lonely soul of humanity than his anti-suicide work.

That episode of Christmas Eve, 1981, was one of 2267 suicide-related calls to the Salvation Army in Calgary that year (5164 the next year; 7261 in 1983). Some were to or from police, ambulances, or frantic families; the rest came directly from desperate people to whom the Sally Ann is the last resort. (There were two other crisis lines in Calgary at the time but the Army's drew the most would-be suicides.) Day and night Ostrom and a staff of thirty to forty trained volunteers try to rescue callers from the emptiness brought on by runaway spouses, unfeeling parents, broken romances, or lost jobs.

Across Canada the Army handles many more thousand such calls per year. Alberta and British Columbia lead the country in suicides per capita. Calgary and Edmonton lead their province with more than one hundred reported per year. Ostrom estimates that for every reported suicide, two others go into the records as "accidental"—because a family doctor wants to shield the survivors from the stigma, or because no one knows the true cause. Over fifty percent of one-person motor-vehicle deaths might be suicides, Ostrom speculates, but they will never be proven.

Certain things he does know. More women try to kill themselves than do men, but roughly three times as many men *succeed*. Among women the highest risk group is ages forty to forty-nine, perhaps related to the menopause. For men it is often ages twenty to twenty-nine, possibly because they feel pressured to succeed in a society that places inordinate value on money and rank. Some who've made it feel threatened; those who haven't made it think they're failures. Whenever the unemployment rate goes up by one percent, Canada can expect thirty-seven more suicides.

The most used (by men) and most effective instrument is a gun. Hanging, pills (commonly used by women, but less effective), and carbon monoxide (from the automobile exhaust) are the runners-up. Friday and Saturday nights are the most dangerous, as lonely people grow lonelier. Spring, perhaps surprisingly, is the most suicide-prone season.

"All around, things are brightening up as winter ends, but people say 'Nothing has changed for me,' " Ostrom says.

Teenage suicides are on the increase. Some of these young people have lost a parent through death or divorce; others are depressed because their peers are doing better in school or have more boy or girl friends. "A fair number of them have low opinions of themselves, and kids feel out of step if all is not happy and bright."

For watchful friends and family, any dramatic change in a teenager's habits—eating, sleeping, a drastic change in weight, school marks suddenly falling off—could be a warning signal.

For two hours the eighteen year old in Ostrom's office stares persistently at the floor. She answers "yes" or "no" without looking up. The woman friend who brought her is frustrated. Finally Ostrom says, "We're not getting anywhere. Something's bothering you but I can't help if you won't talk. Will you come back tomorrow?"

"Yes. But I want to come alone."

The next day she lets out a little of her story. She left her well-to-do Edmonton home a year before. Ostrom pursues the likeliest angle: did her parents reject her? She flares up; how dare he run down her father! The problem, she claims, is her boyfriend—an addict who becomes abusive when he's on drugs.

She has made three abortive suicide attempts. Once, when trying to hang herself from a basement hook with pantyhose, the pantyhose broke. Next, she failed to slash her wrist with a dull razor blade. Then she took an overdose of pills but vomited them up before the damage was done.

They talk for days on end. She's unwilling to sever the connection, but Ostrom is still not getting through. One day he writes her a poem:

> . . . Lift her sad dropping spirits high
> Teach her daily on You to rely
> Help her, Lord, like an eagle fly
> High above the cloudless sky
> Lord, show her You really care
> And her life You wish to share
> Lord, replace the emptiness
> The depression and the meaninglessness . . .

It will never win the Governor-General's Medal, but the girl bursts into tears, deeply touched.

For almost a month she comes daily from 10:00 A.M. until mid-afternoon, leaving the room only while Ostrom deals with other clients and problems. The Army staff lunches with her, talks to her, prays with her.

Now she is in university, studying pre-law. Her life is coming together again. The Army performed no miracles. It simply fulfilled a role that those closest to a troubled person sometimes can not: it stood by her patiently, friendly but not judgmental, and let her know that someone cared. The rest was up to her.

Ostrom—although secure in his soul and never remotely suicidal—can emphathize with the lonely and the displaced. Officers are forever facing new beginnings because the Army regularly boots them from pillar to post.

After getting his commission in 1970 he spent a year in Carleton Place, near Ottawa. Then with Dorothy, the bride he'd met in training, it was off to The Pas, Manitoba—which can be a form of purgatory in winter. That particular winter, he recalls, had eighty days of below-zero temperatures. Dorothy was sick most of the year.

Omnipotent Toronto then shipped them to Brandon, for six months. After that: "Ed, we'd like you to go to Neepawa. Just two months while the auxiliary captain there is on course getting his captaincy." The day before they were due back in Brandon, a new assignment came through: Kamsack, Saskatchewan.

In training college there were two postings every cadet dreaded. One was Kamsack, because it was so small. The Ostroms arrived in pouring rain. The building looked as though it hadn't been painted in years.

"I think my wife felt like crying, but we stayed. They called it a temporary appointment. It turned out to be four and one-half years, the longest we've stayed anywhere."

Next they went to Ed's home town, Meadow Lake—an unthinkable posting because the Army rarely sends people back home: too many personal connections. But they stayed two years and it went well, after the people got used to having the little Ostrom boy as their pastor.

Then off to Portage la Prairie. It was everything Ostrom wanted. A local radio station gave him a Sunday afternoon gospel show—the kind of job he'd dreamed of before the Army beckoned. The corps began to grow under his touch. He helped start a religious education program in local schools. He was elected president of the ministerial association. Then: "Ed, we're sending you to Calgary!"

Among officers there is a wry little joke, a Salvationist's version of Murphy's Law: whenever things are going best is when the Army's likely to move you. It had happened to Ostrom. Eight postings in twelve years—and now they were plucking him out of this perfect spot!

Just then the radio station offered him a full-time job and Ostrom nearly took it. But he hung on, for which he is everlastingly grateful. For the first six months in Calgary his job was mostly welfare work and he was bored. Then he branched into suicide prevention. He hasn't been bored since.

Why did this beautiful girl across Ostrom's desk try to kill herself with an overdose? She is in her early twenties, elegantly dressed, artfully (albeit heavily) made-up, and she grosses $3,000 a week.

Her husband, at university in another city, and her parents, to whom she regularly sends a large cheque, think she's doing wonderfully well at her job. And so she is. What they don't know is that she's a high-priced call girl.

Now, she has come to loathe it. Her pimp is forcing more and more "tricks" on her and taking ever-increasing cuts of the fees. This is brand-new territory for Ed Ostrom but the woman is being torn apart by her life, so he helps her find a hiding place. For a while she changes her name.

Finally the pimp gives up and the girl—rid of her glitzy clothes and make-up—reassumes her name, gets a job in a department store, and joins a church.

"She'll be lucky to earn $300 a week now," says Ostrom, "but she's happy."

Ostrom spends much of his time training volunteer workers. There is a constant turnover because the work is demanding and not everyone can do it. Ostrom and his partner, Salvationist soldier Richard Hollingsworth, look for Christians (not necessarily Salvationists) of all ages with a genuine concern for other people.

Their training is reinforced with refresher courses. In 1983, for example, they attended a three-day seminar, with films and other material from Alberta's Suicide Information Centre. It began with a look at the volunteers' personal attitudes toward suicide and dying. Do they, for example, consider a suicidal person crazy or irresponsible? (Such people are *not*, necessarily.)

How do you assess a potential suicide over the phone? Ostrom cited some key factors: note the caller's age and sex, as related to the suicide-prone groups. Any suicide attempt before? If so, the odds are he or she will try again in two or three months. Is there a method at hand (such as a shotgun)? Does the caller have any human resources (family, friends, doctor) to fall back on? Any evidence of alcohol or drug abuse which can enhance a suicidal situation? Any evidence of stress?

Then the volunteers spent a day at role-playing: one as a potential suicide, one as counselor. It was exciting and sometimes frightening, but at the end they were better equipped to do their job.

Ostrom also visits many schools. After one lecture in which he described typical teenage suicides, a fourteen year old came up to murmur, "I know a girl like that."

"Really? What's her name?"

After a few minutes of evasion she admitted, "That girl is me."

She had already tried slashing her wrists and overdosing on aspirin. She lived in a group home and her schoolmates, in a well-to-do neighborhood and all with parents, teased, "You've gotta be an *oddball* if you don't live at home!" Her social worker, when the girl threatened suicide, told her, "Don't be stupid!" The Army took her under its wing. She is getting better.

Ostrom's favorite case, perhaps because it is so bizarre, began with repeated calls from a middle-aged man who had in times past been under psychiatric care. For seven years he had scarcely stirred from his apartment. On rare occasions he ventured out to the doctor or druggist.

He lived on welfare which came by mail. The druggist cashed his cheque, the local grocer delivered food, and the recluse shoved money under the door to the delivery boy. After seven years the apartment was a mess. So was the man, except for his hands which he meticulously scrubbed in disinfectant.

Occasionally he called crisis lines, threatening to kill himself, but in time even Ostrom's volunteers gave up on him. Ostrom didn't. He left orders that a call from the man be transferred to him at any hour. Sometimes these turned into three-hour talks in the middle of the night.

Slowly the man unfolded a snake-pit of problems. As a soldier with a peacekeeping unit in the Middle East, he had been attacked by homosexuals in his unit. Back home and married, he had beaten his wife, after she danced with another man. She ultimately divorced him on grounds of cruelty. Now he was laden with guilt, and saw blood every time he looked at his hands.

Finally Ostrom said one night, "If you have faith in God we can deal with your guilt."

"Don't talk to me about God. *Show* me God!"

"How do I do that?"

"Well, come and take me for a hamburger. Talk to me."

Ostrom does not suggest that God appeared that night over a Big Mac, but the man's willingness to step out of his solitude was a start. They sat in the Army van, talking and praying. A long-time doctor friend then took the recluse under his wing.

Today the man lives in another city, keeps clean, attends a church, and sings in the choir. He still has problems but he doesn't talk of suicide any more.

Was he ever *really* serious about killing himself?

"Want to see something?"

The captain fetches a lethal six-inch butcher knife that the man had kept constantly beside him in his apartment. As we look down on it in silence, there is a tiny glimmer of satisfaction in Ostrom's eyes. Not many of us can hold in our hands the tangible evidence of having saved another human's life.

2

"I Have Found My Destiny"

And yet . . . saving lives, physically, spiritually, is what the Salvation Army is all about. It was rooted in the beginnings, in the passionate heart of the founder himself.

William Booth was humanitarian, evangelist, and crusader all rolled into one, but in England in the 1860s that was not enough. To change society a man had to be a kind of soldier too, so Booth made himself general of an army—a marching, hollering glory-be-to-God-and-Hallelujah kind of army. Its enemy was Sin. Its weapons were brassy hymns, hellfire-and-damnation sermons, and food, shelter and salvation for those who had none.

Booth's army met the enemy head-on in saloons, slums and brothels. For years his troops were heckled, beaten and abused but they prevailed. Today there are twenty-five thousand officers in eighty-six countries plus soldiers and adherents in the millions. Times have changed. The troops are more sophisticated, the tone is less strident, but basically Salvationists are still what the General wanted them to be: soldiers of the Lord.

The General is still revered, even more than in his lifetime. His face looks down from the wall of many an Army office across the land. It is a strong commanding face, the beard flowing free like a Biblical prophet's, the eyes kind but unyielding like the Army itself. He has been dead seventy-two years but his fiery spirit still courses through the ranks. To understand the Salvation Army today it is essential to understand General Booth.

His life *was* the Army; all other events in it were but a prelude. He grew up in poverty in Nottingham after his father, once a wealthy builder, speculated away the family fortune. At thirteen he worked

The General.

in a pawnshop to help support his widowed mother. Time after time he watched desperate people hock their last possessions against another day of life.

At fifteen the boy was entranced by the fervent Hallelujahs and Amens of a Methodist Bible meeting. He began holding open-air meetings himself. Once he marched a squad of ragtag boys into the best pews in Nottingham's Wesley Chapel, to the consternation of the Methodist minister. As an appointed preacher he gave his first formal sermon at seventeen.

One day six years later he met pretty twenty-three-year-old Catherine Mumford at a tea party. She was the perfect match for Booth: daughter of a lay preacher, steeped in theology and brimming with compassion. Once as a child, seeing a drunk being marched to jail with a jeering crowd in his wake, she marched beside him to show that somebody cared. At twelve she was secretary of a juvenile temperance society. On the day she met Booth she was forcefully defending abstinence during a heated argument on drinking.

They married three years later. Slightly built, immaculately dressed, so gentle that some mistook her for timid, Catherine Booth was a lioness. With her quiet strength and religious conviction—a son once wrote of her: "The light upon her face shone from the windows of another world"—she was an Army in herself. She was William Booth's full and equal partner.

In 1858 he was ordained a Methodist minister but Booth was never meant to be a conventional churchman. He preached in church and out, sometimes to crowds of two thousand. Other ministers deplored his flailing evangelism and ordered him to slacken off. Instead he resigned and went on the revival circuit.

East London in those years was the cesspool of England. The American Civil War had disrupted British trade, making unemployment proportionately worse. The workhouses—ghastly places where, sometimes, men and women slept in a naked mass on the floor—were filled. Nearly twenty-five thousand were on relief. Men, women and children often starved to death in the streets.

"A region of narrow filthy streets and yards," reported a writer of the day, "and, alas, many of them occupied by thieves' dens, receptacles of stolen property, gin-spinning dog holes, low brothels and putrescent lodging houses, a district unwholesome to approach and unsafe for a decent person to traverse even in the daytime."

Sewage was dumped directly into the Thames; smallpox and cholera were rampant. Gin was cheap. Beer shops were legally open from 4:00 A.M. to 10:00 P.M. England had raised a generation of drunkards; even children were reeling out of the bars.

Into this pest hole strode William Booth one July evening in 1865. He stopped to listen to a gospel missionary meeting outside the Blind Beggar pub. The leader asked if any bystander would like to speak. Booth did. He was tall, gaunt, pale with a billow of black hair and beard, a great wedge of nose and eyes that, a contemporary said, "looked right into your soul." His voice was sonorous, compelling, almost hypnotic. The crowd fell strangely silent. So did the missionaries. Then they eagerly asked Booth to lead a special mission soon to be held in a circus tent.

The gospel tent was his milieu. The people he wanted—derelicts, drunks, prostitutes—were at home here as they never could be in a church. They came from curiosity at first, then conviction. Booth

Artist's version of William Booth and son Bramwell, taking their message into the lowest dives of London's East End.

"Anything would do for a meeting place." Artist's version of the early Booth preaching in a stable.

used simple language, often repeating his sentences to hammer home the point. He filled his sermons with drama and anecdote. He could hold a crowd on his words for an hour.

"Oh Brother Booth!" a follower cried. "If I could preach and floor the sinners like you, I wouldn't thank Queen Victoria to be my cousin!"

Night after night Booth went home, haggard and spent, but aglow with enthusiasm. "Kate!" he cried to his wife one night. "I have found my destiny!"

Tales of his conversions swept through the East End: of how Peter Monk, the tough Irish prizefighter, had been saved; of how

Jack Allen, a coal porter, came to the meeting ragged, black, and full of sin and, in the end, was on his knees crying, "I do believe, I do believe!"

At first even Catherine Booth wondered if her husband "was going ahead of the teaching of the Holy Ghost." Then one night she went to his meeting. Later she said, "I saw 20-30-50 of the biggest blackguards in London broken all to pieces on a single Sunday night. I spoke to them, applied the tests of the Gospel and I was bound to say, 'This is the finger of God!' "

Certain others thought it was the work of a crackpot. Booth's Christian Mission suffered continual abuse, partly because it was different, partly because it was luring customers from the pubs. He and his followers were pelted with stones, tomatoes, eggs, garbage, tar and whitewash. They did not waver. Hired goons beat them and their converts. They carried on. As they knelt in prayer screeching mobs poured beer over their heads. The Mission group shouted "Hallelujah" [from the Hebrew: 'praise to Jehovah']. Thugs cut down the guy ropes, bringing their tent down on the kneeling audience.

"Go along, my brothers," bellowed Booth. "Go outside and pull up the tent while I carry on with the preaching."

Anything would do for a meeting place: a theater, the room behind a pigeon shop, a carpenter's shop, even a music hall with adjacent saloon. The saloon was scant comfort to his enemies; it took a dedicated drunk to enjoy his ale with Booth thundering hellfire and salvation into his ears.

He converted a market place into a meeting hall. When somebody suggested spreading asphalt on the stone floor, Booth said, "No, the poor people feel the cold quite as much as the rich. We shall have a wooden floor and the place shall be heated. No one gets a blessing if they have cold feet and nobody ever got saved while they had a toothache."

With that same practical streak Booth enlisted music and converts to help save souls. Church music of the time was plodding and funereal. Why? he demanded. "Music belongs to the devil, does it? Well, if it did I would plunder him of it. . . . He's a thief. . . . Every note and every strain and every harmony is divine and belongs to us."

So he gave his people music, although it was sometimes less than divine. He gave them the brass and drums they knew and loved. Let the neighbors complain about the noise (as they often did). Brother Booth was packing in the converts.

The people did not so much come to hear him, Booth once told his wife, as to hear the "Bills and Dicks, the prize fighters and bird and dog fanciers" who had been converted. His meetings began to feature a "converted burglar," "a converted pigeon flyer," "Gypsy Smith" or

Artist's version of the early ministry: William preaching from a soap box in London's wretched East End; Catherine welcoming a penitent sinner into the fold.

"Elijah Cadman, the converted [chimney] sweep." The meeting's chairman would introduce, as in this eyewitness account, "a milkman who has not watered his milk since he joined the Mission."

"HURRAH!" cried the crowd.

"Friends," the milkman said, "you all know me. You know what a miserable wreck I was six months ago. Look at me tonight. And what's done it? Salvation!"

"HALLELUJAH!"

"I take my wage home to the missus now. I don't get up in the morning with a head as heavy as a ton of coal."

"PRAISE THE LORD!"

"I gets up with a merry heart and sometimes sing. . . ." And here the milkman launched into this variation of a Mission favorite:

> I will tell you what induced me
> For the Better Land to start
> 'Twas the Saviour's loving kindness
> Overcame and won my heart . . .

And the audience, off-key but hearty, joined in. Then the leader cried, "God can make a honest milkman of *you* if you will let Him!"

Mawkish, yes, but the wretches of England wanted that Better Land and the Christian Mission seemed to offer it. As the years passed Booth knew he needed some stronger format to control and direct his mixed and growing movement, and to unify its stand against its enemies. It came somewhat by accident.

One day in 1878 Booth, his oldest son Bramwell, and their foremost aide, George Scott Railton, were reworking a report. The cover page read, "The Christian Mission under the superintendence of the Rev. William Booth is A Volunteer Army." At the time England had a citizens' "volunteer" army that was something of a laughingstock.

"Volunteer!" exclaimed one of the Booths (historians disagree on which). "We are not volunteers, for we feel we *must* do what we do, and we are *always* on duty." The founder crossed out "volunteer" and wrote in "salvation."

From that came all the military terms of today, plus a few—"assault party," "open fire" or "opening shots" (to begin a meeting)—that have fallen by the wayside. Uniforms like those of London policemen became mandatory. Catherine Booth, who also preached sometimes, designed the women's straw bonnet with great flaring brim to help ward off beer, ripe tomatoes, pots of urine, and other guided missiles. Many British and a few Canadian Salvationists still wear a modified version of it.

Some of Booth's countrymen criticized his military format, but he had his reasons. His recruits needed moulding even more than those of regular armies. Most of them came straight from the streets—if not the gutter. Booth not only had to instill good conduct but actually instruct them to take baths, eat nourishing meals, and sleep with the window open. Overall, he had to muster from this well-intentioned rabble a strictly-disciplined force that could withstand the onslaughts against it. Only an army would do.

As the Army grew so did the persecution. In 1882 alone 669 Salvationists were brutally assaulted. Some were jailed almost every day on phony charges of disturbing the peace or causing an obstruction. A girl officer was trampled and killed by a horse and cart driven deliberately into her open-air meeting. The "skeleton army"—gangs of toughs with obscene songs and a "Beer, Beef and 'Bacca" flag—dogged the Salvationists' heels. The churches and much of the press were indifferent. A noted professor and champion of Charles Darwin, T. H. Huxley, called the Army "organized fanaticism" and Booth a rogue and a despot.

But ordinary people continued to flock behind it. There were wondrous sights to brighten their dreary days, such as Captain

"Happy" Eliza Hayes sweeping into Marylebone in a two-seater coach, playing her violin while Welsh Tom sat on the roof beating a drum. There were revival posters that cunningly lured the people with promises of something more:

EXHIBITION
of living wonders. Men who were
once as wild as LIONS
savage as TIGERS
and stubborn as old
JUMBO!!
who were found prowling through
the black JUNGLES of sin but captured
by our troops and tamed

"Ridicule as we may the doggerel hymns, the incoherent prayers, the wild harangues, the violent gesticulations and the rude sensationalism of a country fair introduced into public worship," wrote W. T. Stead, a newspaperman of the time, "the fact remains that the Salvation Army has saved members of the very lowest of the community from vice and crime."

Stead nevertheless thought that Booth was harsh. If any of the Hallelujah Lassies, as they were known, were killed by mobs, he said, the General should be indicted for manslaughter.

"You would never make a general," Booth chided him. "A general must not be afraid to spend his soldiers to carry a position."

That was how Booth saw it: a war with casualties on both sides. Like most generals he was worshipped and hated. He was sometimes irritable and always demanding. But he cared deeply for his people and there was humor in him too. Once when a major, Theodore Kitching, admitted to an error, Booth snapped, "What fool made you a major?"

"Your son, General," smiled Kitching. The old man looked startled, then burst out in a laugh.

Being the General's son or daughter had its drawbacks. Although Booth never exactly forced them into his Army, he expected them to serve, and seven of the eight did (daughter Marian was an invalid). Bramwell, a serious and intense boy, partly deaf, had grave misgivings about his ability to be a Mission preacher. But at thirteen Booth took him into a pub and said, "These are our people. These are the people I want you to live for and bring to Christ." Bramwell began helping at children's mission meetings and was a full-time Salvationist at eighteen. He even developed the family flair for theatrics: he once began a sermon by sitting bolt upright in a coffin

A Booth family portrait (but not the complete family; there were eight children).

with "Death, where is thy sting?" He eventually became the second General.

Ballington, the second son, commanded the Army in the United States and then, to his father's grief and utter disbelief, broke away to found the Volunteers of America, a religious sect. Catherine launched the Army in France; then she too, reluctantly, followed her husband out of the Army to another religious group. Herbert held commands in Canada, Britain, and Australia before he also resigned. Emma and Lucy went to India.

Evangeline, born on Christmas Day in the same year the Army was born, was the General's joy. She could have been an actress but turned her dramatic talents to Salvationism. She stirred passions wherever she went. Once she was stoned in the streets and hustled bleeding into court on a trumped-up charge of disorderly conduct. Again, she addressed a meeting in the rags of a London flower-seller. Evangeline eventually commanded the Army in Canada where once she rode up Toronto's Yonge Street astride a snow-white horse. In 1934 she became the fourth general.

Booth himself never stopped marching forward. Like his troops ever since—*unlike* some churchmen of his day and ours—he was

Evangeline, the dramatist of the children, liked to act out the plight of the poor — here, a ragged London flower seller.

concerned with this life as well as the hereafter. In London alone there were 60,000 prostitutes, 76,000 habitual criminals and 30,000 neglected children on the streets. So Mrs. Bramwell Booth at twenty-three established the first rescue home for girls fleeing from prostitution. Emma and Evangeline set up the Cellar, Gutter and Garret Brigade whereby Army cadets lived and worked in the slums, scrubbing, nursing, and preaching.

Phosphorus matches, which nearly everyone used, produced the hideous "phossy jaw" among match factory workers (the chemical ate away the bones of the face). Booth started his own factory, producing the new safety matches until the rest of the industry fell into line. Then he promptly sold the factory for a dollar.

The General, going home one bitter night in the late 1880s, discovered hordes of men huddled out under the bridges, covered with rags and newspapers.

"Bramwell!" he thundered the next day. "Do you know that there are men and women sleeping out on the bridges?"

Yes, Bramwell admitted, but what could the Army do?

"Well, go out and do something, Bramwell, do *something!*"

So, the first Salvation Army shelters came into being.

Then Booth brought out his book *In Darkest England and The Way Out*, an indictment of the awful social conditions and a blueprint for their cure. It was a revolution in social thinking. It recognized alcoholism as a sickness. It proposed soup kitchens for the hungry, a "poor men's bank," probation for first offenders, industrial settlements for the poor, and day care for the children of working mothers. It called for an immediate public subscription of £100,000. The first edition of ten thousand copies sold out the first day. Within four months £102,559 was subscribed.

Booth saw some of his proposals come true. Others came long after when the world, often prodded by his Army, caught up with his vision.

In later years he traveled afar, visiting his outposts. He was respected by churchmen now, and a favorite even of high society. On his eightieth birthday in 1909 there were warm greetings from kings, queens, and prime ministers. But he never stopped fighting for the poor and the weak.

In 1912 as he lay blind and dying he called Bramwell to his side. "The homeless children," he said. "Oh, the children! Bramwell, look after the homeless. Promise me!" And the faithful Bramwell promised.

William Booth died on 20 August 1912. The next day the Army announced: "The General has laid down his sword."

But he had merely passed it on.

3
Heralds
of Hope

On this golden June afternoon, Cadet Miriam Crews of New Glasgow, NS—she with the smile that would charm the angels—is as tenderly beautiful as any other twenty-year-old on her graduation day. *But she is in the Sally Ann!* Whatever became of those plain hefty girls in coal-scuttle bonnets and thick sensible shoes? Everything about her—trim tailored uniform, black high-heeled pumps, perky air-hostess hat with flared brim, fashionable glasses framing her dark eyes—defies the Salvation Army stereotype.

Before she darts backstage to join her fifty classmates, she lingers with family and friends in the audience in Toronto's Bramwell Booth Temple. "I've got butterflies!" she says nervously. And no wonder. This is no ordinary graduation into some vague future. This is a commitment for life, and a dream turned real. Moments from now she will become a Salvation Army officer. Ever since she was a little girl, daughter of officers and preaching sermons to her Barbie dolls, she has waited for this day.

She is not the only one with nerves. Everyone at this great family gathering of parents, brothers, sisters, friends is keyed up. The place is all smiles, embraces, glad cries. On stage, the scarlet-coated Canadian Staff Band, cream of Salvation Army musicians, floods the temple with joyful sound. Hear the sweet cornets, showering their notes like shiny pennies on the upturned faces below! Feel the throbbing pulse of the drum! This day, 18 June 1983, is a day for rejoicing. Today these new graduates from William Booth Memorial College will pick up the General's sword and march into battle.

Backstage, Lorraine and Henry Legge are ready. For two years they too have waited and worked for this day. They have turned

Graduation day for the Heralds of Hope: Lieutenant Susanne Fisher of Bermuda flashes the Army salute. Background: Lieutenant Miriam Crews (in glasses) and Lieutenant Joan Canning.

their backs on the kind of affluence that some Canadians scrabble a lifetime to achieve (Henry's salary alone was $35,000). From this day forward they will labor for God and the Army at a wage far below the official national poverty level.

To some, their choice seems madness. When the Legges enlisted, a friend exclaimed in disbelief, "Henry, there must be a catch!" But there is not. They *want* to be here. Their faces reflect that inner radiance that seems to be Salvation Army issue.

They are not religious fanatics nor teenagers rushing impetuously into the unknown. He—thirty-eight, tall, moustached, thick dark hair just above the collar (but not below; the Army doesn't go *that* far)—is a university graduate and former teacher. She—twenty-nine, petite, blonde hair stylishly coiffed—was a district manager for Tupperware products. They are the new Sally Ann breed—better educated, more worldly-wise, perhaps more questioning than cadets of a generation ago, yet with all the Christian faith and charity of old.

Consider classmate Wendy Ward of Victoria, B.C.—twenty-six (the average age of today's trainees), slim and exquisite with hazel eyes, curly hair, and a model's high cheekbones. In fact, she once *did* model uniforms in a Sally Ann fashion show; this Army marches with the times. She's a fourth-generation Salvationist but she did not automatically bolt from high school into the ranks.

"I had to think it through," she says. "I wanted to be proud of it." She studied pre-law at the University of Victoria but dropped out, dissatisfied; took a two-year Bible College course; worked as an executive secretary. Always she held to her faith, and she played the alto horn in Army bands as she has done since age fifteen. Now she knows the Army is "a lifestyle I want" and she *is* proud.

So is bearded Bill Mollard, twenty-seven, who as a university science student was "totally non-Christian and into a heavy scene of drinking and drugs." He was vaguely thinking of a PhD in chemistry when he met his wife-to-be, daughter of Army officers, on a tennis court. To that point he thought the Salvation Army was "just a place where you bought used clothes." Today Bill and Darlene Mollard are ready to march together.

And there's Susanne Fisher from Bermuda; Song Dae Lee from Korea; Anne Maurais, a Quebecoise—fifty-one in total, the Army's hope for tomorrow. Their dark blue serge uniforms are immaculate; white blouses and shirts crisp and spotless; silver "S" gleaming on their lapels. Each one drapes the Army tri-colors from right shoulder to left hip. In golden letters it cries their class name: "Heralds of Hope." What better epithet for the task ahead? Now and forever-more, they will bring hope to the hopeless.

On stage the first-year class, "Servants of God," is seated under an Army flag blazing with red for the blood of Christ, blue for the holiness of life, yellow for the fire of the Holy Spirit. "Blood and Fire"—the phrase is etched in every Salvationist's brain.

The Heralds stride forth, each with Bible in hand. On behalf of her class, Wendy Ward recites the covenant that each must sign: ". . . to proclaim the Gospel of our Lord and Saviour Jesus Christ . . . to live to win souls and make their salvation the first purpose of my life . . ." There are hymns, Scripture readings, more hymns. The cadets repeat an eleven-point declaration of faith to Christ, then make their vows.

"Do you regard it as your duty to bear this witness everywhere, to strive to lead mankind to its only Saviour and for His sake to care for the poor, feed the hungry, clothe the naked, love the unloveable, and befriend those who have no friends?"

"We do."

At last, one by one, the marrieds in pairs, they step before white-haired Commissioner Arthur Pitcher, leader of the Salvation Army of Canada and Bermuda.

"In the name of God the Father, God the Son and God the Holy

Spirit I ordain and commission you as an officer of the Salvation Army with the rank of Lieutenant. May God bless you!"

He hands them a certificate. They snap him a brisk salute—right hand clenched shoulder high, index finger pointing to Heaven—and shake hands. There is some confusion over that blasted salute; Salvationists in Canada rarely use it. Should it come before the handshake or after, before commissioning or after? Among them, they manage to work all possible variations. The audience and Commissioner chuckle indulgently. This is no day for nitpicking. The music swells into the closing hymn, "Soldiers of the Cross, arise; Gird you with your armour bright . . ."

Now, for the rest of their lives, Lorraine and Henry, Bill and Darlene, Wendy, Miriam, and the others *will* be soldiers of the Lord, waging a holy war against all the world's evils and despair.

For nearly all of them it has been the most arduous, restricting, often frustrating two years of their lives. Getting into the Army is *much* harder than getting into university. The candidate must be a senior soldier between nineteen and thirty-five if single, twenty to thirty-five if married. The age rule is waived in exceptional cases with permission from international headquarters. Generally, though, the Army feels it would be unfair to graduate persons of thirty-eight

Commissioning and posting of new officers, 1982: then-Commissioner John Waldron gets the salute from an entire family.

or older, often with growing families, into the low pay and shorter career they would face at that age. Older people can take short courses and become auxiliary officers, with more limited responsibilities.

Grade 12 education or equivalent is also a must, and some work experience is preferred. And, of course, the applicant must be of sound moral character—judged initially on the recommendations of the local Corps officer, and by close scrutiny of the candidate's conversion into the Army church. The first and main condition of soldiership is to be saved from sin: accepting Jesus Christ as one's Saviour. The person who *truly* surrenders to Christ, not merely paying lip-service, is converted—an inward spiritual change from the path of selfishness and sin. The Army has accepted many reformed drunks, a few ex-convicts, and (with permission from abroad) the occasional divorced person.

Given these basics, the officer-to-be must complete the Minnesota Multiphase Personality Inventory (a psychological test) and a battery of reports on marital status, educational background, and state of health.

If this passes the screening board the Army gets down to *serious* business: a full-fledged application. This includes an IQ test, recommendations and comments from five officers in the applicant's home territory, a very thorough medical (an officer's work is extremely taxing), and a more exhaustive report on the conversion and holiness experiences. It is the Army premise that all humans are sinners but salvation from sin should lead to holiness of life. That holy life is one of constant fellowship with Christ.

In the more mundane realm of economics, a prospective officer must start out with a modest bank account. Tuition is a nominal $250 for singles and $400 for marrieds; the rest is subsidized by a levy on all Salvation Army corps across Canada. The candidate needs at least $2,000 for a uniform and incidental expenses over the two years.

Those who successfully run this gauntlet (it takes at least three or four months) must then complete nine correspondence-course lessons on Scripture, doctrine, and Army leadership and service, while awaiting the next autumn's training session in Toronto or St. John's.

Rigorous though it all is, applications are on the rise. Last year the Army had more than one hundred applications and put a total of seventy-five cadets into the two colleges. Some think this was a response to the recession—any safe berth in a storm—but Captain Linda Bond in the candidates' office disagrees.

"Young people see that officership is not easy, but they *want* to be challenged," she says.

Young people, perhaps. But why would an urbane couple such as the Legges give up their comfortable though Christian civilian lives for the Army's harsher stuff?

Part of the answer is in their upbringing. To anyone reared in the Salvationist faith, the Army is forever in the soul. Like most Canadian officers today, Henry and Lorraine are from deep Salvationist backgrounds. Her parents in Toronto and his grandfather, a Newfoundland fisherman, were laity. Henry's father was an officer in Newfoundland (where the son was born) and in Ontario.

Their parents held them as babies beneath the flag and dedicated them to God in the Army—the Salvationist counterpart to christening. At age eight they signed the junior soldier's pledge with its commitment to service and renouncement of cigarettes and alcohol. At fourteen they became senior soldiers and signed the Articles of War, a full-page document that states in part: ". . . I do here and now and for ever renounce the world with all its sinful pleasures, companionships, treasures and objects, and declare my full determination boldly to show myself a soldier of Jesus Christ . . ."

They promised to abstain from smoking, drinking, addictive drugs, profanity, the reading of obscene literature, and from any deceitful or fraudulent business conduct. "I do here declare my full determination, by God's help, to be a true soldier of the Salvation Army till I die."

A true soldier Henry was, but like many an Army officer's child—especially in the turbulent Sixties, which tugged at Salvationist children as others—he shied away from officership. With no money for university he chose a one-year free-tuition course at teachers' college. Later he taught Grades 5 and 6 in Toronto schools, earned an Honors BA in psychology by taking night courses at York University, served as school guidance counselor, taught music and always received good reports from his school principals.

And yet . . . the *call* kept nagging inside him. The Army's musical training for young people had made him a skilled trombonist. He played and sometimes toured with the Canadian Staff Band. He attended Toronto's North York Temple ("temple" and "citadel" are interchangeable terms for an Army church) where he met Lorraine Brownlee in 1969. They were engaged in 1973, the same night that Henry's young sister Betty and her husband, Doug Lewis, were commissioned as Army officers. Lorraine wanted to be an officer too but "we married, got comfortable and postponed it."

They had a $130,000 house in Thornhill, an affluent suburb north of Metropolitan Toronto. Henry occasionally played the stock market, and ran a small photography business on the side. Lorraine worked variously for Eaton's, Bell Telephone, the Army's Bethany Home for unwed mothers, as well as becoming the Tupperware manager with a flourishing clientele and company car. They hired a nanny to help out with their sons Stephen, David, and John-Michael.

"People thought we had really 'arrived,' " Henry reflects. "But I was becoming restless. I liked teaching but I wasn't as happy as before. I was toying with the idea of teaching abroad."

One June Saturday in 1980 they attended a commissioning in Toronto's Massey Hall, Lorraine in the audience and Henry in the band.

"Commissioning is an emotional event," Legge says. "It tends to make you feel guilty if you're *not* in the Army."

This one, like all others, ended with a strong appeal for uncommitted members of the audience to step forward and promise their lives to Christ. Several did. Afterward the Legges met for coffee before Lorraine went on shift at the Bethany.

"Would you have been surprised if I had gone to the stage?" she asked.

"Not a bit, because I was thinking of exactly the same thing!"

At that moment they sensed the hand of God—as do nearly all Army officers who look back on their decision. "There's no doubt someone or something was prodding us," Henry says firmly. "It wasn't the beginning of our struggle, it was the end." On Monday morning they applied for training.

As the Legges phased out of civilian life, their friends were variously baffled and complimentary. "It's a noble thing you're doing," said some. Henry and Lorraine did not feel noble, nor that they were making a major sacrifice.

True, they could not expect riches or high rank, especially at Henry's age. Rank—up to and including major—depends on length of service, not merit, and has no bearing on the weekly allowance (the Army doesn't call it "salary"). On graduation a cadet becomes a lieutenant at $84 a week for singles, $140 a week jointly for a married couple (who always bear the same rank). Each child under five adds $23 a week or, between ages five and sixteen, $27.50 a week to the parents' stipend. After twenty-five and, again, thirty-five years' service, there's an extra $3 to $8 a week.

After every three years' service, the allowance automatically goes up one dollar a week. At the same time, with more mandatory study courses and seminars, the lieutenant automatically becomes a captain in five years; a major, after another fifteen years. The ranks of lieutenant-colonel, colonel, commissioner and general (of which there is only one, world-wide) are by special appointment.

The system counters civilian life's in-fighting for pay and promotion, but produces strange anomalies.

"A junior officer with four children makes more than I do," says training college principal Lieutenant-Colonel Brown, wryly but without rancor. "And our civilian janitor here makes more money than any of us—and drives a better car."

The Legges on graduation with three children were eligible for just over $200 a week (1983 rates) or $10,500 a year—nearly $2,500 more than Lieutenant-Colonel Brown, but $12,000 less than Statistics Canada's so-called "low-income cutoff"—the basic deemed necessary for a family of that size. On Henry's mandatory retirement in the year 2010, with his children grown and if he and Lorraine are then majors, their joint income (at 1984 rates) would be a mere $8,112.

Yet they expect to live comfortably, educate their sons, and take modest yearly holidays. There will always be a free and furnished Army house, including utilities. Tailored uniforms, of serge or wool-and-polyester (so dark blue that some officers call it "the black") will cost a mere $108-$115, half of what Salvationist soldiers pay.

There's a free car, if their work requires it; or an allowance for their personal car. They'll have excellent medical, dental, and group insurance plans and, on retirement, $20,000 in lieu of equity in the house they will never own.

The day after they were accepted for training, Henry learned he was on the short list for a school vice-principalship (a job that can now pay around $47,000). He could still have backed away from the Army.

"It was almost a test, a chance to ask ourselves 'Are you *sure?*' " he says. "But our decision was so clear to us that nothing short of a hit on the head with a baseball bat could have made it clearer. We believe the Lord speaks to us, not with a voice but through our conscience. And it kept saying 'This is where you should be, this is what you should be doing with your talents.' If we had chosen to ignore it, we would have been saying, in effect, 'Get out of our lives, God!' If you are a believer, you must act on it."

After sixteen years as a breadwinner, thinking fast on his feet in public and getting a university degree in his spare time, Henry found college studies a breeze. The discipline was a pain. To a man who'd been head of his own classroom, it was galling to be told when to study, when to go out, when to stay in. Compared with high schools and universities, this Army is a nitpicker—like *any* army. Its training is based on the premise that officership requires dedication and self-discipline: none of the trainees can ever again do exactly as they please.

Sunday is reserved for devotions: shopping, going to a restaurant, doing laundry, or "overusing" TV is frowned upon. Saturday is usually free. Every other day is laid out to the minute: when to eat, when to pray, when to spend time with the children (who are in college day-care centers or regular neighborhood schools while their parents study), when to watch the TV news, when to do homework. During study hours in Newfoundland there is no doing of laundry or taking showers, and "all room doors are to be left open for the purpose of supervision."

As in any army, privacy is limited. In Toronto, apart from breakfast in the private quarters, all meals are in a communal dining room. (Children dine with their parents.) The tiny rooms for singles and small apartments for families are subject to snap inspections.

"This is a *battle* school," stresses Lieutenant-Colonel Brown.

Most battle schools permit, if not encourage, a healthy interest in sex. The Army recognizes sex, but puts it on the back burner, which requires considerable self-discipline for normal red-blooded young people in today's society. A Salvation Army officer dropout recalls the frustration of his training days and muses, "It's a wonder more single female cadets don't get pregnant!" (How many, if any, do, is a statistic not available from Army headquarters.) A college manual allows "that there may normally develop an interest between men and women cadets [but] public display of affection is not in keeping with Christian propriety."

Visiting between singles of opposite sex in either's room is banned. The manuals even spell out the Army's drill for people who want to fall in love. "When a cadet desires to have a courtship with a fellow cadet, candidate or officer officially recognized, both parties should write a letter to the Principal with a copy to the Section Officer," states the Newfoundland manual. "Official correspondence will not be granted until after the first year of training unless courtship was officially recognized prior to entering training.

"A dating couple should restrict the frequency and length of time spent together during the week to a maximum of three times (for example—from 9 P.M. to 10:30 P.M.)." A cadet may become officially engaged after graduation.

In spite of all this, and in spite of a heavy curriculum of Biblical and theological studies, counseling, corps procedures, public speaking, Christian education, and seminars on everything from addictions to communications, cadets *do* fall in love, court, and marry as soon as the Army law allows.

They also have innocent fun. They tape each others' doors shut. They move every stitch of clothes and stick of furniture from a classmate's room to points unknown, should that one be so unwise as to go out. At Toronto college, Obadiah, the resident skeleton, makes sporadic appearances: once, in the principal's office in full

Student's room in the Army training college in Toronto.

uniform; once leering from the women's lavatory and nearly shocking a pregnant (married) cadet into early labor.

The Legges, being too old for tomfoolery, were diligent students. Although Henry had been an ardent bridge player as a teacher, he played no more, lest he offend those who interpret all card-playing as "gambling." In their second year they were promoted to Cadet-Sergeants with a supervisory role over some of the first-year class. Their marks never dipped below eighty percent and Henry won the top-student award for their session.

They refused to let the system impinge on their family life—and on that point the Army willingly bends. The rules say 6:00 P.M. to 8:00 P.M. is "family time," followed by two hours of "scheduled time" for parents (study or other activities). But the Legges apportioned those four hours as they saw fit. They also made sure they had a good babysitter before agreeing to attend a college evening activity. Overall, youngsters in Army colleges spend more time with or near both parents than many children outside.

"There are a lot of things about the place I didn't like," Legge summed up at the end of training. "But you know if you can endure it and get into the field, you'll be all right." He could even accept the reasoning behind the discipline: "It explains why Army people respond so quickly and effectively during an emergency."

As the year ended every cadet wondered: where will I begin my life's work? In the late spring of 1983, as every spring, the trainees knew from the Sally Ann grapevine which officers were retiring or moving. They hung a big map of Canada in the dining hall, marked the openings on it, and speculated endlessly (no *betting* of course) on who might go where. There was no guarantee they'd get what they wanted.

"People coming out of battle school should be prepared to go anywhere," says Lieutenant-Colonel Brown, who with other senior officers makes the assignments.

Wendy Ward who "dearly loves to work with people on a one-to-one basis" seemed a natural for more of the same. Bill Mollard said, "I don't think there's anywhere that God can't use me," but hoped to work with teenagers going through his own youthful turmoil with drugs and alcohol. For Miriam Crews what mattered most was that in seven months she'd marry classmate Tim Leslie and they'd be somewhere together.

The Legges dreamed of their own corps in a small community where, as Henry put it, "we'd be Mr. and Mrs. Salvation Army," dividing its many duties between them.

"That's the front line!" he said enthusiastically on the eve of graduation.

It is evening, 18 June. A bright silver star gleams from each crimson-trimmed shoulder bar of the fifty-one new lieutenants. Now, the grand finale: postings. Here in Massey Hall, three thousand friends and relatives—old and young, many in uniform, many stylish and affluent-looking couples in civvies—are fanning away the heat with a forest of programmes. Henry Legge's mother—who all through their training kept her son and daughter-in-law fortified with little gifts of chicken and home-made cookies—is brimming with pride. She is now the mother of two officers.

The Staff Band is playing sprightly marches. Beside them onstage, fifty-one empty chairs await. Suddenly the lights go down, a spotlight darts to center stage, the music roars, and the blood-and-fire flag comes leading the way. The Army *does* know how to put on a show.

Into the spotlight march the Heralds, the couples struggling to stay in lockstep while not falling down two badly-lit steps. Their names boom over the sound system. There are cheers, *squeals*, the kind of reception generally reserved for Michael Jackson or Princess Di.

"Off to the front line": Lieutenant Henry Legge and Lieutenant Lorraine Legge, with sons Steven, David, and John Michael, receive their marching orders from Commissioner Arthur Pitcher.

They get down the treacherous steps intact, and snap flawless salutes at the Commissioner. More hymns and prayers. The crowd is on fire with full-throated song, clapping in the choruses. In the front row a graying woman twirls and slaps a beribboned tambourine with such *elan* that we know she soldiered with a band in some distant time and place.

The suspense is electric. It's like the Academy Awards. At last the Commissioner gets down to the main event: appointments. His little jokes are warmly received by this partisan audience.

When Wendy Ward steps forward he smiles, "You're from Victoria, Wendy? . . . You like the west? . . . (The audience beams; probably she'll get a BC posting.) . . . Well, we're sending you to Guelph, Ontario . . . (Gasps). Well," the Commissioner grins, "it's west of *here* . . ." (Actually, it's a dream posting: she'll be Guelph's first youth officer, a job tailor-made for her talents.)

Miriam Crews is off to Liverpool, NS, only two hundred miles from home where her parents are Army majors, a mere thirty miles from her fiancé who's assigned to Bridgewater. (Does this tough Army have a soft center after all? Does it secretly love lovers?) Bill and Darlene Mollard will take charge of the South Burnaby, BC, corps. Anne Maurais, the only French-Canadian graduate, goes to Quebec City. Song Dae Lee, to no one's surprise, is posted home to Korea.

Couples with children bring them on stage and the Commissioner has a grandfatherly word for all. The Army is, among other things, the biggest family on earth. At last the Legges and their sons stand before him.

"We're posting you to Erin Mills, in charge!" The corps, barely four years old, is in the vast municipality of Mississauga just west of Toronto. There'll be work and challenge galore for Mr. and Mrs. Salvation Army. Henry and Lorraine have their wish. They are off to the front line.

4
"Will
It Last?"

As they marched to the "front," Henry and Lorraine Legge were a mere one hundred miles from history: the spot where two of their spiritual forebears helped launch the Army in Canada a century before. The front line then was London, Ontario, where one night in 1881 Jack Addie was pining for some of that good old whoop-and-holler praise-the-Lord-and-turn-a-cartwheel evangelism he'd learned from Salvationist Gypsy Smith back home in England.

As Addie, a moon-faced lad of eighteen, entered a cottage prayer meeting for an extra dollop of religion, after a relatively hushed service in the Askin Weslyan Methodist Church—no brass bands, no tambourines, no barn-burner sermons—he suddenly thrilled to a familiar sound. A tall young stranger with a smudge of a moustache was singing a Salvation Army song!

"Who are you?" he burst out after the service. "Where are you from?" Joe Ludgate was who he was and Salvationist England was where he was from.

"You're the fellow I've been looking for!" cried Addie.

"And you're the fellow I've been trying to find!"

Ludgate explained how he had been a proper sinner back home before he was saved. First, he had acquired the depraved and shocking habit of reading *novels*. Then, at age fourteen, he had turned into a drunk.

Together they held their first Salvationist meeting in London's Victoria Park one Sunday in May 1882, with a few conscripted singers. As Ludgate later reported in the *War Cry*, "At the close the Lord crowned our efforts by saving a poor drunkard." Soon Addie, a

Although not the first Salvationists in Canada, Jack Addie, left, and Joe Ludgate are best remembered in its history. Fresh from England and yearning for William Booth's fiery Christianity, they got the Army off to a permanent start, in London, Ontario.

draper in a London clothing store, and Ludgate, a presser in a tailor shop, were holding regular meetings indoors and out. They concocted uniforms: blue tunics from the tailor shop and helmets like those worn by English "bobbies," adorned with Salvation Army shields and the admonition "Prepare to meet thy God."

But they were not the first Salvationists in Canada. A dozen years before, James Jermy, an English cabinetmaker with Salvationist roots, had preached a few outdoor sermons in Hamilton and St. Catharines. In 1881 English Commissioner George Scott Railton, who had witnessed the naming of the Army with the Booths three years before, stopped off in Halifax on his way home from launching Salvationism in the United States. He became so caught up in spreading the good word that he missed his boat and stayed on seven more days.

In Toronto a handful of Salvationists met in February 1882, before Addie and Ludgate. But these Toronto beginnings were so faintly recorded that the Army usually calls London its Canadian birthplace.

In the Booth tradition, Ludgate and Addie took their message straight to the altar of Sin—in London's case, a stretch of twenty-two saloons known as Whiskey Row. They stuck to it through the hoots and jeers and curses of the drunks until the town's biggest boozer, Whiskey Mason, joined the Army. Then scores of others crowded forward. Obviously these peculiar soldiers knew how to put the boots to the Devil.

The fire of evangelism flashed through Ontario. The Army charmed so many citizens of Bowmanville that a local bylaw forbade swearing in the streets. Vivacious Captain Abby Thompson, first commanding officer of the Kingston corps, became eastern Ontario's darling in the single year she was stationed there. Although only twenty when she arrived with other officers from the United States in 1883, she was a born leader, with a talent for cajoling rowdy crowds and making the hecklers eat out of her hand.

The newspapers were full of her exploits. A soap manufacturer created a brand of "Abby Soap." A yacht was christened the "Captain Abby." Her colleagues called their local barracks "Abby's Temple." There was even a rumor that she'd be made chaplain of the Senate in Ottawa—not as preposterous as it sounded, because Sir John A. Macdonald, the member for Kingston, attended some of her meetings.

"The Army is in our midst, fully equipped with banners, bands and all other paraphernalia of spiritual warfare," editorialized the Toronto *World*. "The sincerity of the movement is not to be doubted. The question is 'Will it last?' These movements depend on emotional excitement which is in its very nature transitory."

If the *World* could have seen into the hearts of ordinary people it would never have doubted. The Army met a need. It was emotional, it was entertainment, it welcomed the humblest of humans, and it was contagious. Even the nicknames smacked of fun and joy: Captain "Happy Tom" Cathcart and "Hallelujah Wife," Captain

"Glory Tom" Calhoun, "Sledgehammer Bill" (a blacksmith with a speaking style straight out of the forge).

"Happy Bill" Cooper—widely known and revered as a reformed alcoholic and ex-wife-beater—led marches interspersed with cartwheels. When his audience dwindled, he delivered his sermon while standing on his head, a ploy that invariably drew them back. Three woman officers stood Paris, Ontario, on *its* head, wearing long red

In the mere year (1883) she served in Kingston, Ontario, before returning to her native United States, vibrant Captain Abby Thompson was the darling of eastern Canada.

silk dresses with "The Salvation Army" inscribed on their bosoms and "Hallelujah" boldly lettered on the hems.

Any tactic—the "Hallelujah Runaway," for instance—was fair game in the Lord's work. In the midst of an outdoor meeting an officer would suddenly take off at a dead run, like a man berserk. His soldiers pounded after him. *What on earth . . . ?* Naturally, no crowd could resist. By the dozens, by the hundreds, the curious sinners chased after the galloping Salvationists—until they found themselves sucked into a meeting hall with a blood-and-fire sermon raging around their ears.

The "Hallelujah Wedding" was another crowd-pleaser. Canada had never seen its like. Consider the Belleville, Ontario, nuptials in January 1884 of Joe Ludgate—yes, the original Joe, a captain—and Captain Nellie Ryerson. About one thousand people, including the police magistrate and judge, paid fifteen cents a head to come and cheer them on.

At 3:00 P.M. the Hallelujah minister and Captain Ludgate arrived at Bridge Street Church, to loud huzzahs from the assembled throng. Tambourines whirled and drums boomed as the band led the congregation in a Salvationist song, "O how happy they are," to a hit tune of the day, "Tramp, tramp, tramp, the boys are marching."

Then came an "experience meeting"—basically a giving of testimony, including Ludgate's own. There were tales of conversion. A "Hallelujah tailor" told how he hadn't hit the bottle for nine months, inspiring "Happy Bill" to spring up and sing "He's given up whiskey drinking" to the jingle of tambourines.

Finally the bride in blue uniform arrived on the arm of the local bank manager, and the marriage went ahead in fairly conventional fashion. The couple launched their honeymoon by going to prayer meeting in the same church that night.

By the end of the decade the Army had won followers and admirers from coast to coast, with its soup, salvation, and tambourines. Even Toronto's *Saturday Night* magazine, self-appointed arbiter of the nation's social conscience, intoned: "We may smile at the incongruous crowds that carry banners and shout hymns to the music of tambourines and drums, but we know . . . that the Salvation Army does much good in reclaiming drunkards and providing places and methods of worship suitable for those who do not feel inclined to show their rags and uncouthness in a fashionable place."

But not without pain. As in England, there were enemies in other religious groups and among the saloonkeepers whose best customers were being leached away by salvation. And the Army's very exuberance contributed to its grief. In an age when a lady's quivering glance over the top of her fan was the ultimate in flirtation, it *was*

With tambourines and squeeze box, this nineteenth-century Army group is ready to seek out sinners. Center rear: Happy Bill, "Saved Through the Blood of Christ."

upsetting to see bold young women flashing their bloomers in cartwheels down the main street.

As a churchman scolded in an 1884 pamphlet: "If I were to go into the lanes of the city beating a big drum, with one of my elders beating a little one, accompanied with several of the women of the congregation, playing tambourines and fiddles, what would be thought of us?" The Army's highly visible role for women was, he said, "not only inconsistent with the position in which it has pleased God to place women, but also with that modesty which is an ornament to her sex. . . . Their late hours and all-night meetings of both sexes together do not promote good order or the morals of the community."

Also, the Salvationists were awfully noisy and, by Jove, the law was not going to stand for it. In Acton, Ontario, Captain Minnie Milliken was jailed on a charge of "beating the snare drum on the street." In Brockville an officer and cadet were jailed ten days for *singing* in the streets. At Brampton, the offense of holding an open air meeting drew ten days with *hard labor*. In Lakefield a soldier was jailed two months for "beating a tambourine," while in Lindsay twenty-seven Army men and women were crammed into one small cell in the local police station, after marching down the street playing a sacred song on New Year's Eve.

Where the law left off the mobs took over. One Sunday a little band of Salvationists was holding services with men of the Twenty-ninth Regiment on the outskirts of London. A crowd gathered to view the fun. Two drunks began to fight and anti-Salvationists seized on the opportunity to start a brawl. Each time the Salvationists tried to sing, they were flung down to the cries of "Kill them! Kill them!"

Finally an officer galloped into the mob with drawn sword. The Regiment formed a double ring around the Salvationists until they finished their worship; then marched them safely home.

Other champions sometimes cropped up when the Army got into a pickle. In Lindsay a man with a musket announced at an Army rally that he would shoot anyone who interfered. It was the most peaceable rally in weeks. In Toronto a mob in Queen's Park turned ugly—understandably enough—when Salvationist preachers warned them they were on the sure road to Hell and eternal damnation. This time a band of husky young Roman Catholics came to the rescue.

But mostly the Army stood its ground alone while its enemies pelted the warriors with soot, flour, soap suds, fish, rotten vegetables, hot pans, knives, forks, and crockery. A Toronto Salvationist reported that "one of the devil's agents had tried to get us to close our meeting by putting pepper on the stove." In Woodstock, Ontario, a sharp stick hurled from the crowd almost blinded a woman officer.

Nowhere was the Army more savagely treated than in the province of Quebec. French-English relations were at a low ebb anyway and Protestant-Catholic differences were particularly acute. The "attack," as the Army called its arrival in Montreal, began on a December Sunday in 1884. The officers, after prayer indoors, marched out past thousands of Montrealers, who variously cheered, cursed, threw rocks and chunks of ice, or called out "God bless you!"

The outdoor meeting in Victoria Square had scarcely begun before the Salvationists were arrested and driven in sleighs to the police station. Out on bail and back in their hall for an evening meeting, they were still harassed by mobs.

"After several seats had been broken and the windows smashed, [they] took their departure from the hall to follow us home," reported a Staff Captain Madden, a mere boy, judging from his picture in the War Cry. "Having no protection at night they handled us quite roughly. By God's help and the help of some friends we got inside without any serious injury . . . Hallelujah!"

In the end the court ruled that Salvationists had as much right to parade as did Catholics. The Army presence simmered in Quebec until 1887. In March that year a home-made bomb—a bottle filled with explosive powder—went off while Quebec City Salvationists prayed in their meeting place (its windows already repeatedly smashed). A telegram to headquarters told the tale:

> Attempt made to blow up the French barracks during the meeting last night. Great explosion: windows smashed but nobody injured. Devil raging.

In August, as part of fifth anniversary celebrations, the Quebec City corps stubbornly planned a march up one of the main streets, Rue St. Jean, despite the warnings of friends. As they neared the Basilica an angry mob rose from hiding. In the barrage of stones and clubs, twenty-one Salvationists were injured. One man's head was slit with a knife; the drummer's eye was gouged out; the commissioner was saved only because a quick-witted friend snatched off his distinctive hat.

In November another mob of six hundred heckled and harassed an Army parade and stoned the barracks. The police were almost powerless. Three nights later three thousand rowdies gathered to plot mayhem for the next Army march, and went away singing, "We'll hang the Salvation Army to a sour apple tree."

Quebec City's mayor swore he would settle the matter in the courts, and if the Army were found legally entitled to parade he would back it with as much military force as it would take. A tedious succession of deferments kept the case out of court for months. Eventually the tensions cooled but the Army never grew strong in Quebec City and finally closed its church corps in 1920, although a hostel and clothing shop carried on.

By contrast, western Canada embraced the faith with wild enthusiasm. In 1886 the six-member Northwest Brigade rode the new railway (three days and three nights from Toronto) into Winnipeg. A few Salvationist settlers were ahead of them: a sister in an Army bonnet met them at the station, springing into the air with jubilant cries of "Glory! Here they are!"

It was a fair sample of the welcome to come. Although the temperature dropped to -43 F in the next few days, the brigade stubbornly hit the frozen streets with music and copies of the War Cry. Within a month they telegraphed head office:

> Send more officers over to help us. Thermometer 30 degrees below. Salvation boiling over. The whole Northwest a blaze of Salvation.

In the East the Army had pioneered Salvationism. In the West its officers were pioneers in *every* sense. Staff Captain Arthur Young, head of the brigade, pushed on by wagon and horseback through the emptiness to Edmonton and Calgary. In that whole great expanse he saw about one hundred people, most of them in Calgary itself. The trail, he wrote in the *War Cry*, was a "rough beaten track" marked out by small mounds of soil, an iron rod jutting up from each. From time to time he and fellow-travellers bedded down in one of the three or four log-cabin stopping places along his eight-hundred-to-nine-hundred mile route:

"Did I go to a nice room and sleep between nice sheets on a spring bed? Oh no! I had the choice of the open prairie or the floor of the hut, so I joyfully chose the latter." He spread a rubber ground sheet, pulled off his muddy boots, made a pillow out of his vest, rolled himself into his two blankets and fell asleep amid the wood and tobacco smoke.

Other officers "invaded" Manitoba's smaller towns—Morden, Neepawa, Minnedosa. By 1887 pioneer Salvationists had reached the coast. The West was won and never was heard a discouraging word. British Columbia and especially urban Vancouver offered familiar big-city conditions and needs that the Army could readily identify and handle. The prairies, although friendly, never gave Salvationism a fervent following.

One of William Booth's schemes for easing the misery of city people was to put them on farm colonies. The prototype in England helped launch others abroad. Canada had two such (short-lived) ventures, in Coombs, BC, and Tisdale, Saskatchewan, settled by members of the English colony and by experienced farmers from Ontario. Here, their faces glowing with anticipation, the Cannon family is on its way to settle in Tisdale.

Praise the Lord and Hallelujah! This painting by Canadian artist Robert Harris shows an early Army march down the streets of Charlottetown.

"The rural conditions of the prairies, with the population scattered over a large area of farmland, seemed to defeat the ingenuity of the Army's officers," writes Gordon Moyles in his excellent Army history, *The Blood and Fire in Canada*. "In the second place, although perhaps less significant, the Salvation Army was never able to rid itself of its Englishness. Prairie residents, unlike those of British Columbia, were largely of non-British origin and among the Ukrainian, Polish, Scandinavian, Russian, and German settlers, most of whom owed staunch allegiance to their own churches, the Salvation Army found few supporters."

The pattern still holds. A recent census shows more than twelve thousand Salvationists in British Columbia and less than thirteen thousand in the three prairie provinces combined.

The Maritimes, meanwhile, were as hospitable as the West but Newfoundland was a shock. The Army reached there in 1886, drawing so large a crowd that the police, in trying to disperse it, were themselves battered about. Street marches, with police escort, were thereafter limited to Sunday mornings.

This failed to protect the Salvationists in their everyday rounds. Once they were waylaid by a crowd wielding hatchets. Newfoundland women attacked officers with scissors, darning needles and knives. A Salvationist girl was repeatedly trampled and manhandled by a gang while local women looked on crying "Kill her! Kill her!" A doorkeeper at the Army hall was permanently crippled. The Citadel itself was so persistently stoned that hardly a pane of glass remained.

Yet within a decade the Army was accepted, admired, even "respectable" everywhere. By the end of the century its evangelism had simmered down; it was on the way to becoming a more established church. As such, it was more palatable to many admirers, and less threatening to many other churches. At the same time, its social services were gaining strength: homes for "fallen" women, for men just out of prison and for the aged; hostels; a missing persons' bureau. In Toronto in 1892 the Army founded the first League of Mercy, for hospital visitations, which subsequently spread through the Army world. Salvationists were beginning to acquire their reputation of "good people."

Now in an average year the Army provides a million beds and nearly two million meals for Canadian transients; runs twenty-two homes for the elderly; pays twenty-eight thousand visits to prisons and courts. Year round, the League of Mercy (civilians, soldiers, and Army officers) takes friendship and the *War Cry* to nearly a million shut-ins and hospital patients. Year round the Army shelters countless unwed mothers, battered children, alcoholics, mentally handicapped, and terminally ill.

From a time of ridicule and rejection, the Salvation Army has become indispensable, a fact and a necessity in Canadian life. Two provinces are particular strongholds. One, not surprisingly, is Ontario with its dominant population and that Britishness that Moyles describes. The other *is* surprising. Nowhere in Canada is the Army so revered, nowhere is Salvationism more fervent and fiery than in one of the provinces that hated it most—Newfoundland.

5

Oh,
This Is the Place
Where Salvationists
Gather

At 7:00 A.M. Lieutenant Ross Bungay, in maroon sweat shirt and jogging slacks, is running the few hundred yards down-road to his Arnold's Cove citadel. Church doesn't begin until eleven and it is not unduly cool this September Sunday, but Bungay is going to turn up the heat. On Sunday *everything* must be just right.

Newfoundland *is* the Army in Canada. Toronto is headquarters but Newfoundland is home. It has more Salvationists in total, 45,120, than any other province or any other region of its size in the world, and has poured thousands more into the rest of Canada. This is Salvationism's mother-lode.

From the nineteenth century until not long ago, each major church on this island ran its own schools. In the 1890s the Army, too, began educating its children, which helped entrench it as a major faith. Now, Newfoundland is the Army's heart and its outports are the soul. In these villages clinging to the island's perimeter—rocky hills at their backs, sea at their faces—there is little need for social services. The people take care of their own. In a Newfoundland outport the Army is *church*, above all, and Sunday service is the major event.

Which is partly why Ross Bungay is jogging this morning: to unwind. Being a corps officer is a draining job. Bungay pours himself into it every day but Sunday to him is like the championship game to an athlete, the day he has trained and prayed for, the day he gives his personal best to the people he serves.

He is in his early thirties, compact, bearded, dark hair cut in page-boy fashion, dark eyes intense and gentle. His arms and shoulders are uncommonly powerful, from lifting ninety-pound weights two or three times a week and from five years as a lumberjack. Bungay can hoist bags of cement that would stagger the average man.

It still seems to him a small miracle that he—an ordinary outport boy who once strayed from his Army—is back in its fold *and* leading a congregation. *And* in an outport where every sight and sound and smell and heartbeat is an echo of home.

If he were to veer uphill off the road this morning he could see it all. The shimmering cove itself, leading out to Placentia Bay. Boats at anchor. Homes for eight hundred people, mostly of wood or aluminum siding in white and greens and yellows, perched all up and down the hills. Post office, school (non-denominational now), bank, movie theater, grocery stores and the big fish processing plant where most men and many women of Arnold's Cove work. Fire department and municipal building, small fish plant, hardware store, cemetery, three churches besides his own.

Here, the Army shares the population with other faiths, but in Bungay's home town, Seal Cove-Fortune Bay, nearly everybody is a Salvationist.

"We go back there sometimes for a Sunday, myself and Mrs. Bungay," Ross is saying in that fine dancing Newfoundland accent with its lilt of the Irish, "and the place is *black* [with Army uniforms]! The whole shebang at eleven o'clock, out to the Army! All singers too. In Seal Cove if a woman's not tone-deaf, she's a songster."

There was a time when Bungay was not among them. On Sunday morning he'd be nursing his hangover from the dancing and drinking of Saturday night. His family were staunch Salvationists but like many boys of his time he drifted away from the Army. "I lived quite contrary to my upbringing but I never did escape."

The Army kept tugging at his sleeve. As a crewman aboard a fishing trawler out to sea one Sunday night, he heard his Uncle Archibald Bungay giving spiritual testimony over a radio station on shore. It seemed like a message to *him* and Ross was touched, but stayed with his rough life.

He took to the woods. Again and again—in a letter from Cousin Harold Bungay, a cadet at the training college in St. John's; in another broadcast by Uncle Arch; in the sure knowledge that his parents were praying for him every day—he felt the irresistible pull of Salvationism and the faithful folk of Seal Cove.

In 1976, his fourth year in the bush, he watched seven converts, mostly rough loggers, yield their lives to God in an Army church one night. "That began to eat away at the personal notion I had, that religion and faith were for senior citizens." A few weeks later he, too, was at the mercy seat—the penitent bench beneath the lectern at the front of every Army hall—for confession and forgiveness.

"Four days later, amidst the noise of my chain saw, I prayed and praised God, and preached in some sort of way. While there was no one to actually listen, I could imagine a congregation, and the overwhelming sense came that I *must* preach."

He turned away from drugs, booze and cigarettes. The smoking was hardest to shake. Some of his mates sympathized and tucked sticks of gum between the pages of his Bible to help him kick the habit. When he graduated from training college, the people of Seal Cove were as pleased as his own family. "When I go back, they invite me to speak. They monitor me, they run a measure on me. I'm one of the several officers they've turned out and I'm under a trial and a test."

This morning he proudly shows off his citadel, a long white former warehouse with a view of the cove. The local people bought and refurbished it for $90,000 (Army territorial headquarters helped out with a grant and a low-interest loan). Inside it is airy and white with warm wooden pews, a raised platform with podium, the mercy seat and beside it the holiness table draped with a crimson cloth, emblazoned in gold with words known to Salvationists around the world: "Holiness unto the Lord."

As Bungay leads the way to a big basement that will become meeting rooms for Home League (the Army women's auxiliary) and Sunday School, he runs a knowing eye over the citadel's underpinnings. He is a handyman. In an earlier post his citadel flooded every time it rained so Bungay, impatient with local inaction, dug a drainage ditch and laid weeping tile himself. Another time the cemetery needed a fence so he struck a deal with a local Anglican: the Anglican had timber, Bungay is a virtuoso with a chainsaw, so in exchange for his labor Bungay got one free log for the Army from every Skidoo-load.

Back at the Army's three-bedroom frame bungalow he shows the painting and fixing he's done, because he can't abide things unpainted and unfixed. He plucks Sheldon, age fifteen months, from a rubble of magazines hauled down from high places while his wife Brenda lays out a mighty breakfast. To be well-fed among Newfoundland's generous cooks, Ross says, "You just have to sit by and look pitiful."

Last night he worked on his sermon, then turned on the TV baseball game.

"I don't think the General would mind if I watched the Expos," he said.

"He'd probably watch them with you," said Brenda.

Now, uniform pressed and brushed, he walks back early to the citadel to compose and prepare himself for the service. At home Brenda, a Newfoundlander too, prepares a huge turkey dinner for after church, humming and singing hymns in her sweet clear voice. At training college her voice marked her as a superior talent, given some professional training.

But there will never be time to study music. An Army wife's days overflow with home, children, and church. For now, Brenda is content. She is in charge of the Arnold's Cove songsters, and every night something else goes on, often in her basement: youth group, Christian education, senior Bible study, corps cadets, choir practice, women's fellowship, men's fellowship. . . .

By 10:45 A.M. some fifty of the Cove's two hundred adherents—an average Sunday congregation—are trickling into the citadel. Townsmen, fishermen, a husband home from an offshore oil rig; friendly, well-dressed, a trifle shy. Sunbaked faces but no rubber-booted Newfie-joke stereotypes.

Several are in soldiers' uniforms, the foremost being Corps Sergeant Major (CSM) Llewellyn Guy, fisherman. The CSM is senior elder of the Army church but "Uncle Lew" is more than that. He is Mr. Salvation Army of Arnold's Cove.

The day before, we had driven over by the small fish plant to seek out "Uncle Lew" (respected elders in most Newfoundland outports are called "Uncle" and "Aunt"). He is sixty-three, bald, bespectacled, and the picture of goodness. Not one sour glance or mean thought mars his lean kind face. When vandals tore down one of the new iron railings on the citadel's front steps, decent Uncle Lew could not comprehend such mindless destruction.

We coax him to tell how the Army began in Arnold's Cove. It was 1895 when Henry Guy, his distant relative, held the first open-air service on a hill overlooking the cove. Today Uncle Lew's wife hangs her washing right on that hallowed spot.

"As long as I can remember there was Army in our family," he said.

The Army appointed its first officer in 1900 and officers were treated with reverence.

"When I was a boy you tipped your cap to the minister and gave him his title," Uncle Lew said. "If I'd said 'Hello Ross' in those days, Grandfather'd have whipped me! Oh yes, my son [in the outports "my son" is synonymous with "friend"], you had respect of place."

All the same, it was the locals who kept the church strong and if it wasn't a Peach it was a Guy. Henry Guy was CSM until 1918. Malcolm "Uncle Mackey" Peach succeeded him for twenty-five years, including twelve lean years when there was no officer. That was during the Depression, when the Army suffered like everything else and the Home League shut down because the women couldn't afford the ten-cent monthly fee.

Uncle John Peach, the next CSM, was illiterate but everybody said he preached a "hot" sermon.

"We had no learning. I don't imagine any of them fellows went over Grade 4," said Uncle Lew, who got to Grade 3 himself before he started work at age nine. "I was working on a highway, carrying what they called 'small steel' to a forge. Only $1.80 a day but I had to get it to help Dad."

He stared out the car window at Newfoundland's hard-scrabble grass and little trees, remembering. "The people lived in humble homes. They shared, y'know. The table, as the sayin' goes, was always spread. They worked hard but there was always time to chat and there was always that time for worship."

In 1943 Uncle Lew became Young People's Sergeant Major; in 1957, the CSM. There was no officer again until 1968 so Lew preached three Sunday services himself. "Oh I should say, it's different comin' up with the gospel message today as it was back there. Different in speaking today, different in pronunciation."

At the time, he was working down the telegraph line as a cook. "You had to think about your sermon during the week. I'd get home Sunday morning just about the time it got light. I'd take the morning service and maybe Sunday school.

"You speak as you feel and I guess what learning you had, you give them. Maybe it's like the fella playin' music, if nobody knew notes it was fine, but anybody knew notes it was different! Then the night service and the taxi waitin' for you at 9:30 and you'd go to work again. . . ."

On the way home this day, he let drop another memory: of how once in an abandoned Catholic church in the neighborhood he found a barrel-stave wrapped in red flannel. It was where the people had knelt to pray. "It was worn through from years of use. To me that was sacred. It wasn't my church but it was my God."

No wonder the congregation beams affectionately back at him this Sunday morning, as he awaits the Bungays on the platform, smiling down in his Sergeant Major's uniform. The same families of generations past are still the backbone of the corps. Harvey Peach hand-painted the Salvationist crest on the outside wall. Congregation and songsters are full of Peaches, Guys and their relatives. The band—eleven brass, two accordions, two guitars, bass drum, kettle-drum—is led by Clyde Guy, town clerk, Uncle Lew's son and self-taught musician.

"He couldn't tell you a chord on the accordion," says Ross. "No, my son, he would not be able to tell you where a G was! Time and again I've heard him say, 'I can play it once but I can't play it twice.' He don't know where he's goin', just that he's goin'!"

In their backroom office Ross and Brenda bow in prayer. Ross flicks and fusses his uniform with a lint brush one more time and they stride out to the oom-pah of the band.

"Welcome to the house of the Lord again!" Brenda begins from the lectern. "To those of you who are visiting we extend a warm welcome, and hope that as you worship with us the Lord will indeed enrich and bless you."

The band strikes up and the hand-claps pick up the beat: "O glorious hope of perfect love, It lifts me up to things above...." Who cares if the music skids a half-note off-register now and then. It is a hearty, happy sound.

A voice from the congregation leads in impromptu prayer. From the platform Uncle Lew murmurs a reverent flow of Amens and Thank you, Lords. The juniors sing, with Brenda leading; the congregation claps through the "glory, glory, hallelujah" refrain. Then she leads the excellent adult songsters, in close-knit harmony—so good that, at the end, Ross impulsively calls for applause.

A female voice from the congregation calls out: "He's a friend and companion, I thank Him for saving me and I thank Him for keeping me another week. And if you're here this morning and you don't serve this Jesus, well let me tell you, you're missing out on the greatest opportunity in life. Why don't you give your life over to Him...?"

"Amen!" cries Uncle Lew.

"... May you seek and find Him and may He bless you."

"Praise the Lord!"

Others offer "testimony"—a reaffirmation of their faith in their own words. Bungay holds it all to about ten minutes, but an evening of testimony can easily run to midnight.

More songs. There is a rolling lilt to the music. Any stranger with a semblance of church heritage can pick up the tunes in a minute. They are buried in your consciousness: tunes your mother sang, tunes from other churches in other places, even tunes with a music-hall rhythm.

Ross steps forward with his sermon. His face shines out his pleasure. When he speaks, it is clear that Lieutenant Bungay is *right* for Arnold's Cove. Oh, they'd accept a St. John's boy for their officer, or maybe even a Mainlander. They'd be courteous, and in time he might work his way into the community. But Bungay? Well, you know he's *from* here; he's been through hard work and weather; he knows that the land and water are everything and the Mainland is a place apart.

"Brothers, I know some theologians who do great with the book but who do nothing with the living. It's true! God doesn't wait for you to get a headful of knowledge. God blesses you in your ignorance, blesses *me* in my ignorance and if he didn't bless me that way, comrades, I would not be here this morning. . . . That's the way the Lord blessed me. I had no time to fill my head with the facts. And, praise God, like the old saying goes, 'I'll not miss Heaven by eighteen inches with a headful of knowledge and a heart that has not been transformed!' I let the knowledge that I have of Jesus Christ guide my footsteps. He took my filthy rags and He gave me a pure robe of His religious holiness. . . ."

"Hallelujah!"

Bungay tells a workingman's tale about a new church with a ceiling forty-five feet high. Looked like a flawless piece of work until they turned on a spotlight: "And when that light hit the ceiling you could see flaws even at forty-five feet! And the builder said, 'No workmanship will stand a high intensity light!' And the minister says, 'There's one bit of work will, and that's the work of grace.'

"One of these days when you and I get to Heaven we're not going to be inspected with a forty-watt bulb. We're going to be inspected with the high intensity of the holiness of the Lord Jesus Christ. Every little white lie will be an ugly stain. Every little bit of selfishness will be an embarrassing spot. Every immoral deed will be a flaw in the fabric of our lives. If we serve God faithfully in the storms and in the shadows and if we serve God faithfully in the sunshine, when we get to the spotlight of God's grace we'll be able to stand there without fear."

"Hallelujah!"

They close with the stately cadence of "I'm Going to Live the Way God Wants Me to Live." And the people file into the sunshine, renewed, refreshed, ready to serve the Lord for another week in Arnold's Cove.

"My association with the Army has been intimate since the age of fifteen, but I was never a Salvationist," Joey Smallwood is saying. He leans back in his leather chair, shirtsleeved, his sharp birdlike gaze peering from horn-rimmed spectacles. Through the window at his back is a splendid view of Signal Hill. Joey has earned the view: twenty-three years this island's premier, the man who led Newfoundland into Confederation, loved by many, hated by some.

Now, at eighty-three, he works on his multi-volume encyclopedia of Newfoundland in this big cluttered office in St. John's. Still the fans and supplicants flock in. Joey pauses to autograph a book for two young women ("That autograph will be worth $1,000 someday") and pose for their Instamatic.

"I was the oldest of a family of thirteen children," he begins. "Most of the world was poor. Newfoundland was a poor little poverty-stricken rock. The oldest child of a very poor family had to get a job."

Joey is hitting his oratorical stride, with pregnant pauses and the calculated whack of desktop for emphasis.

"And so, having outrageous ambitions to be a newspaper reporter, I earned $1.50 a week as a printer's devil on a weekly newspaper. Weeeell . . ." He unrolls the word like a red carpet.". . . at $1.50 a week and walking to work every morning there was the problem of eating in the middle of the day. And I solved it, or at least the Salvation Army solved it. They had a soup kitchen on George Street—I can see it now in my mind. Besides soup you could get a cup of tea and some bread, with maybe a little jam on it. It was not aristocratic food, but their soup kitchen was just what I needed. It cost eight or ten cents a meal, six days a week, so almost half of my $1.50 went to the Army."

He pauses with impeccable timing, setting up the laugh he is about to earn: "Which means, I suppose, that I was one of the earliest contributors to the Salvation Army. From there on to this moment, I have had the warmest possible kind of feeling for the Army."

As premier he kept a picture of General William Booth in his office. Well then, Mr. Newfoundland, tell us why the Sally Ann so captured this island's affections.

"Life was simple and lonely," Smallwood says. "There weren't many ministers, not enough to serve all those little communities. In comes an evangelist, holds a service in a fish store or on a wharf. No church, but the people are given somewhere to go."

Smallwood grew up a Methodist, studied Methodism and claims one of the world's largest collections of books on or by founder John Wesley.

"By the 1890s and 1900s the great evangelical drive of Methodism had become diluted and . . ." (Fist smashes into palm) ". . . in came the Salvation Army doing exactly the same thing! The Methodists got so angry but it was just what *they* had done to the Church of England and what the Church of England did to the Roman Catholics. And where do the Pentecostals get some of their people today? The Salvation Army! Which indicates there is always a need for the evangelical. The Salvation Army today is incomparably more respectable than it used to be."

By "respectable" Smallwood means, of course, more traditional. Which may seem strange to a Mainlander listening to the morning service at Arnold's Cove, yet that service is mild compared to the

Army's evangelical past. And among the five citadels in St. John's—notably St. John's Temple, a $1.5 million architectural gem with pitched roofs, soaring windows and comfortable padded pews—Sunday services are even more restrained. The temple caters primarily to three hundred mid-upper class families including lawyers and judges, with a few sleek sports cars in its parking lot.

"Most people here are your native St. John's man—a 'townie' as opposed to a 'Bay bye'," says Major Kevin Rideout, the pastor. "The style is different. If you took out the uniforms and the brass band, any Anglican or United Church person could feel at home here."

Other local citadels have stronger degrees of Sally Ann evangelism, for newly arrived "Bay byes" (boys from the Bay, *any* bay). St. John's also has those familiar Army services unneeded in most outports: Harbour Light, thrift store, Grace Hospital and a rescue mission for down-and-outers. This last is the Springdale Corps, near the waterfront, with Sunday services especially for people who aren't comfortable anywhere else. Its parishioners have included certain ladies of the night who, in their heyday, were a bigger tourist attraction than Signal Hill.

Springdale's welfare service caters to as many poor and despairing people as any other Canadian city. Ninety-five percent are Roman Catholics, the largest religious denomination downtown, but this makes no difference to the Army.

"You have to try to save the next generation," says corps officer Captain Everett Barrow. "We try to get the kids into church, any church, not necessarily ours."

Newfoundland schools are integrated now and most Salvationists bowed gracefully to the change. Integration gave Army outports some badly needed access to large high schools. But it also tossed their children together with others of different or no religions; others who smoke, drink or use drugs. Enlightening, yes. Exposure to temptations of the flesh, yes.

Major Bill Ratcliffe is the kind of man who glitters when he walks. He stands well over six feet, with blond hair, white smile, craggy good looks, infectious humor, and bottomless energy. An aura of leadership hovers around him. He could have been chairman of IBM, president of the Royal Bank, or prime minister of Canada, had he set his mind to it.

He has never wanted to be other than a soldier of God, like his officer-father. "I think of him now and wonder, 'How can I ever be like him?' He was the ultimate—compassionate, tender, discerning. As I get older I long to have those attributes."

Many would say that Ratcliffe has them in abundance. From 11:00 A.M. to 2:00 P.M. on a typical weekday, his shoe-box office at

Major Bill Ratcliffe is pastor, friend, and surrogate father to nearly four hundred Salvationist students at Memorial University, St. John's. (Photo by Bill White, Memorial University)

Memorial University in St. John's is a refuge for up to 150 students. They drift through to say hello, cache books, eat lunch squatting against a wall or arrange a private meeting. He is the Army's only full-time university chaplain in Canada and, with nearly four hundred Salvationist students on campus, his days and evenings are crammed.

"It's *very* exciting," Ratcliffe says. "It's no hardship for me to spend ten or twelve hours a day with teenagers, no hardship at all. I just enjoy teenagers. I'm not putting on an act. You can't fool them. If you think you can, you're the one who's being fooled."

He is their pastor, friend and surrogate father; easy and colloquial, neither too intimate nor condescending. Most of them are fresh from the cocoon of the outports. Suddenly, from a community of a few dozen they are adrift among thousands who are infinitely more worldly in terms of drinking, smoking, and drugs.

"When I came here I was not quite seventeen," says Edith Rideout, a small redhead with a soft voice. She is from Seal Cove-Fortune Bay, the solid Salvationist outport that produced Ross Bungay. "I didn't know *one* person in St. John's. It was very lonely."

Now, for kids like her, there is Ratcliffe. He helps them find boarding houses, often with other Salvationist students. "I don't want them to live exclusive lives, divorced from society, but they have enough to cope with on campus. I like to think that they go back at night to a place that has some stability, some love perhaps."

He packs their weeks with meetings of the Salvation Army Students Fellowship club, guest speakers on everything from cults to euthanasia, barbecues, swim nights, roller skating, ice skating. There's always something to do when others are having beer bashes.

Ratcliffe spends whole evenings phoning Salvationist students in the city (names supplied by outport corps officers or anxious parents): "Haven't seen you in the office yet. Where are you living? How are you doing? What'd you have for supper? Do you need a ride? Do you want to come over to the house?"

The Army gave him a home as fine as any corporation executive's, with a big basement where he hosts up to eighty Salvationist kids of an evening. "We don't provide big feeds. A drink and a biscuit is all. It's the fellowship that's important."

Above all, he ministers to their inner hurts.

"I guess my daily prayer is that I will be available, that I will be compatible, that I will be seen as a person who is caring. My credibility is essential and of course they know that what they tell me I don't even tell my wife. I've lived in a number of societies around the world—it would take a bit to shock me and I think they know that."

There's not much that Bill and Marion Ratcliffe haven't seen. They met at training college, graduated in 1956, served in Newfoundland, and went to Pakistan for ten years. As the only whites in a Pakistani village they lived in mud huts, slept outdoors on the hot nights and depended on the guards at each corner of the village to protect them from marauders. Ratcliffe learned to read and write three regional languages and became principal of the school.

Life was primitive and often dangerous. Flipping through their photo album, he pauses at a picture of an elderly Pakistani. "He was being attacked by three guys with a knife. I took the knife away from them and sent them packing." He tells the story not for its heroics but for the punch-line. "When I asked him why he was fighting back, he explained he was protecting his piece of pavement, next to the garbage cans, where he would get his next meal!"

When the Indian-Pakistan war broke out the Ratcliffes were caught in the middle. For a while they took to the trenches; eventually Marion and the children were evacuated. Ratcliffe still can not talk easily of that time, but wants to serve there again someday.

For now the university post is his meat and drink. "Every task I've been given in the Army, I've always said there aren't enough hours in the day. People have said, 'I'm sure you'll get bored.' I've never been bored in my entire life."

It's indoctrination time for a fresh crop of cadets at the St. John's training college. Major Margaret Hammond is telling them how to respond in church when people come to the mercy seat. "Be sure to take your Bible. Don't pounce on your prey! . . ." (She's trying to ease their earnest attention with a little humor, and it works.) "Be very discreet: usually a man should minister to a man, a woman to a woman, because physical contact can be misinterpreted. Remember that tears are good therapy but not necessarily a sign of repentance, not a sign that you reached that person's mind."

Assistant Principal Major Ira Barrow offers tips on door-to-door visitation. Be courteous, he tells them. Don't walk on the lawn. Don't set up negative feelings. And that goes for personal hygiene: use deodorant and breath mints.

If you see them peeking at you from behind the front curtains, don't pretend you didn't. Smile and nod. Look for children's toys, a new car in the driveway, ideas for conversation-starters.

"They may ask you about *your* family," Barrow says earnestly, "but get the conversation back quickly, because that's a device the Devil has to get you off-track." All the same, he adds, don't be a hard-sell evangelist the first time in a stranger's house. "Your message is: 'I care about you,' and you build a relationship for future conversations."

Then Principal Major David Hammond gets to the very core of the Army's being, with a lecture on evangelism.

"Write it down on your paper, on your walls: 'a passion for souls' is essential to a Salvationist," he implores. "The fire of God in our souls will conquer anything. When the fire of evangelism goes out we begin to die!"

So now, on a September Sunday night, those cadets are in the outport of Dildo for a taste of that old-time religion. The school gym is packed to the rafters with people from five outports. The founder himself would have loved a night like this. The band is large, loud and professional; the beat, a rollicking double-time, even faster than in Arnold's Cove.

And the cadets? Inspired! Some are leaping on their toes, arms flung high. "Praise God!" "Amen!" "Hallelujah!"

They lead off the testimony, to coax the timid in the crowd. "I was a prodigal daughter!" a young cadet cries. "I was an alcoholic!" a male classmate from Calgary calls out. "I look over this crowd and say, 'thank God I'm home.' I was away from home a long time."

It begins as a trickle: the cadets kneel at the mercy seat, one by one. A fervent blond boy comes away in tears; a friend throws an arm around his shoulder. Suddenly that trickle turns into a flood. From all over the congregation they come—soldiers, laymen, a young man and woman, old men—to kneel at the mercy seat. The whole front of the gym is crammed with them, and with the officers and cadets who come to kneel beside them with prayer and support. And the torrent of music goes on.

At last they stand and move away, clasping hands, some with arms around each others shoulders, a young woman red-eyed and tear stained, maybe from the catharsis of her decision, or the enormity of it, or maybe from a burden lifted.

And the drums crash, the brass shrills out to Heaven, the tambourines are a swirling blur of ribbons, and the voices soar triumphantly into the closing hymn:

> My Jesus, I love Thee, I know Thou art mine
> For Thee all the pleasures of sin I resign . . .

Oh yes, my son. The fire of Sally Ann burns bright in Newfoundland.

6

The Holy War: What Salvationists Believe

In the ferment of an outport Sunday night there's not the slightest doubt that the Salvation Army is a church. Elsewhere in Canada, to the Army's occasional chagrin, the non-Salvationist is frankly puzzled.

Church, sect, or social agency? Some Salvationists speak of "church" but more often call their place of worship a "hall," "temple," or "citadel." It may literally be a hall, or a conventional-looking church, or a streamlined wonder with pitched roof, acres of glass, and a round or sexagonal inner sanctuary. Instead of a "pulpit" it has a "reading desk" or lectern. It does not practice baptism or communion.

Against this seeming-confusion their social work is clearly imprinted on our consciousness. We rarely think of the Army in religious terms. "They do good work," we say, and leave it at that.

Yet they are *clergy*, above all else. The Army was a founding member of the World Council of Churches. (It suspended full membership in 1978, protesting the WCC's granting of funds to the Rhodesian Patriotic Front: it could not condone the use of violence, even to fight the evils of racism.)

Every Army officer is an ordained minister, able to preach a sermon, marry you, or bury you. To some degree every Army church service has the ingredients of a Sunday in Arnold's Cove: prayer, Scripture reading, songs (occasionally called "hymns"), a sermon (sometimes called the "message"), testimony, and a collection. By its own definition the Army is "a fellowship of people who have accepted Jesus Christ as their personal Saviour and Lord and whose common aim is to induce others to subject themselves to the lordship of Christ."

Salvationists rarely proseletyze or "push" their religion on outsiders, in the context of their social work.

"I like to feel that we have enough diversity of programs so that if you are not terribly religious you can still find things that attract you," says Major Bill Ratcliffe in St. John's. "Maybe after a while you look around you and say, 'My word, if *he* goes to those Bible study and prayer sessions and is still a human, there can't be too much holier-than-thou about the Army.' "

Nevertheless they are eager to share their faith, and sometimes wonder if they downplay it. "Here is the dichotomy," says Commissioner Arthur Pitcher. "We're committed to a wide spectrum of social service. We can't afford to weaken it. But there is danger of clouding our reason for doing it. So it is time to make it clear that we are a spiritual organization with great social outreach as an expression of our love for God and our love for people."

Partly for that reason, Pitcher proclaimed 1984 as the "Year of Evangelism." Also, he thinks Canada like most of the world is "in a moral morass. The time is ripe for the Salvation Army to identify itself as having a message of salvation and hope and redemption."

Is the Army really different from other religious or social service organizations? Theologically, it is in the mainstream.

"If you took our eleven points of doctrine and put them before an Anglican, he would feel quite comfortable with them," says Pitcher.

Those points show that Salvationists believe: in one God, in the Holy Trinity—Father, Son and Holy Ghost, in the immortality of the soul, resurrection of the body, a last judgment and "in the eternal happiness of the righteous and in the endless punishment of the wicked." The Bible, Old and New Testaments, is "the source from which all Army doctrine is derived" but few if any Army people take it all literally. Today's adherents, unlike many in William Booth's day, do not accept a hell of fire and brimstone presided over by a scarlet person with a forked tail.

Although the points of doctrine do not mention the virgin birth, many Salvationists accept it. Even the Army's non-observance of baptism and communion came only after a long and agonizing internal tussle. For several years founder Booth, who came from the Methodist Church, continued to practice the sacraments. This drew increasing criticism from his own ranks and beyond. Traditional churchmen were outraged because Booth insisted on the equality of women, and for women to administer the sacraments was unthinkable in Victorian England.

At the same time, Booth's own officers, notably George Scott

Railton, vehemently insisted that there was only one true baptism: the baptism of the spirit. All ceremonies that seemed to set a priest or a ritual between God and the soul were a hindrance, he said. In time the Booths agreed. After fourteen years of soul-searching, William Booth in 1895 laid down the new rules, although emphasizing that Salvationists do not *disclaim* the sacraments. As a result, most

The infant dedication ceremony, "hallowed by the profoundest sentiments of love and loyalty."

(but not all) of his followers have been comfortable without baptism and communion for generations.

"The language of the [infant] dedication service is now venerable with age and hallowed by the profoundest sentiments of love and loyalty," writes John Coutts, formerly a major in the British Army, in his book, *The Salvationists.*

"It is the same with other symbols too: the flag . . . the sound of a brass band . . . the informal delight in God which characterizes Army worship at its best—all these are evocative symbols that convey the mystery of God's presence. For sacraments are above all drama, and the Army, finding little meaning in the old classics, has sought to invent new dramas of its own. But like other Christians, Salvationists who find their own symbols profoundly meaningful do not always remember that to the uninitiated they may appear odd, alien or downright daft."

"Our difference is that we are positively spiritual," says Commissioner Pitcher. "We feel that the spiritual sacramental position—whatsoever you do in word or deed in the name of the Lord Jesus—is much more vital."

Beyond the visible differences in form of worship there is, thinks Captain Iain Trainor of Halifax, a more fundamental one: that God *made* Salvationists different.

"Paul in describing Christ to the Corinthians said that the human body is of many different parts, each with a function," Trainor says. "I suggest that the Christian churches are like that too; that each has a different gift. Perhaps intellectualism is the Presbyterian; emotionalism the Evangelical; ceremony the Anglican. And we believe that God raised up the Salvation Army for the salvation of the world. We have been likened to a Protestant version of the Trappist monks. We bring practical Christianity to people."

The analogy may be simplistic but the Salvationist *does* try to live his faith each day, much as he feels Christ would live His. It is an appealing stance, to an onlooker. Time and again those who have rejected churches, refuted God, and spurned prayer, look at the Army—gritting its teeth and dirtying its hands at the bedrock of humanity—and whisper inside, "If *this* is what Christianity is all about, maybe I should try it."

Ron Pumphrey grew up in a poor Catholic family in Harbour Grace, Newfoundland. His father, a World War I veteran working in the Bell Island mines as a cook, remembered the Salvation Army as "good people" but Ron and the other Catholic kids used to tag behind a local Army soldier and provoke her with their chant:

> The Salvation Army made the Devil run
> Up the stock pile and down the Number One

The "Number One" was a mine tunneled out under the sea. At fifteen Pumphrey worked there himself, while picking up his schooling in bits and pieces. He had a poetical bent and was no good at sports. "I was an ugly-looking son-of-a-gun too. Big red pimply nose. I kept this mirror in my pocket. 'Please teacher, can I leave the room?' She thought I had bad kidneys but I'd go to the toilet and take out the mirror and see if my nose was any worse."

He was not the sort to back away from the world, so he became a warrior: drank hard, fought hard—"I had to make sure I was very argumentative and got in the first blow"—and became a Newfoundland celebrity as newspaper columnist, publisher, radio broadcaster, and St. John's alderman.

Over the years he fought Catholicism more than he accepted it. About 1980 he became a Christian in the gospel sense and went looking for a church. He liked the Army music and the compassionate officers in St. John's Springdale Street corps ("this naked church, people coming in from the streets, the smells of urine and stale clothing were nauseous"). Still floundering, he knelt one day at home and asked for guidance.

"At that moment I said I'm going to *join* the Springdale corps. I couldn't tell a major from a captain but I *knew* this had to be it. This was a revelation from God. My mind and spirit were absolutely satisfied. It was a very cold January day, a mauzy day as we say in Newfoundland. I was filled with tears, I was absolutely enraptured. And as I walked into the dressing room off the bedroom there was a burst of sun that absolutely transfixed me."

He wrote in his kitchen calendar, "The Day I Met God." With an enormous effort he stopped smoking, and began studying for soldiership. "When I was a kid trapped on this island, I yearned to get out into the world," says Pumphrey, now fifty-three. "But I have never sensed this excitement. All other excitements were finite. This is not."

Pumphrey the warrior will not be out of step in the Sally Ann. Of course, he has already discovered that the Army prefers its troops to avoid physical combat. Soon after his conversion Pumphrey came out of the temple to discover a hit-and-run driver had wrecked his car.

"The next day when the cops called and said 'We have the man' I reverted to the flesh. I said to myself, 'I'm gonna have him, face to face.' "

He phoned the man, began bellowing, then to his utter astonishment heard himself say, "I hope you weren't hurt . . .?" The man was half-crazed with personal problems; when he wrecked

Pumphrey's car he was on his way to drive into St. John's harbor. Pumphrey ended up befriending him.

Auxiliary Captain John Miller was beaten and had his car stolen while serving on the Six Nations Indian Reserve in Ontario, yet asked to be posted back when his term was up. Salvationist Ken Clarke was mugged by three youths while taking a late-night walk in Ottawa.

"If I could have got my hands out of my overcoat pockets in time I'd probably have bopped them back," he says. "But in a day or so I cooled off and my reaction was to look into a program to help street kids."

Yet this is not to say the Army is impotent. Once at an open-air meeting in Toronto's Phillips Square a violent drunk smashed down a chair amidst a little group of the faithful. One of the uniformed soldiers, a karate expert, instantly seized the man's arm in a nerve-numbing grip, gave him two sharp agonizing kicks in the shin as a warning, then gently led him aside and defused him with conversation.

"We will defend ourselves if we have to," says Major Maxwell Ryan, pastor of Toronto's downtown temple, "but we know that abusive people are acting abnormally and we try not to strike back."

The same gentle persuasion is the Army style on controversial issues. It never gets into partisan politics. It refuses to attach its name to extremist civil liberties causes, although it is often quietly working behind scenes to cure the same ills.

"Our mission is to the people of a country, whatever its political stripe," says Pitcher. "We have to be free to move across all political boundaries."

The Army speaks out against Sunday shopping at the civic level, lotteries at the provincial level, nuclear war internationally—but always from a moral rather than political stance. It condones abortion only if it will save the mother's life or prevent serious physical or mental injury. It is painfully grappling with the reality of homosexuality in today's society.

For an organization so far ahead of its time in most aspects of social change, the Army has been fairly unforgiving of homosexuality. One official guideline views it as "a serious threat to the integrity, quality and solidarity of society as a whole"; deviance rather than predilection; a sickness that could be cured. If a homosexual renounces and abandons the lifestyle, perhaps with the aid of medical, social and psychiatric treatment, he or she *might* be considered acceptable. But, says *Chosen To Be A Soldier*, a ninety-one-page summary of regulations, "homosexual practices unrenounced render a person unacceptable as a Salvation Army soldier, just as acts of immorality between heterosexual persons do." In short: homosexuality is a sin.

Latterly, the Army seems to be struggling toward middle ground.

"We should seek, in the spirit of Jesus Christ, to understand and help the homosexual," says a recent Army positional statement, "differentiating between homosexual acts and the innate tendency which may or may not lead to that activity. Psychological deviance in sex, so long as it does not express itself in homosexual acts, is not blameworthy nor should it be allowed to create guilt . . ."

"We have to believe in redemption," adds Captain Linda Bond, in Toronto, stressing that these are her personal views. "All we need is an assurance that the [homosexual] person has been delivered from his problem. And if God, who can make an adulterer a good man, can not clear up a homosexual, then I don't think He is God."

The Army would never turn away a gay person in need of help. However, no *practicing* homosexuals—say, a couple living quiet and otherwise exemplary lives—could become Army officers or soldiers. This has driven a number out on their own.

The young man's voice over the phone was at first wary and barely audible. He identified himself only by first name and asked that I not use the name of his Toronto-based group. He is a founding member of some thirty former or still-active Salvationists, male and female—and they are gay.

In their beginnings, two years ago, they were involved in litigation with the Salvation Army, because they had been using a variation of the Army's name. They have a new name now, with no Army connotations.

"Basically we are a support group," he said. "We're not recruiting and we don't want to convey that perception. We are just helping people deal with their sexual orientation and the conflicts it brings up—the rigid moral beliefs of an Army upbringing combined with the feelings they are going through about themselves."

They meet sometimes for Bible study or discussions, and they have a phone line where others can call in to talk about their struggles. One particular difficulty: after they leave the Army they have few or no social contacts, because all their prior social life has been Salvation Army. Some call in from phone booths, terrified of being found out by a spouse or a fellow Army member.

"In theory, you can remain in the Army as long as you are not a *practicing* gay," the man said, "but in fact it isn't always that simple."

Some of the group, he says, have tried to talk about it with their corps officers but the latter won't discuss it. Even so, the man adds, the Canadian Salvation Army's attitude toward homosexuals is not as unyielding as in the United States.

"As far as our organization is concerned," he says, "the Army is just ignoring us."

Although the Army keeps a relatively low profile on most controversial issues, compared to some churches, Salvationists feel a sense of achievement.

"At the risk of sounding biased," says Major Don Ritson, now of St. John's, "I know of no other organization that provides so much opportunity for people who want to serve God and their fellow man and hope to make this world a better place in which to live."

In *Chosen to Be A Soldier,* an entire chapter is devoted to holiness, a state almost as difficult to explain as it is to attain. The Army believes that salvation does not stop simply with God's forgiveness of sin and sinners. It must be followed by a new standard of living.

The Army therefore styles itself as "both a revival and a holiness movement." An entire 1983 issue of the *War Cry* was also devoted to the subject. Theirs really *is* a holy war.

What *is* holiness? A writer in that special issue said in part: "It is a quality of life which is marked by love, genuine concern for others before self; by purity, an integrity which shuns every form of duplicity; and by humility, a joyous sense of self-forgetfulness which is the essence of freedom."

"Christlikeness" is the best description, concludes the Army handbook. A holy life is constant fellowship with Christ. Anyone emulating His life and character may be deemed holy. "It is marked by the glad acceptance of the greatest commandment of all, the commandment to be loving, even towards people whose attitudes could provoke to unconcern, bitterness, self-assertion, enmity, strife and the like . . ."

The average Salvationist grapples with the concept in all humanity. "Holiness is almost like a magnifying glass," said Lieutenant Ellen Whatman in a sermon to the Hazelton, BC, corps one summer Sunday in 1983. "The closer we get to it, the closer we see our own errors, the flaws in our character."

Conspicuous holiness, adds Major Bill Ratcliffe, "is not what Christianity is about. It's living life to the fullest, in a world that's trying to cut you off at the knees!"

God and Christ are friends and daily facts in the lives of Salvationists. They speak so openly and naturally of the Deity ("The Lord called me," "The Lord put it all together"), that it is hard even for non-believers to feel scorn or embarrassment. If anything breeds skepticism, it is that tendency to attribute to the Lord those things that others would call coincidence. (Other Christians do this too, but it comes as more surprising from an Army so pragmatic on most matters.)

In Saint John, NB, for example, Salvationists tell of—what? A miracle? John Tremblay, a young civilian worker in the men's social center, was immersed in work one day when a hobo of the old school came in—complete with bundle slung over his shoulder on a stick. His name was Yuri and he was filthy from days on the road.

"Take a shower, take this form and get fresh clothes," Tremblay said briskly, his nose in his work. There was a heavy silence. Yuri haughtily shredded the form, wafted the scraps in Tremblay's face and stalked out.

Tremblay was so upset he went off by himself and prayed. That night he drove thirty miles home as usual, including a ferry ride across the Kennebecasis River. Next morning on the road outside his house was—Yuri.

"You're not!" cried Tremblay's wife, reading his mind.

"I *must*," the young man said. He hailed the hobo and asked his forgiveness. Would Yuri care for a lift into the Army center for meals, clothes, a shower *(if he wished?)*. Yuri accepted graciously. In a day or so he moved on, clean and regal.

Was it coincidence that brought the man almost to Tremblay's door? Or a miracle that gave Tremblay a chance to make amends? Salvationists in Saint John are sure it was the hand of God.

Whether or not you accept miracles, theirs is an amiable and often enviable relationship with the Almighty. In Halifax Captain Betty Lewis—a lively brunette, and the sister of Lieutenant Henry Legge—has been known to invoke God's help in finding a parking space, when she's rushing her kids somewhere by car.

"Oh, Lord, please give me a space!" she'll say. And her son Todd, unimpressed with her driving ability, murmurs, "Oh Lord, it's my mother, give her *five* spaces!" They are a devout family but they see nothing inconsistent in worshipping God *and* being His friend.

"It is a serious mistake to be so preoccupied with living *for* God as not to have time for living *with* God, adoring Him, listening to Him, worshipping Him and consciously resting in His love," says *Chosen To Be A Soldier.*

The Archbishop of Canterbury once remarked, "Every Salvationist has in wonderful measure the gift of joy. . . . I don't think I've ever seen a gloomy member of the Salvation Army."

Is the joy real? How can so many people be so happy so much of the time?

"If you preach the forgiveness of sins, and preach that God through Christ can bring you peace and joy, there's no reason why you shouldn't live it," says Major Stuart Booth, of Quebec City. "And I think the reason there *is* joy is when people have released a burden."

Joy to the contrary, adds Booth, Army officers endure a lot of stress. On the one hand they strive for personal grace; on the other they do daily battle with every kind of sorrow, pitfall and temptation. The path of holiness is not an easy one, and some fall by the way.

7

The Everlasting
Salvation Machine:
Dropouts and Dissent

One evening in early 1984 I phoned Reverend Jim Girling,
now a United Church minister in Turner Valley, Alberta, to say I
wanted to discuss why he'd quit the Salvation Army.

"I wish somebody from the *Army* would ask me that!" he said,
with a trace of asperity.

He hastily added that he is not bitter but later, when we met, it
was clear that the experience still gnaws at him. "It took me a long
time to get over it," he admitted. Given the Army's and its officers'
deep mutual commitment, a parting inevitably leaves scars. According to Girling, "The Army has lost excellent people, hundreds of
them." Army headquarters acknowledges only that some drop out
from time to time.

Girling is a serious man of early middle age, with neatly trimmed
moustache in a lean intelligent face. He was born in Calgary and
drawn to Salvationism by a brother in Vancouver. He entered
training college in 1966 and there the friction began.

"Training was not a happy experience for me," he recalls. "I
asked questions, I rebelled, I couldn't see the sense of controlling our
time and movements down to the last minute. Frequently I was told,
'We have a negative report on you, Girling.'"

At college he met Dorothy, his wife-to-be, a third generation
Salvationist whose officer-parents had divorced (her father is still in
the Army). Even she, with her Army background, was surprised by
the barriers to courtship (more so fifteen years ago than today).
Once Girling phoned her at the college from a booth in a nearby
shopping plaza, to get a bit of private conversation.

They married after graduation and spent seven years in three different posts. Those frequent reassignments bothered him: "There's no way you can build anything in a corps in just two years." He also reached the point where "I couldn't go through another Red Shield campaign." Normally, a percentage of Red Shield collections by a local corps would go back to that corps for its needs. His third and last corps, Brockville, Ontario, was solvent, Girling says.

"We don't need it for the band or the corps," he told his commander. "Can't we funnel it all into welfare?" He says he was refused.

Most of all Girling missed the sacraments (although he knew the Army's stance on them when he joined up). He grew increasingly disenchanted. After deep and agonizing thought, Girling finally resigned. Naturally there were no benefits or pension after such brief service, so he and Dorothy "left without a dime." He says that he was then "treated like dirt" by most Army people for having left the fold, although certain officer friends stuck by him. This does not sound like the Salvation Army most of us know, I pointed out.

"Sometimes I think they treat outsiders better than their own," Girling said.

He spent a year working in an Ontario iron foundry, was invited to take services in a small United Church, went on to get degrees in theology and has served, reasonably happily, for eight years. Time has even mellowed his memories of the Army. His wife sings in a Calgary Temple and he's in touch with many of his old friends again.

"We enjoyed our stay in the Army for all its frustrations," Girling insists. "It's still the most practical of all churches in many ways. And I think the Army has tremendous opportunities."

Some friends think he'll go back; that the Sally Ann stays forever in your blood. Girling says it's out of the question unless the Army some day accepts the sacraments. Maybe, he reflects, back then as a young man he was "worshipping the uniform" when he signed up for training. Maybe the very idea of being in the Army kept him from seeing the realities.

"One thing is for sure," he adds emphatically. "We won't ever let ourselves fall in love with a *denomination* again."

Jim Girling's case is not necessarily representative—obviously, he was a burr under the Army's saddle—but some of the things that bothered him are concerns also to many within the ranks. Officers who deeply love the Army criticize it among themselves but airing dirty linen in public is considered bad form.

The Army can be surprisingly thin-skinned. In England one officer left the ranks because, friends say, a book he wrote (with the

Army's full knowledge) brought down on his shoulders too much displeasure from above. Yet the book, to a layman, is a well-written, honest, and only mildly-critical appraisal of an institution that the author clearly loved.

"There is great loyalty to the Army among us," says Captain Betty Lewis in Halifax. "There's an Army joke: to be so loyal your blood runs red, yellow, and blue."

"I don't think you could survive unless you generally supported the way things are," adds Major Ken Evenden, national information officer, in Toronto. "But officers often get together and put the Salvation Army straight."

This happens in formal fashion at week-long triennial conferences, where representatives from each division make suggestions for change. These are translated into study papers, recommendations are presented to the Army brass, and action of some sort is nearly always taken, Evenden says.

Others will tell you the Army still has a distance to go: that its leaders are overburdened (sometimes because they won't delegate authority) and that leadership therefore tends to come from the grass roots, and is merely channelled at the top. That the Peter Principle (wherein persons automatically reach their level of incompetence) applies to the Army as to any other organization. That the Army gets bogged down in the thing William Booth eschewed: committeeitis.

Dissent is not new to the Salvation Army, nor surprising, considering the individualists it attracts and its chafing rules. From the very beginning a few renegades and free spirits have stood apart within the ranks. Some have bolted.

Lieutenant Walter "Happy" Bailey, one of the Canadian pioneers with Addie and Ludgate, dropped out to join something called the Hozanna Banner. Evangelistic splinter groups were common at the time, some of them based on or in competition with the Salvationists: the Blue Ribbon Army, the Lord's Army, the Gospel Army, and the Saved Army.

Three of General Booth's own children left the fold around the turn of the century, much to the old man's grief. In the 1890s Brigadier Peter Philpott of the headquarters staff and Abner Sumner, acting editor of the *War Cry*, ultimately joined by nearly fifty other officers and four hundred soldiers, clashed head-on with a fourth Booth offspring, Herbert, who was then commandant of the Canadian Territory.

The gist of their complaints, widely publicized in the press of the day, was that high-ranking English-born officers were getting favored treatment at the expense of low-ranking Canadians and that the Army had become too traditional and "churchy" to the neglect of its evangelism. Legitimate concern was mingled with selfish motives among the dissidents, writes Army historian Gordon Moyles. In the end Booth refuted the major charges, but quickly reorganized Army administration and set up an inquiry to examine the plight of officers in small corps. Philpott, with others, formed a Christian Workers Church similar to the Army, and later set up his own non-denominational church in Hamilton.

In the late 1920s a different upheaval shook the Army to its roots. General Bramwell Booth, in his seventies and ailing, showed no signs of stepping down. The Army had been ruled by only *two* Booths for sixty-three years. Was it fated to an endless succession of them?

Regulations dating back to 1878 empowered him to choose his successor, but a 1904 amendment said that the High Council of commissioners and territorial commanders could vote out any General for such reasons as dereliction of duty, gross misconduct, or physical or mental illness. Many around Bramwell felt the old man should authorize a democratic system of electing future Generals. It would permit him to step down gracefully now. He refused.

In November 1928 the Council after much soul-searching and pleading, voted him out. Bramwell and his lawyer fought the decision and lost. In February 1929 Commissioner Edward Higgins was elected the Army's third General.

"It was sad because, you see, Bramwell had really gone into his dotage," says retired General Clarence Wiseman, a Canadian who headed the world-wide Army in the 1970s. "Years ago I met one or two who were on that High Council and I know it hurt them deeply to have to take that kind of action."

Four months later Bramwell Booth died. The public—persuaded by sensational news stories that a sick old man had been hounded to death by a heartless hierarchy—turned cool to the Salvation Army. Public giving declined in Canada, as elsewhere, and it took the Army some years to recover.

In recent times officers have dropped out, or been let out, sometimes because—like Jim Girling—they discovered too many aggravations in the life, sometimes because they cracked, physically or emotionally. Marital breakups occur, even in the Army. At least one senior officer was discharged because he left his wife for another woman; in that case the wife remained in service.

Near Toronto in 1978, an Army brigadier committed a bizarre suicide after twenty-eight years' service, much of it among prisoners.

"He carried the burden on his heart," the then-Commissioner John Waldron sorrowfully told the press. "I can only believe something snapped."

It was little wonder that in the turbulent 1960s, registration dwindled in Army colleges and, in the Toronto area, a most un-Army-like phenomenon called Creation Two flickered on. Like one of the strobe lights so beloved by the Sergeant Pepper generation, Creation Two illuminated and distorted the scene around it, and excited the people in it before they returned to reality.

How laughable, how thoroughly *freaky* the disciplined Sally Ann must have seemed—high haircuts, London Fog raincoats, Midnight Blue neckties, Late Victorian virtues—to that make-love-not-war generation with its sandals, easy sex, and loathing of the establishment. The wonder was that rebellion within the Army was so mild and self-contained.

Creation Two was the nearest the Army came to flower people—*too* near, in the view of some. It was a theater company of some fifteen young Canadians and Americans with Army people—including at least one ex-officer and the son of a divisional commander—at its core. Its founder and artistic director was a charismatic young Salvationist, Louis F. Capson, writer, artist, and actor.

Capson, who grew up in Fredericton, first caught the Army's eye when he entered a Salvationists' art competition. His entry, though not a winner, was vivid unforgettable expressionism, totally unlike the rest. In 1969, at twenty-five, he began lecturing in theater arts at Toronto's York University. He had a BA from the University of Victoria, and a Master of Fine Arts from the Yale University school of drama. Capson had already written four plays and one film script, directed several others and served a term as speech instructor at a college in Connecticut.

Creation Two rented a house in Toronto's Yorkville—at that time, the Canadian counterpart to Greenwich Village in New York, and a Mecca for the young and restless—and put on noon-hour drama in parks and shopping centers.

"I was trying to get beyond all the artifices, all the endless kinds of packaging, that sometimes inhibit people from really understanding a dramatic experience," says Capson, who in 1984 was completing a two-year teaching contract at the University of Winnipeg.

Major Kenneth Evenden visited them frequently and encouraged their work. They were not irreligious, he recalls; rather, they felt they were putting the Army right, bringing it back to God and to faith.

"Their street drama was very effective stuff," he says, "and their Christian witness was quite straightforward."

Gradually Creation Two began to speak out against things its members disapproved of, including the dictatorial structure of the

Army as they saw it. At one point they drew up a manifesto calling on the Army to repent, and sent copies to the newspapers.

"I could understand and sympathize with some of their points," says Captain Iain Trainor of Halifax, who came out of training college during those years. "They were misguided but very intelligent and sincere. They said the Army was no longer what it had once been, which was true. But it could never go back to the past and that was part of the fallacy in their belief."

"Louis railed at the authoritarianism of the Army, but he demanded a much greater discipline of mind, time, and skills than the Salvation Army ever did," adds Evenden. "His plays got wilder and wilder, and became screaming frenetic expressions of his ideas."

Creation Two found its ultimate expression in September 1972, with the six-day staging of a musical, *The Everlasting Salvation Machine* in Toronto's St. Lawrence Centre for the Performing Arts. It was Capson's thirteenth play in three years and the Toronto *Globe and Mail*'s mixed review observed, "His subject matter shows signs of mental fatigue but his production techniques have been honed to a fine edge."

The Everlasting Salvation Machine, with a cast of twenty-two, portrayed an Army with overtones of Nazi Germany. As Capson explains it now: "It wasn't written to change the Army or anyone in it. It was written to explore what that structure does in terms of the gospel of Jesus Christ or the Scriptures. If you have a surrogate group doing what each individual should be doing in your neighborhood, then somehow we've missed the point. When you have a group of mercenaries to buy off the pain that other people should be experiencing, by doing their own good work, then you're in trouble. That essentially was the thesis of the play."

By this route, Capson arrived at his Nazi Germany analogy. He suggests that there is a parallel between socialism which leads to totalitarianism and the kind of work the Army does. "It promotes a kind of lazy attitude toward the person on the street. I don't object to the work, I don't object to the fact that people are helped. I just object that something is lost in the responsibility inside the Army. It doesn't stop to think, at times, of the structure behind it. And it loses its way, and becomes just another suburban church."

More than one contemporary officer also worries that the Army is becoming "just another suburban church"; that it may have drifted from its original goal to "comfort the afflicted and afflict the comfortable." But the form of *The Everlasting Salvation Machine* left most of them cold—particularly parts that had a Sally Ann girl doing a strip tease, peeling an Army flag from her scantily clad body, and a cadet stabbing a training college principal to death with the point of an Army flagpole.

One of today's officers, a girl herself at the time, found it "disgusting." A non-Salvationist broadcaster reacted with "bewilderment soon followed by boredom . . . the frenzied style too unreal and unconvincing to be absorbing. . . ."

The *Globe and Mail* was sweet and sour: "The Everlasting Salvation Machine grinds on too long . . . people tend to protest too much too loudly in their religious agonies and ecstasies. There is nothing like an interminable hell-fire sermon on humility to make one's mind wander to thoughts of golf. When he climbs down from the pulpit, Capson can be quite amusing. 'Pose for the Citizen,' a scene in which the Army gets out there on its soap box and sells salvation like a mountebank hustling a cure-all cordial is excellent satire. . . ."

Creation Two's dénouement came at an Army holiness meeting one Sunday morning in Toronto's Varsity Arena. The guest, General Erik Wickberg, had just finished his address and then-Commissioner Wiseman stood to lead the nearly five thousand people in prayer. Suddenly a band of dissidents marched in with placards to surround the mercy seat, some shouting their protests.

The congregation was shocked. Some wanted to have the intruders evicted. The General was taken aback. But Wiseman, in what many regard as a masterful move, was by his own account "inspired to call our young Salvationist people out."

"These lovely young people here don't agree with everything," he called out. "That's all right. But we love them. And I want all you young people to come out and surround them and let them know that you care for them and pray for them."

The response was electric.

"I've never seen anything like it—young people rose up from all over the Arena and knelt around them," Trainor says. "They expected to be thrown out of the Army but we who opposed them let them know that as people they were important to us. They were broken not by opposition but by love."

A few young dissidents knelt in prayer themselves. A father went to put his arm around his son. And although Creation Two continued as a theater group for several years, the effect of its protest ended that day.

"It certainly didn't do the Army any harm but I fear it did some of them irrevocable harm," says Evenden.

"They tried to start a revolution and revolutions never change anything, only the players," concludes Trainor, who went through his own time of youthful dissent. "As I grew older and became more aware of God's call, rebellion seemed to me a very selfish thing. It was time I started helping people. There was enough pain and suffering in the world without adding to it."

But Trainor and others, including some high-ranking officers, believe the Army benefited from 1960s unrest, and perhaps even indirectly from Creation Two.

"The Salvation Army is a child of change," says former General Wiseman. "We have had a constant diet of change since our inception. The Army has been able to adapt, sometimes a bit tardily. And I see no reason, providing that we keep within the theological parameters that have been established for us by God, why we can't continue to adapt to change."

"Out of turmoil and questioning comes growth," adds Trainor. "I firmly believe that if we don't continue to question, we will become what Creation Two said we were: a sausage machine."

8
Not-So-Ordinary People

Their blue tunics are unwrinkled, their white shirts sparkle, their faces are unfailingly cheerful, no matter how grotty the situation. Are these soldiers of the Lord surrounded by some invisible shield that makes them impervious to the dirt and grime and despair of other mortals? Do they hurt, cry, laugh, make mistakes? Or are they indeed stamped from some universal Sally Ann officer-machine?

They are, suggests one Salvationist, "ordinary people serving an extraordinary God." In fact, they are a curious blend of the average and the not-so-ordinary. In some ways they are like the rest of us: short, tall, lean, fat, vulnerable to misery, beset by human frailties. They include former criminals, alcoholics, street kids, and business executives. Captain Iain Trainor of Halifax, as an example, once designed cars for General Motors. He gave it up, he says, because once after a few drinks at lunch he made a mistake that could have killed people.

Some officers dine with flowers and candlelight. Others sit at the kitchen table because, through rank, location, or luck of the draw, there is no dining room in the home the Army provided them. None, of course, have drinks before dinner or wine with meals (some serve fruit juice instead). Partly because of this they dine early; there's no time spent unwinding over pre-dinner cocktails.

They spring up each morning, unencumbered by hangover or ten-minute spasms of smoker's cough. The Army woman, readying herself for the day, dons stockings or pantyhose of discreet charcoal hue and skirt that falls respectably just below the knee. There's no Army directive on cosmetics but every officer goes easy on the lipstick and eye shadow.

"My mother used to say, 'Never paint a rose but if the backfence needs a little whitewash it's all right,' " says Lieutenant Wendy Ward of Guelph. "Basically, we feel the uniform is special, and nothing should detract from it."

At work, like any other employees, they make jokes or gripe about head office. There are tensions between the evangelistic types and the administrators, as between creators and administrators everywhere.

Some use fractured grammar; others have advanced university degrees and wide-ranging tastes in literature. One officer mentions his library of two thousand volumes. Another drops easily into her conversation quotations from William Ernest Henley's *Invictus* ("I am the master of my fate, I am the captain of my soul") and Saint-Exupéry's classic *The Little Prince*.

"We have the same stresses, the same sexual urges as other people," says a vibrant young captain, who frankly admits that she'd like to get married, but with single women outnumbering single men ten to one in the officer ranks, the odds are against it.

Even if the mature female officer finds a likely prospect twenty years her junior, she can't have him, contrary to current fashion in secular society. Nor can an elderly male take a young bride. No more than fifteen years' age difference between partners is preferred, although that was bent at least once, when a certain General wanted to marry a younger woman. The rule prevents a vigorous fifty-five-year-old man in a demanding field post from being burdened with a seventy-five-year-old wife, or a sixty-five-year-old man dragging a forty-year-old wife into premature retirement. It also lessens the hazards of such lopsided marriages breaking up.

All of this suggests an idyllic picture of honest clean-living Disneyland folk. In fact most Army officers and soldiers are as good as we like to think they are. Their orders instruct them to avoid debt, eat healthful meals, get enough sleep and exercise, read at least one serious daily newspaper, and live amicably with their neighbors. At work, soldiers are expected to not place undue emphasis on money, holidays, or promotion, but always to stand ready to help their fellow workers. They are required to avoid excess of all kinds, even in such worthy pastimes as sport and music.

Ken Clarke, a Salvationist businessman of Whitby, Ontario, spent four years heading up the Ministries Enrichment Program, a multi-million dollar fund-raising effort. He learned the Army inside out so he could answer any tough question from prospective donors. As a committed soldier, Clarke could be forgiven a certain bias— but by the same token, he doesn't have it in him to lie.

"I tried to set aside my romantic ideas, and be ready to see the good, bad, and ugly," he says. "I called a spade a spade—well, that's

a bad colloquialism for the Army!—and I had very little disappointment. Pretty well everything enhanced my admiration. Most of the
officers, *most* of them, are caught up in that romantic idea of the
Army too. They all believe in the Army's cause, and continually
promote it through their actions."

In patterning their lives on Christ, they ask nothing of others that
they do not demand of themselves. The poorest of families knows
that Army people are not wealthy do-gooders out slumming. An
adulterer or an alcoholic knows that, if he tries to reform, the Army
officer beside him will be a living example.

Which is not to say there are no temptations. "There are bad
marriages or marriages under strain, but the Army doesn't like to
talk about it," one officer says.

If the Army is reluctant to talk, it is because it reveres marriage
and hates to admit even the occasional failure. Prospective Army
brides and grooms are urged to tell each other of any prior sexual
experience and, during courtship, to "not allow impulse or passion
to obscure judgment to encourage unworthy conduct. . . . The
realization that kissing and caressing are really the preliminaries to
the full expression of sexual love will necessitate self-restraint."

Before marriage, they discuss health impediments, how they feel
about money handling, and whether they want children. To wed
under the Army flag they must agree to five Articles of Marriage,
among them: that they have not sought marriage purely for their
own happiness and will not let it lessen their devotion to God or the
Army.

So much does the Army treasure healthy marriage that it formed
in Canada the first pastoral care program in the Salvationist world. It
is an effort to improve the quality of marriage within the ranks *and*
outside where, statisticians say, four out of ten marriages this year
will end in divorce and two more will be troubled. It includes
pre-marital education, marriage counseling, and marriage enrichment.

"Marriage counseling is the end of the line," says Lieutenant-
Colonel Cyril Boyden, a gentle Englishman who, with his wife Helen
of thirty-three years, runs the program. "So we are trying to improve
and hone skills in counseling. But we want to get to marriages even
earlier, and so we have moved to marriage enrichment."

Eventually officer teams will fan out into the community to
instill in Salvationist couples an appreciation of communication,
negotiation during conflicts, and each other's strengths, weaknesses,
and needs.

"We are not trying to impose standards, but we want to make our
congregations *caring* congregations," Boyden says. "We see no alterna-

tive to the family. We see it as crucial to society. As marriage goes, so goes the family; as the family goes, so goes the community."

Army life with its long hours and heavy emotional burdens can be hard on a family. Many of the physical and emotional drains of the job are imposed by the officers' own and their parishioners' expectations.

"On the street where you live, everyone expects you to be able to handle everything," says Captain Betty Lewis of Halifax.

"If you call me in the afternoon and find me in, I feel a bit guilty, as if I should be out visiting a hospital," says Captain Wayne Pritchett, pastor of the St. John's, Newfoundland, Temple. At age eight Pritchett felt sure he would be an officer like his grandfather. In his Newfoundland hometown, Gambo, he would put on his Uncle Abraham's uniform, assemble a group of "sinners" (as many of his ten brothers and sisters as he could dragoon) and preach from the top of the stairs: "It doesn't matter if you have a hole in your shoe! Pride should not prevent you from coming forward!"

Pritchett gave his first formal sermon at fourteen and loves the pulpit. "But every time you stand there to preach there's an extreme drive, a need to be liked. People are wondering 'Does he really practice what he preaches?' "

Urged on by these inner drives and the demands of the job, Army officers tend to be workaholics.

"A corps officer in particular can never do all the things that need to be done," says Major Ken Evenden of Toronto, a thirty-three-year man. "Smart ones schedule time with the family. According to regulations, an officer is supposed to take one half-day off per week. I try to take off all the time I can, yet I never take what other [non-Army] people get."

Since Salvation Army officers don't drink, smoke, swear, tell dirty jokes, watch risqué movies, go to dances, or cheat on their spouses, what's left to do *except* work?

Like millions of others they play golf, go camping, go skiing. Evenden is a bird-watcher. Lieutenant-Colonel Albert Browning, a divisional commander in Newfoundland, collects twisted driftwood, finding or carving from it the shapes of birds and animals. Another officer ties fishing flies as a hobby.

"We wouldn't expect to see a Salvationist at an X-rated movie, but we wouldn't be upset if he attended *The Sound of Music*," says Lieutenant-Colonel Edwin Brown of the Toronto training college. Some officers screen films at home on video cassette recorders rather than risk censure for attending *any* movie. Few can afford a VCR on an Army salary but they can bring one in from civilian life, or receive it as a gift.

Much of their social time is spent with each other.

"The quality of time we spend in groups is great," says Evenden. "We have a riotous time. Salvation Army officers know how to have fun." Much of that fun is the do-it-yourself kind that an earlier generation of Canadians enjoyed before TV and spectator sports overwhelmed us. Impromptu skits are a favorite diversion. Once, at a conference, groups of officers had one hour each to devise a drama or an opera, and stage it with whatever props they could find. Some of the jokes were based on the day's guest speeches and the result, Evenden says, was "sidesplitting, sheer creative humor."

Salvationists love to laugh. They joke about that near-mythical figure, The General: not founder Booth but any current General, whoever he might be, in faraway England. In Arnold's Cove, Newfoundland, Lieutenant Brenda Bungay seizes a dinner plate from the slippery fingers of her small son: "Don't break *that*, it's the General's!" (In fact, years ago, all Army property *was* registered in the General's name.)

Two chaste women officers gleefully told me of the Dutch Salvationist, who related to her flock in the Amsterdam red light district a story about the Christmas spirit of giving. One hooker was so moved she announced she would that night, in keeping with the season, give all her customers a freebie.

Despite the Army's warts, and nagging rules, most officers feel they have uncommon freedom in their jobs.

"I have enormous latitude to do what I think needs to be done in any given situation," says Major Bill Ratcliffe of St. John's. And Regina's Captain Peter Bielby is so unlike the Sally Ann stereotype that his account of how he got into the Army has overtones of *Guys and Dolls*.

Although his waistline now crowds his belt, Bielby once was, by his own account, a powerful and menacing young man: "... 165 pounds of muscles, I pushed cement, I pushed gravel, I'm tanned black, and I got two little beady blue eyes."

Dark hair slicked back, dark eyes glittering in a square face, he launches into the story of his conversion with a pseudo-scowl. It's a pose: the captain is full of mischief, loves to entertain, and has a heart bigger than his ample stomach. The tough-guy role is convenient cover, lest anyone accuse him of being a softie.

"I never went to church in my life. I was a street kid, I went through all the orphanages, I was expelled from schools, I was classified as incorrigible. I don't think I was. I think I just had a dummy bunch of social workers who didn't recognize a hyperactive kid who needed to be loved, who really wanted help and didn't know how to say the word 'help.' "

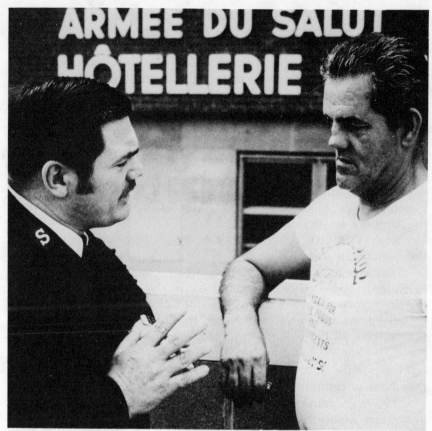

Captain Peter Bielby (now of Regina) in his previous posting at the men's hostel in Montreal.

A Salvation Army couple befriended him and loaned him books.

"Well, I knew the kind of books they gave me, the guy would get saved at the end. So I would read all the things he did and skip the last three chapters and hand it back saying 'thanks very much for your book.' "

Although Bielby's vocabulary is perfectly normal, he falls into a street-guy vernacular as he warms to this tale. (Later he will confess with a beetling glance, "I have the habit of stringing people along, so I have to sort of watch; they never know if I'm serious or not.")

"Then they started slipping me books about guys who get converted in the *second chapter!* That wasn't very fair because before I realized what happened—arrrrgh! I'm reading this religion! But I remember one day sitting in a garage, and I said 'Bielby, you're pretty smart but you've gotta be pretty dumb. You may have all the steaks in the fridge, but you don't have nothin'. Awright, God, I don't know how you gotta do this act, but do it!' And suddenly from a position of hate I was able to tolerate. Instead of wanting to lash out I was able to say, 'I'm gonna let you live, you may be interfering with my turf but you're allowed to walk over it.' Amazing! People couldn't figure out why me, who'd always been in isolation, was letting people talk to me.

"I remember one night I was in a gymnasium and a friend said 'Hey Pete, you wanna drink?' and I said 'Nah, not tonight' and he said 'C'mon we got a bottle of *Seagrams!*' And I was not an alcoholic but I liked to pound a few back and I said, 'Nah, I don't want no drink tonight.' 'Whatsa matter?' 'Nothin's the matter.' 'So why wontcha drink?'

"Well, I always believe in direct answers so I said, 'Because I accepted Christ as my saviour today.' And he started hollering to a crowd of people, 'Hey, Petie got religion, Petie got religion!'

"Well, I coulda *died!* All my friends, all the people I wheeled and dealed with, people that owed me thousands of dollars 'cause I used to do a few little things, y'know. And they're all saying 'Hey, he got religion, we don't hafta pay our debts!' and I'm saying 'Whaddya mean, 'course you gotta pay your debts, whether I got religion or not I gotta live!' "

Bielby, then in his early twenties, set out to catch up on his education. "My favorite thing in school was being pushed ahead. Every year they pushed me on a grade, to get rid of me. So when I got saved, I didn't know anything. I started memorizing from school books. *You* know what eight times eight is, *I* didn't know what eight times eight is. If I wanted eight I just *took* eight!" He slogged through night school, then applied three times to the Army training college before he was finally admitted.

"It wasn't a good experience for me, I was a square peg in a round hole. I did not take kindly to authority." He was frequently in hot water. But he graduated in 1967, has served diligently and has become hooked on self-improvement. His walls are covered with certificates and diplomas—courses paid for by the Army—everything from pastoral counseling to management at McGill University. He is particularly proud of the latter: "All I used to know about McGill was riding a Harley Davidson through it!"

"The Lord has been very good," Bielby says, turning serious. "The Army has never stifled my individuality, never limited my ability to function. At times I have been classified as a maverick, and uncooperative. I certainly *can* cooperate. As long as people agree with me, there's no problem whatsoever." And Bielby grins his impish grin.

His wife Carol, a former teacher, is as elegant as he is

Captain Peter Bielby talking with one of the men on the program at the Men's Social Service Centre, Regina.

rough-hewn. "She shares most of my enthusiasm, and has the ability to make me think a second time. She's my honest broker."

Bielby has uncommon empathy with life's losers: old pensioners with no homes, younger men and women from hard places and hard times. He sweeps with gale force into every new posting, cleans up, paints up, devises or scrounges better facilities, starts new programs. As director of men's social services in Regina (where there is no Harbour Light) his charges include alcoholics.

"We put them with normal people. We take them to wrestling. Now some might say, 'Aw, *that* ain't normal!' But it's learning to express yourself in a socially acceptable way in a certain segment of society. They learn that you don't have to be drunk to go to wrestling, you don't have to be drunk to see the Riders play at Taylor Field, you don't have to be drunk to see the Toronto Blue Jays. . . ." Here Bielby cocks an eye at a Toronto visitor. ". . . 'Course it *helps*, mind you. . . .''

When he arrived in Regina the center's occupancy rate was fifty-two percent. In less than a year he upped it to ninety percent. And Peter Bielby has saved as many souls, lifted as many hearts, and serves his God as well as any other man.

Bielby has had four moves in fifteen years, about par for the Army. It's uncommon for officers to stay in one place more than four or five years. The Army feels they'll go stale without frequent new challenges, responsibilities, and chances for personal growth. Aside from that, if an officer dies or falls sick, it can set off a chain reaction of moves on very short notice, with others, or their assistants, being shuffled all down the line to fill the gap. There is no pool of spare people for such emergencies.

Some officers choose to believe that every move is predestined by God, which probably makes the merry-go-round easier to accept. Others, knowing that the Lord's hand is guided by Personnel and the Field Secretary, exchange an old Army joke:

Officer: God, I just learned about my new posting by reading the *War Cry*. That's not fair, God!

God: That's all right, my child. *I* didn't know either until I read it in the *War Cry*.

Most moves are geared to late June, when children are out of school and another crop of cadets graduates from training. In late May they find out *if* they'll be moved. After a week of wild rumors they find out where. Roughly three weeks after that, they say farewell to yet another home.

In the new house they use the Army furniture, linens, and kitchenware left by the previous tenants. All the homes are comfortable and at least adequate. The rule book sets out standards: a four-bedroom house, for example, rates a total furnishings limit of $14,000 (although there's an annual allowance to replace or upgrade, as necessary). Every last item, with specifications and maximum price, is in the book: from $1,000 for a chesterfield to $25 for 100 feet of garden hose. Within these limitations, and with their few personal effects, Army wives try with varying success to imprint their styles and personalities on the place.

The losers most often are Army children.

"They move from pillar to post, and a great deal is expected of them," says Major Bill Ratcliffe of St. John's. "They walk in as an appendix of their parents' appointment and are expected to behave in a very orthodox fashion."

Over the years, as a youth officer in various postings, Ratcliffe has paid particular attention to officers' children, sometimes taking them to lunch without their parents ever knowing about it, "helping sort out some of the frustrations they had as individuals living in a glass cage."

On the one hand Army kids are tugged by the hopes and expectations of their parents and their Christian community. On the other hand they may be considered curiosities by their peers, who for generations have jeered:

Salvation Army, save my soul,
Send me to Heaven in a sugar bowl!

Or, "Hey, do ya save bad girls? Well, save one for me!"

Some tell non-Salvationist friends that their parents are in "the army" without specifying which one. A major remembers buying his son a pair of eighty-dollar Kodiak boots, which he could ill afford, because the boy's high school classmates were ragging him mercilessly about wearing "Sally Ann" boots (implication: from the thrift store).

"Oh, I got the jeering as a kid," recalls Captain Iain Trainor. "I played in the band, I believed in my Church, I *wanted* to play but I dreaded having my schoolmates see me. Because if they did, they'd follow behind me singing 'OOM PAH PAH, OOM PAH PAH.' So, most of my friends were Salvationists. We did everything together. It was like a life apart. And it was from that that I rebelled when I grew older: I discovered new friends, drinking, all that heady stuff. Life caught up with me."

When his daughter Shelley was in Grade 6 she wanted to attend her school's afternoon Christmas party and dance. The Trainors said maybe when she was sixteen but not at age eleven. The school ordered her to take a math class instead. Her parents kept her home, rather than see her penalized. The next day, when others were assigned to write a composition on the Christmas party, Shelley had to write how she felt about not being allowed at the dance.

"I hit the roof," Trainor says. "The teacher apologized. So next time we let Shelley go but explained to her teacher why she could not dance. The teacher announced in class that boys must not ask her to dance because the Army does not believe in it. Naturally, there was a lot of jeering."

"I live in a residence of 105 guys," says a student at Memorial University in St. John's, where Salvationism is of course better known than on any other campus in Canada. "There are two or three other non-drinkers and non-smokers, but I'm the only one for religious reasons. So I'm considered a bit of an oddball by some. They press you to take a drink, to test you. I guess it'd be a good opportunity for giving witness. . . ." But you get the feeling that he has his hands full just coping, without exposing himself to the further ridicule of testifying to his Christian beliefs.

Yet classmate Terry Gilbert, twenty, a computer sciences student with a mercurial sense of humor, encounters little ridicule and considerable respect.

"I don't push the Army but try to gather the nerve and willpower to show myself as a Christian of the Salvation Army type. People seem to feel I'm a friend who won't 'hurt' them in any way but respects them, in some cases in spite of their lifestyle."

It's hinted that officers' children get favored treatment; that their appointments are not always based entirely on merit. If so, that isn't inducement enough for all of them. Some flatly turn their backs on an Army career. More than one officer tells with anguish of a son or daughter who opted right out of Salvationism and sometimes out of Christianity.

"It's hard being a good officer and a good parent," sums up Betty Lewis. "If you don't hold your kids at fourteen or fifteen, you'll lose them." Her four sons are involved in all the Salvation Army youth activities but they also love hockey so she ferries them to games like any other "hockey mother." They also love to kid around.

"They're expected to phone home if they are going to be late. Once Todd couldn't find a phone and I scolded him for it. Then *I* was an hour late getting home. He said 'Oh Mother, haven't I always told you to call? What happened, couldn't you find a phone?' "

Betty Lewis loved and respected her Army parents but when they came to her school in uniform when she was a teenager, "I would just die." So now she sympathizes when her son, going out in his bandsman's uniform, looks both ways down the street to see if his friends are watching.

"It's one thing to proudly wear the uniform among people who all love and respect you, but for a young person among his own kind, it's harder."

In the end, the parents' attitude is reflected in the children. Captain Lewis loves the peripatetic life, and her sons reflect it (they get good marks in school, despite the constant moves). She loves her dual role as housewife and as divisional director of Salvation Army Guides and Brownies.

"I'm not a women's libber. My husband is a chauvinist and I make sure I cook good meals and bake cakes and keep the house nice—so I can have my career. Even if I were not a Salvation Army officer I would be working. I love my children but I want to be in touch too."

Army women, she says, "feel we are called to be officers every bit as much as our husbands."

And there's the rub: Army wives often appear to be mere appendages of the male. A wife always adopts her husband's rank. If a female captain marries, say, a male lieutenant, she automatically steps down to his rank. While he is called Lieutenant John Doe, she is officially *Mrs.* Lieutenant John Doe. When he retires, she automatically retires too, whether or not she's of retirement age.

Theoretically there's no reason why a woman can't become the General, but there has been only one in Army history: Evangeline Booth. In early 1984 there were four women Commissioners, worldwide, but none was in Canada. Why are no women holding

Evangeline Booth, probably taken at the time she served as Commissioner of Canada.

even the job of Divisional Commander anywhere in Canada, ask many of the bright aggressive young women in the ranks? Why has there been only one woman commissioner in the Canadian Army's history—again, Evangeline Booth?

The stock answer: the Army is a partnership, requiring a woman as a helpmeet in those major posts. Very well, say Army feminists, so why not let the *male* officer—the husband—be the helpmeet?

The lack of total equality is all the more visible in view of Catherine Booth's equal partnership with her husband, and her remarkable pamphlet, *Female Ministry*, published in London 125 years ago. With William's full support, she set Victorian England on its ear with a reasoned, masterful case for what was then near-heresy: women's right to preach the gospel. Such phrases as "Why should woman be confined exclusively to the kitchen and distaff, any more than man to the field and workshop?" and "We think it is a matter worthy of consideration whether God intended woman to bury her talents and her influence as she now does" would not have been out of place in recent times.

To give the organization its due, Army women preach more sermons and do more important and involving work than the women of most, if not all, other denominations. The ministry of such as Christine MacMillan on Vancouver's Skid Row, Marguerite Lloyd in the London Children's Village, and Lorna Oliver of Grace Haven in Regina shines beside that of any man, in or out of the Salvation Army.

9

"The Children, Oh the Children!"

She scoops the baby into her arms so deftly, so lovingly, you would think Captain Lorna Oliver is the mother. In a sense she *is*, although this slim dark young officer with the gentle watchful eyes is unmarried. In Regina's Grace Haven on this spring afternoon, she is surrogate mother to six small boys and girls, two teenage unwed mothers, and the baby, whose fifteen-year-old mother is at this moment in school.

The scrubbed and cheerful old house on Scarth Street is one of a multitude of ways that the Army ministers to children, still mindful of William Booth's deathbed plea. Grace Haven takes unmarried mothers for pre-natal and post-natal care but, unlike thirteen similar Army homes, it also welcomes battered children plucked from unhappy environments and awaiting the pleasure of the courts.

The baby-child-adult mix works surprisingly well. The young unweds see, in the children, what happens to babies who grow up in a less than ideal home. The children, mostly from large families with a constant baby population, happily change diapers and give bottles. For them it is a comfortable reminder of what a home *could* be.

Most of them are Metis. Regina has the largest Metis and Indian population per capita of any Canadian city. Many have drifted in from overcrowded reservations, full of hope—only to find behind the bright city lights the same old despair. Few of the children brought to Grace Haven have known a normal childhood. One ten-year-old had never had a Christmas tree or presents. Guns and alcohol have been part of their daily lives. One girl has seen three suicides in her family. A boy tells the captain off-handedly, "My house is full of holes 'cause we shoot the ceiling with the .22."

Lorna Oliver is one of a few in the white man's world they really trust because she, too, is Metis. She never knew her own parents. At thirteen months she was adopted by a Salvationist couple in Edmonton and grew up in their loving foster home. She worked in a chartered accountant's office, went to Army training college and has been an officer for ten years, mostly with unwed mothers and troubled children.

Now school is out and a nine-year-old explodes into the Haven. He is still scarred from an earlier time when adults around him used to play a "game": tossing him into the air as though to catch him—then letting him drop to the floor. He and his eleven-year-old sister have been here nearly two years. Their mother is in jail and the courts have not yet decided on their future.

When he came to the Haven as a tough never-say-die little scrapper, Lorna Oliver had to constantly reassure him that he would not be beaten. Sometimes he fled at the sight of a strange man; to him, males signified drunkenness and abuse. Now he no longer tries to bite or punch the staff in his temper tantrums. Today he says affectionately, "Remember I used to call you Mother when I first came here?"

"Yes," the captain says softly. "But you know I'm not." Sometimes she even doubles as their mother at Home and School meetings, but she dares not let them grow too dependent on her. One day they must go back to their parents or to a foster home.

"I know," he says agreeably. "You're my pretend mother."

His sister, on arrival, kept all her fears bottled up. Finally the captain broke through and helped her untie the knots inside her. In one year the girl has made up two and one-half years of lost schooling. Now she can say, "I'm happy!" and mean it. Now she turns to Lorna with her hurts. She too is physically scarred from the past, and comes home crying when other kids call her "Scarface."

"Never mind," Lorna says. "Lots of others have scars, they just don't show."

One day the girl ran home from school, scared and ashamed of her first menstruation. The captain patiently explained the onset of womanhood, as any mother would. Her surrogate daughter, who was just beginning to enjoy being a child, grumbled, "It makes me sick!"

At night the children of Grace Haven have a quiet time for homework, reading, or TV. Many of them are only now learning how to play. Before, their spare time was spent cooking, doing housework, caring for younger brothers and sisters while their parents were out. Here they are part of a real family, even to the volunteer big brothers and sisters from the community who take them on outings or home for Sunday dinner.

"Here, they become normal children again," Lorna says. "I think, I *hope* a lot of what we do will stay with them after they leave."

"It Is Better To Build Children Than To Repair Men." The plaque on Major Ron Butcher's desk, a gift from his own children, puts his life's work in a nutshell. Here at the House of Concord in Langley, BC, they try to rebuild boys before they grow up into bitter twisted men.

"I don't think even the Army fully appreciates what we have here," Butcher enthuses, and maybe he's right. You must live here a while to understand the magic of Concord. "The money spent on this program is of much more value than on any adult system, because these kids are salvageable."

His "kids" are boys of fourteen to seventeen, on probation from the courts but not yet hardened offenders. Here they get a second chance before they slip inexorably into a lifetime of crime. Most have had twenty to thirty brushes with the law, and have quit or been kicked out of school. Many are of average intelligence, or higher, but twenty percent are below a Grade 3 level of literacy. Some can barely read. One sixteen-year-old arrived unable to sign his own name. Ninety-eight percent are on drugs or alcohol. Some are violently anti-social.

"But," says Butcher, "when they come here they look at their feet when you talk to them. When they leave, they look you in the eye!"

The Army has two other Houses of Concord—one in London for older boys, one in Toronto for prisoners on the last one-to-nine months of their sentences. There are many other kinds of "halfway houses" in Canada. What, if anything, is different about the Army's?

"Maybe we invest a little more of ourselves," suggests staff psychiatrist Colin Stewart. "It's that greater element of *caring*. People from other institutions and provinces come here to study us—royal commissions, for instance—and they invariably comment on our caring."

Concord is a sort of family, the support system some boys never had because the father left home or was never there.

"When they come up against a shattering time in their lives, a divorce maybe, they have no one to turn to," Butcher says. "So they get drunk, or toke out on dope, to avoid facing reality. Our caring turns them around. Sometimes they say afterward, 'You were too easy on me. You shoulda kicked my backside up between my shoulder blades.' "

Concord *is* patient but very firm. Underneath Butcher's easy good humor is a streak of steel, polished during a seven-and-a-half-year hitch in the Canadian Navy, where he ended up a petty officer. The navy was the making and nearly the breaking of him. For this fourth-generation Salvationist, raised in the relatively sheltered environment of an Army child, the navy was a shock.

"Suddenly, on Sunday there was nothing to do. Nobody said 'Go to church.' So I hit the bottle pretty hard. I became a lone drinker. I thought I wanted to be a career man in the navy, and in my estimation there was nothing lower in the world than a padre. Yet deep down I knew God wanted me to be an Army officer. The more I fought this conflict, the more I drank."

Finally he took his discharge, enrolled in university and spent weekends with Christian friends.

"The Lord put it all together," Butcher says. He graduated from the Army college in 1957 and most of his service since has been in prison or prison-related systems.

About two hundred boys a year—forty-two at any given time, and there is always a waiting list—pass through the complex of one-story dormitories, cottages, workshops and classrooms set among trees and green fields in the Fraser Valley twenty miles east of Vancouver. They arrive watchful and suspicious.

"When are you going to push religion?" they ask warily.

"What do you think I'm doing when I talk about 'caring'?" retorts Butcher. Concord does not try to turn them into Salvationists, although they're encouraged to attend Sunday services. Little by little they relax, trust, maybe even love. As Butcher walks the grounds, tall and trim with gray hair and beard, they hail him cockily—"Hey, Majuh, whattya say?"—but the respect and affection are palpable.

It takes three to four weeks for a boy to recover from a drug or alcohol habit (which is not to say he is *cured*). Concord does it with good plain food, a busy day, and an early night. Bedtime is 10:30 P.M. for those in the dorms; 11:00 P.M. in the coveted cottages, where boys move after good behavior. They're up at seven to a stiff aerobic program. Butcher, a fitness buff, believes if they appreciate their bodies they'll feel better about themselves. The day is crammed with classroom studies and opportunities for such manual training as carpentry, motor mechanics, gardening, and landscaping.

"We emphasize the setting of goals," Butcher says. "They won't all be electronics engineers or airline pilots but they can be good foremen in factories."

At night a boy must take part in at least two activities, including a swim in Concord's pool or a game in the gym. Concord runs on points: a boy can earn them for writing a letter home, playing a game, reading a book, doing well in class. If he quits smoking he gets fifty points; if he starts again he loses one hundred. Fighting, swearing, or going absent without leave (AWOL) loses points for the guilty one and, in some cases, for his entire cottage. That way, peer pressure comes into play.

There are no guards or high fences. If a boy wants to leave someone may try to talk him out of it but will not physically restrain him. If he leaves, he is AWOL, his parole officer is notified, and a warrant is issued for his arrest. A court then decides whether he returns to Concord or goes to a harsher institution.

"We are trying to teach them to make decisions, not just drift," Butcher explains. "But if a boy leaves we look for the reason. Maybe he was homesick. Maybe he just couldn't stand the freedom here, after having been in institutions where he never had to make up his own mind. Or maybe another boy was going AWOL and laid a heavy on him: 'Either you come with me or I'll beat yer head off.'"

His staff (not all Salvationists) are involved and enthusiastic. Ten volunteer tutors give the semiliterates an individual reading program. The volunteers include a doctor's wife, a retired teacher, and a prison mechanic's wife. They neither pity nor downgrade their students, and to boys who have been scorned, or physically or verbally abused, this alone is a revelation.

Some are boys who were lost in the education jungle and sometimes shunted into grades far beyond their capacities. Others have physical disabilities that have gone unnoticed. One small ornery kid had twenty-twenty vision but his eyes were unfocused. He couldn't read from a blackboard so tried to mask it with belligerence. Eye exercises cured him. Another appeared to be ignoring his teachers; in fact, his hearing was so bad he could only distinguish a few conversational tones.

"A kid isn't always a screw-up because he wants to be," says Butcher.

Eventually, nearly all are fitted into Concord's regular classroom, but the turnaround—from semiliterate to literate, or from trouble-maker to the beginnings of a useful human—comes slow and hard. These are not, as in the title of an ancient Hollywood film, angels with dirty faces.

One boy was baffled by the word "siphon." Finally his teacher acted it out.

"Ah!" cried the kid. "Steal gas!" It took longer to explain there are other uses for a siphon.

Another demolished a staffer's car hood with an iron bar; he claimed a psychiatrist in an earlier time had told him to work out his aggressions by hitting a tin can, and since there were no tin cans around Concord . . . Another overturned Colin Stewart's desk into his lap. Yet another literally climbed the wall—up Stewart's book-cases.

The psychiatrist has confiscated a wondrous array of home-made hashish and marijuana pipes: one contrived from a light bulb, another carved from a block of wood, a third from a lead pencil with the lead stripped out. When boys return from a weekend pass they must be searched for drugs hidden in radios, shoes or, as once, a tennis ball.

Girls try to sneak into camp at night, to a warm reception from the inmates. The night supervisor once found a naked girl under a boy's bed. Clearly the culprit would lose big points for this offense—but what name to give it? There was nothing like it in Concord's standard list of sins. Finally they called it, "possession of illegal contraband."

"Sometimes you'd like to put them over your knee and spank them," Butcher sighs. "But mostly you can't help liking them. They're just kids."

The average boy graduates in about four months. Roughly seventy percent go on with education through day or night school, correspondence courses, or a trade apprenticeship. A fifteen-year-old who'd been the terror of his small community was lifted from Grade 7 to Grade 9 in four months, went on to complete Grade 11 outside, and now has a career in the regular Canadian Army.

Another graduate came back after five years at the wheel of his own cross-country trucking rig. ("*That* made a big impression on the kids.") Yet another returned to order fifty cedar coffee tables, made in Concord's own shop, for his thriving furniture business. Still others are making big money in the oil fields.

Then there was the problem kid who phoned, four weeks after graduation. "Just wanted to tell you I'm doing fine, Captain. I'm working and I've just become a Christian."

"After a call like that," Butcher smiles, "I feel ten feet tall!"

A few miles north of London, Ontario, at the front door of another House of Concord, a seventeen year old lingers, a new Adidas bag (symbol of honorable discharge) in hand. He's a grade school dropout who held and lost four jobs in two years, got drunk, broke into a store, and was put on probation. Six months at Concord seem to have turned his life around. He has completed a plumbing/electrical/handyman course and has a job waiting out-side.

Now, at 10:00 A.M., it is time he was gone—but he's not.

Captain Fred Jackson, the administrator, pauses curiously.

"How come you're still here?"

"I'm saying goodbye."

At noon, with his mother waiting to drive him home, he is still "saying goodbye." Finally, reluctantly, he leaves at 3:30.

"You see," he tells Jackson, "this is the first place I ever felt anybody really cared about me."

In downtown London, at the Children's Village on a tree-lined corner of Dundas East, a six-year-old boy one day happened on to a book of wallpaper samples. He had been in a dozen foster homes. As every other day, his small face was unfailingly grim. Now he flipped the pages muttering, "That's what I had in my room with my last mother . . . That's what I had with the mother before. . . ."

"You know you only have one *real* mother," said Major Joyce Ellery, the officer in charge.

He sat very still. She heard him grinding his teeth. At last he turned.

"Maje, you know what I thought?"

"What?"

"Maje, I never knew I had a mother. I thought I never got born!"

A lot of others *wish* they'd never been born, until the Army takes them into its arms. There are three Villages across Canada: Toronto's deals with handicapped teenagers; Calgary's program is solely for emotionally disturbed children; London takes the emotionally disturbed *and* mentally retarded, as young as five and up to the mid-teens. They are referred here by Children's Aid Societies, family doctors, social workers, or parents themselves.

"Some parents nowadays are not doing a very good job at being people, much less parents," says Major Marguerite Lloyd, today's administrator. She has a square, infinitely kind face, a gentle voice, and a firm handshake. She began her career in this Village in 1956, as a nurse and new lieutenant. She moved on to the home for unwed mothers in Vancouver, then the Children's Village in Calgary, and in 1973 back here. It's a tribute to her work that the Army left her in this post so long.

Some of her charges are from large families where the parents simply couldn't cope with a problem child. Others, like the boy who thought he'd never been born, have ricocheted through one foster home after another. It is not necessarily the kids' nor the foster parents' fault. Sometimes a family moves to another province and regulations don't permit the foster child to go along. Sometimes an elderly relative comes to live with them, nudging the child out of the only available space.

"Whatever the reason for leaving, the foster child always *thinks* it's his fault," the major says.

She has a special tenderness for these waifs, partly because *she*

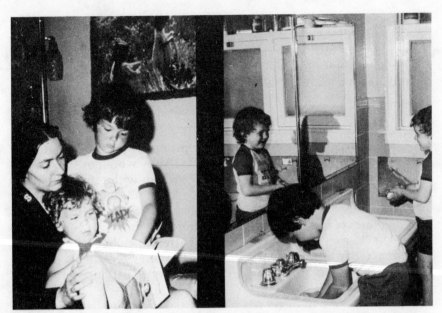

At this Children's Village, some kids find the first real home they have ever known, and a hug and a surrogate mother.

was adopted when she was twelve days old. Her adoptive parents separated when she was five. Her mother had a hard life, working in other people's homes and moving constantly. At sixteen Marguerite had tried several churches and settled on the Army because "the others don't require as much of you."

She worked two years in a children's hospital before enlisting in the Army, hoping to become a missionary nurse. Rheumatoid arthritis put an end to that dream but the Army, seeing something special in her, sent her to the University of Toronto School of Social Work. Like all Salvationists, she sees the hand of God behind these twists and turns in her life. "I have to feel the Lord had other plans for me and this was it."

The Village is a central building surrounded by five cottages set among trees and a small green playing field. Each cottage holds ten children, grouped according to their disability, with a supervisor always on hand. They breakfast here, make their own beds, then attend classes in the main building or an outside school.

Special cases get special attention from a large staff of teachers and counselors, learning something as simple but essential as how to use a fork, or how to color between two lines (which will lead to printing between lines and ultimately to writing).

If a child can't verbalize feelings, they are acted out in play. He has a half-hour to do what he likes: sit in a sandbox with his back turned, smash a block of wood with a hammer, sit quietly rocking beside an adult. One absolute rule is enforced: no one at the Village is permitted to hurt anyone else.

At noon they lunch in the main dining room. The major leads them through a simple grace:

> God is gracious, God is good
> Let us thank Him for our food.

The children can't all walk or talk properly but they chatter as gaily as normal kids. She points out a small boy who looks about six but in fact is twelve—a blond imp so wired-up with tension that he nearly always walks on his toes.

"His mother was heavily into drugs and alcohol before he was born," she explains. "Because of it there are holes in his brain." Maybe he'll never live a normal life. But after lunch he skips forward to embrace her and squeeze the hand of a stranger, then catapults outdoors to take part in a field day run by the patient staff. He is happy.

Marguerite Lloyd never married but she is mother to all of these. Her eyes grow soft in the telling of a seven year old who had been in twenty-one different foster homes. He was angry, withdrawn, and utterly without self-esteem. He reached sixteen before learning his real name (when he applied for a driver's license). At the Village he grew well enough to cope in a group home. From there he got a job and married a girl from a solid family who has become his bulwark. He still keeps in touch with the Village, his first real home.

Many of the kids have volunteer families on the outside. For five years Major Lloyd herself has been sister-cum-mother to a boy. He came to the Village so badly disfigured and emotionally seared from a serious accident that he vented his rage by smashing whatever was at hand. Finally the Village had to turn him over to an institution where he could have round-the-clock care. With that, and some corrective surgery, he improved.

Now he is fifteen. The major has filled his life with little pleasures: a trip to Niagara every winter to see the frozen Falls; a visit every summer to Canada's Wonderland, a funfair near Toronto; trips to the zoo or shopping centers, rides on escalators, Cokes and hamburgers—all the things healthy kids with families take for granted. Sometimes she lets him use her spare bedroom on weekends. Every Christmas they go to see the lights in London's Victoria Park.

Now, on this summer day, she says, "He's ready to go into a foster home at last. That's miraculous!" It is a miracle largely of her making.

When a child is ready to leave the Village the staff treats it as a happy event. "If they don't want to go, then we haven't done a good job," says Major Lloyd. "Everybody fears change, and these children more than most, but they should want to go out and be like other kids."

Each gets a personal scrapbook filled with mementos of the Village years: birthday and Christmas parties, winning a race on the field day. There's a farewell party with presents and a cake. "We want them to realize they can look forward to a happy future."

If they do it's because of the love and security they found here. One six year old talked non-stop when he arrived, as though if he kept asking questions no one would have time to send him away. A few nights later a staffer was tucking him into bed.

"Nobody can hurt me here, right?"

"Right."

"Cause if they tried, you wouldn't let them?"

"That's right."

His face went red and rumpled.

"Why weren't you always with me so nobody would have hurted me?"

There was no answer to that. All she could do was hold him tight.

10

On the Streets

From Skid Row on a clear day you can almost reach across Burrard Inlet and touch the mountains sculpted against Vancouver's sky. Except no one on Skid Row looks up that high. The blue-gray perfection of Grouse, Seymour and the rest is for tourists, lovers, skiers, and expense-account easy-riders in the tall hotels downtown. Here on the Row—only a twenty-minute shuffle from those hotels—the mountains and everything they stand for are beyond reach. Beyond eternity.

The Skid Row people live in fleabag rooming houses or tired hotels. Or, in summer they flop in wrecked cars or under the Granville Street bridge. Or, in winter huddle close to the warm-air ducts of the city heating plant.

The world outside Skid Row—nuclear missiles, jet-setting prime ministers, hockey players with dryblown hair, civil servants with indexed pensions, inflation, recession—is beyond their comprehension. Life for them is *always* in recession. Life is survival, and maybe a coffee and a kind word around the wooden-barrel tables in this small room on Cordova.

This is the Crosswalk, the Salvation Army storefront street ministry. The young officer and her twenty or so volunteers of various religions are kind. They listen. They do not want to use you. They will help, if you want help. It doesn't matter if you are old or ugly or Indian or a whore.

Tonight, as several nights each week, Christine and David and Pauline are going out on the street, reaching out, not just waiting for the shy suspicious Skid Row people to come to them.

Captain Christine MacMillan, thirty-five, is tall and slender with fine facial bones, a flickering of freckles, dark hair coiled beneath her hat in approved Army fashion and deep dark eyes that crinkle at the corners with her smile. She administers the Army's uptown Homestead for women alcoholics and the Crosswalk which she founded in 1978. "Crosswalk" has two connotations: the cross of Christianity, and those two parallel white lines on streets that safely lead you from one place to another. Sometimes it leads the people off Skid Row to better things.

"For some it's frightening to leave this place," she says. "We get to know them. If they wish, we will pray with them individually. We encourage them to get off this way of life, but we don't say they can come only if they go to a Salvation Army rehabilitation center. If they do, fine. If they don't, that's all right too."

Our first stop is a little park at the corner of Carrell and West Hastings. On this warm June night men are slouched against the nearest wall or perched like sparrows on the benches. Unwashed men. Men with hair watered and combed into a glossy cap. Men with furtive eyes and beaten faces from years of begging handouts. Some of them call Christine by her first name, which she encourages. This is no place for pulling rank.

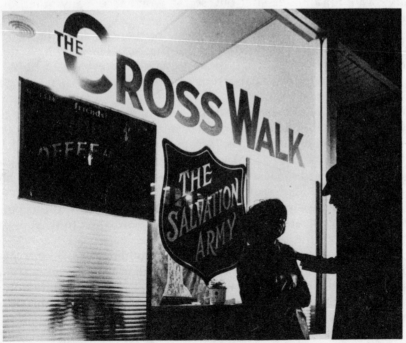

The Crosswalk, the Salvation Army storefront street ministry on Skid Row in Vancouver, founded by Captain Christine MacMillan.

"Some people say the trust is for our uniform but it's more than that," she says. "I think we invest too much in tradition or in a piece of cloth. This is an underground world. It takes a long time to break down the barriers. I've had to sell the Salvation Army through my own personhood, not through my uniform."

She has done a good selling job. One night a man came to the Crosswalk heaving with pain. He had fallen down three flights of stairs and broken his back. The Army rushed him to hospital. "He would not phone an ambulance. Too suspicious. He came straight to us. We are constantly protecting people, *physically*."

Pauline Fell, a widow and civilian volunteer, moves among her "boys," shaking hands and chatting. With her crisp white blouse, neat skirt and white hair, she looks like everyone's granny. The men treat her like the lady she is. Maybe they dimly remember someone like her from some better time.

"Hey! You a friend of Pauline? She's my girl-friend." He is maybe thirty, tall and well-built, with the lean-jawed good looks of a tweed-jacketed Mr. Wonderful from a *New Yorker* ad—and he is wiped out on drugs and booze. He shows the needle marks on his arms. "I'm haywire, y'know? I mean, I'm just haywire." He mutters it over and over, like a damaged record. Maybe he'll go to the Crosswalk for a coffee later but, so far, won't accept any other kind of help.

Along the darkening streets Christine glances down lanes and alleys, looking for fallen drunks and druggies. They are easy prey for the stronger ones in this private jungle. "We have to be very alert. People are often in dangerous situations. We are often trying to break up violence."

Violence goes with the territory. Pauline has befriended a girl who, having stabbed her boyfriend to death, is serving five years and writes regularly to say she has "accepted the Lord." (Maybe she has; Pauline wants to believe it.) Once Christine came upon "this guy with cowboy boots" kicking a pregnant woman in the stomach. She shouted and the aggressor backed off.

"One learns the technique of not getting involved to the point where you aggravate people. You have to know when to walk away. I've had to call the police only twice in five years."

There've been other times when she should have called the cops. Such as the night she found a Skid Row regular in a doorway carving his wrist with the favorite downtown weapon—a paring knife honed sharp on both edges. Passersby were ignoring him. Down the street his girlfriend hung over a car, weeping helplessly.

"John!" the captain cried, and grabbed his knife-hand. He stared through a haze of drugs and alcohol, and turned the knife on her. "Luckily I was stronger than he was. That's when you pray a lot."

She wrestled the knife away. A few days later she saw him again. He remembered nothing of the incident.

Even at thirteen, Christine MacMillan wanted to help people. Her parents were Salvationists whose marriage went awry and she grew close to her grandfather, Alex MacMillan (one hundred years old and still active in Army work, on this night that we walk Skid Row). "He had a heart for people. He used to take me into downtown Toronto, and I remember walking through a low-rental housing project and wanting, not to save the world but to reach out to those people."

She spent several years as a government social worker; set up a community services outreach program for a Toronto Salvation Army temple; set up day-care facilities. "I'm an innovator by nature, I guess." After her Army graduation in 1975 she came to Vancouver and within a year was planning the Crosswalk.

"Loneliness is maybe the biggest malady on the Row."

A message comes from uptown: one of Skid Row's regulars is wandering in the city center ten blocks away. Normally they don't stray so far from their turf but this girl is trouble-prone, Christine explains with a worried frown. "She's somewhat retarded, has a low opinion of herself and when she's drunk men just use her."

She takes the wheel of the Army's blue station wagon. David Jones, a tall young volunteer and, as it happens, an Anglican, slips in beside her.

"Drive straight up the Granville Mall," he says.

"We can't! It's just for buses and taxis and emergency vehicles!"

"That's okay, this is an official car."

"I hope you're right, Dave, or you'll have to come visit me in jail!"

We hurry up Granville without incident, park in an alley, and quick-march down the busy street. All eyes turn curiously on the Sally Ann woman with the long urgent stride and the handsome young civilian. Up here the hookers are almost elegant, sell themselves for money, not just drugs, and say discreetly "Good evening, sir, would you care for some company?" or, if in saucier mood, "Care for a little extra-curricular activity?" A teenage prostitute throws David a long molten glance.

"It's pretty hard to break hookers of the habit," Christine says, glancing them over. "The young pretty ones can make $100-$150 a day, so they don't want to work in an office for $30. We never talk to a girl while she is working the street. They know we are here and they usually come to us when they're in trouble."

Two girls hail us, part of Christine's grapevine. They've seen the missing one. "She was wearing her red dress, halfway off her shoulder. She was pretty drunk!"

"She's probably in bed with a man by now," Christine sighs.

We search a dozen bars, from the quiet to the sleazy. Two scruffy boys yell, "The Salvation Army sucks!" Christine ignores them. Three teenagers snap salutes at us, and fall about in fits of laughter at their wit. Christine keeps a straight face until they pass; then her great infectious grin breaks out. At a disco joint, where a bored and mostly bare dancer grinds her hips in a cage, Christine and I wait at the door while David searches. "Took you a long time to get through there, Dave," she says mischievously.

At the last bar the door flies open. Two waiters drag an Indian girl to the sidewalk and drop her like a bag of rags.

"Bitch!" snarls one, as they turn back inside. She is very drunk, another stray from Skid Row. Christine calls her name and says indignantly, "They shouldn't have treated her like that."

David lopes off for the station wagon. Christine and I hold the girl upright for ten minutes. Passersby ignore us or circle wide as though avoiding a mess on the sidewalk.

"Don't leave me, Christine," the girl whimpers.

"I won't leave you, dear. We're going to take you home."

And we do, to a plain rooming house on the dingy side of town.

And still the night is not over. The New Dodson Hotel, just across from the Army and Navy Store and the Double Happiness [Chinese] Restaurant, is a good ordinary beer parlor where the people of the Row feel comfortable. The waiters have thick shoulders, slicked-back hair and wise old eyes. There are lumpish men gone wobbly and silly after two beers, and young women with gaunt eyes, bad teeth and bodies run to fat.

Everyone knows Christine, Pauline and David. They move from table to table—"Hello, how are you tonight?" "Any problems?" Loneliness is maybe the biggest malady on the Row. Once Christine asked a Crosswalk visitor what she was thankful for. "The mice in my room," the woman said. They were her friends; she talked to them when they came up through the floor.

Tonight Christine befriends a sixty-three-year-old widow who lives in a neighborhood hotel on her war widow's pension. As they say good night she wraps the captain's hand in both of hers.

"It's a beginning," Christine says on the way out. "If women like her would only keep up the contact, we could get them out of here, maybe into the Homestead."

Strolling back to the Crosswalk, we run escort for a native woman who is afraid to walk home alone. Last night her man beat her up; she has the black eye to prove it. Another girl is so drunk she can't remember where she lives. "What's your name, dear?" says David wearily. Her purse turns up an address with her name on it. David drives her home in a red Army van, hoping it's the *right* address.

It is nearly 11:00 P.M. Christine has been on the go since 7:00 A.M. in her double job. But as we cross the emptying streets she murmurs, "Here comes The Seagull."

He is an elderly loner with gray beard and gray fringe circling his bald scalp. His suit was once white. The Row calls him "Seagull" because he scavenges, not so much for food as for *objets d'art*. Tonight his prize is a charcoal drawing of a boy in jeans, rescued only slightly rumpled from a garbage bin.

The Seagull is intelligent, articulate, and eager to talk about music, bands and musicians' unions. "He plays a great piano when we get him into the Crosswalk," Christine whispers. Finally we back away, waving good night with The Seagull still talking.

"Tiring? Oh yes, the long hours," Christine sighs. "But what

Christine MacMillan: "It takes a long time to break down the barriers. I've had to sell the Salvation Army through my own personhood, not through my uniform."

drained me for days, at first, was when one of them died. I still get upset, but death doesn't necessarily mean the end, in my thinking. Maybe it's a relief for them because their life has been so hellish."

We drive toward the city center again. "I don't think I'll go up Granville this time," she smiles. It is quiet and restful in the station wagon, already a million miles from Skid Row. What is it like, working down there every day?

"Initially you're embarrassed. At first I was always aware of buses going up and down the street, people looking out the windows and seeing someone holding on to me, my hat falling off or something, and me looking as much of a fool as they did!" That melting smile again.

"You lose that as you become sensitive to people and yourself. One of the Scriptures that has taught me more than anything is when Christ said to the Pharisees 'I desire mercy and not sacrifice.'"

She threads the wagon expertly through the late-night traffic. "If I look at my life as one of sacrifice, it has limits. When you decide to become sacrificial, you set goals, you set boundaries, in some ways you premeditate what that sacrifice will be.

"When I think of the word 'mercy' I think of something that's limitless. I don't know where it's gonna take me, I don't know where I will end up. And then I look at Christ on the Cross and I think, if His sacrifice were without mercy, I would not be attracted."

She pulls up beside my hotel.

"So, mercy is being pulled out of me. People recognize if you are doing it out of your need to perform 'good deeds' to enter the Kingdom of Heaven. I no longer feel that need. I feel that my salvation is in place. It's *who* I am, not *what* I do. But because of who I am, I want to be a merciful person. So one loses one's inhibitions."

The Sally Ann's angel of Skid Row waves goodbye.

"I wake up in the morning eager to go. I guess that's an indicator that this is where I should be."

Some men will never make it on their own. This small neat thirty-three year old is one of them. The Salvation Army is the center of his universe. He pops out of his single room in the new Men's Social Service Centre in Saint John, NB, just as Captain Ed Peltier happens along, showing off the place.

"Mind if I show this man your room?"

"Be my guest, Captain." Such elaborate courtesy is uncommon in the twilight world of these men with no homes of their own.

"A real little gentleman," the captain murmurs. The room with its single bed, bureau, radio, a few pictures, is as tidy as the little man himself—neater than any we've seen. On the way out we thank him.

"Any time, Captain!" And to me, "My pleasure!"

He has been in the hostel five years or more and will probably be here for life. He is on welfare and is an epileptic but his disease is controlled by medication.

"No point in putting him out," Peltier says. "We're his family. If he didn't have us he might be in jail or in the provincial hospital. We're his *everything.*"

As a youth he was in and out of petty crime. He's been out of it for fifteen years, but the local police still get uneasy when they see him wandering through a downtown shopping center. In fact, it is simply one of his daily rounds. Each morning he pokes his head into Peltier's office. "Any errands Captain? Any mail to go?"

Over the years his behavior has steadily improved.

"I feel good about him," Peltier says. "It may not be success by other people's standards but it's success for *him.*"

That is the criterion in each of the twenty-nine men's social centers across Canada. Some are strictly hostels; others, like this one are licensed as special care homes. All are for men who can't cope on their own, whose success is not measured by society's usual yardsticks, whose contribution to mankind may be minimal but who have been battered in ways that few of us can comprehend. For them, sheer survival is a daily triumph. The Army is their rock and their salvation.

Saint John had one of the first men's hostels in Canada but the strangest was Joe Beef's Canteen in Montreal. In the 1880s it was a combination saloon, flophouse (beds for ten cents) and a menagerie. At various times the proprietor kept bears, monkeys, an alligator, and a buffalo on the premises.

Joe Beef, a burly quick-witted Irishman, was fond of the Salvation Army. Its soldiers with their prayers and the *War Cry* were always welcome in his saloon. In 1893, four years after he died without leaving a will, the canteen became an Army shelter.

The $1.7 million architecturally-designed Army center in Saint John today would disgust Joe Beef: it is spotless, uncommonly bright and devoid of alligators. Part of central Saint John's renaissance which includes a shopping mall/hotel complex in the city core, it holds fifty-six men, about one-third of the demand. "We take those with the greatest need," Captain Peltier says. "They don't like to leave here. Our cooks do an awful good job."

Some are parolees, some are pensioners, some are single men on welfare. Few can afford to live outside and the Army—which needs a minimum of ten dollars per person per day to function—can't afford to keep them for their welfare or pension cheques. Yet it *does*, finding odd jobs for them in the adjoining thrift store, hoping they'll eventually find work on the outside.

"These are nervous shy people," Peltier says. "They like to look you over, size you up. We never force them into anything. We're their family."

Ed Peltier is tall, with gray-flecked sideburns and that lived-in look that hard work and a knockabout life print on a man's face. He grew up on a farm near Huntsville, Ontario, where his grandfather, a drinker, gave shelter to other drinkers or men just down on their luck. After Peltier went out on his own he happened into an Army hostel in Sudbury. He had no interest in the religion but was pleased to find people doing what Grandfather had done. He stayed to work, trained to be an officer, and has helped needy men ever since.

"It's my life and hobby and passion," he says quietly. "If somebody offered me a million dollars to change I'd turn it down. Well, I *hope* I could. Because I'm completely fulfilled."

In the basement "Friendship Room," a drop-in center for street people run by the Toronto Temple Corps, a small circle of officers, soldiers, and civilian volunteers bows in prayer before taking to the streets for "midnight patrol." Outside, the howls and catcalls from the Yonge Street Strip announce a typical rowdy Friday night.

The half-dozen blocks of what once was Toronto's proudest thoroughfare are crammed with hookers, drunks, gays, young boys wearing gloss lipstick, schoolgirls in pasted-on jeans that chart every crease and curve of crotch and rump, peddlers, street musicians, bullies, bluffers and a few bemused tourists. Elbow to elbow, they surge and swagger aimlessly through the blink of neon. Cars creep bumper to bumper, occupants yelling, radios at full blast.

Street patrol, Toronto: soldier Alan Drury (now in officer training) offers information to young travelers while soldier Hee Lam Leung looks on.

Into this cacophony the Army marches, two by two, to patrol the Strip, its back alleys, a bus station, and an underground parking garage where street waifs and derelicts sometimes seek shelter from the elements. Their mission: find anyone who might want friendship, a prayer, a bed for the night or coffee and a sandwich in the Friendship Room.

"Yonge Street feeds on loneliness," sighs Alan Drury, a recent education graduate from the University of Toronto. Slim and serious, he towers over his mate, Edward Udoh, but Edward's huge white smile makes him ten feet tall. He is the son of Army officers in Nigeria and a York University student in honors French and political science.

Soldier Joe Elkerton, early twenties, broad of hip and chest, moves with the confident rolling gait of one who knows his turf. Until he joined the Army six months before, he was a street kid. He knows the Strip's habitués, their vices, their scams. Beside him, her bonnet barely up to his shoulder, marches Mrs. Major Pat Ryan, the downtown corps commander's wife. What is the mother of four grown children doing out in this human jungle?

"I wouldn't want to come out here *alone* tonight," she admits. But like every Army veteran, Pat Ryan has steeled herself to a less-than-perfect world. Her quick bright gaze misses nothing: the disheveled man carrying a signboard (yes he tells her, he would like a coffee later); the prostitutes posing beside a drugstore; the gray-haired man in a crumpled heap beside the Eaton Centre, ignored by passersby.

She kneels, expertly checking his pulse. He has fallen down drunk and gashed his forehead. She stirs him awake while Elkerton calls for the Army's blue van.

"What's your name, sir?... Jerry? Where's your home?... Newfoundland. All right, we're going to fix that head and get some coffee into you."

Jerry perks up and tries to kiss her hand. She gently fends him off until the van whisks him away to a hospital detoxification center.

Down the street a belligerent drunk, fresh out of prison, pours abuse and obscenities on Major Max Ryan and young soldier Doug Crighton, another recent recruit from the streets. The bearded major, slim and straight-backed, coolly stands his ground, but there is no reasoning with this man. As they turn away the drunk jeers provocatively at big Crighton, "Hey, Fatso, what's your name?" Drury and Udoh close in, watchfully.

"Alan?" the major says, with a meaningful nod. And Drury, who has a way with the worst of people (and subsequently went into officer training), sets out to defuse the drunk with conversation.

A crowd of hooting youths swarms around Ryan.

"Wanna buy some pot? It's good for you!"

Ryan grins wryly and counters with an invitation for coffee at the corps. An elderly man huddles in a doorway with his belongings in three plastic bags. The Army takes him back for coffee and finds him a bed. They discover that his "belongings" consist of girlie magazines and empty bottles.

Max Ryan at his own request gave up the prestigious job of Army literary secretary to minister to an inner city congregation, ranging from very rich to very poor, and to these street people. Five nights a week as many as one hundred crowd into the Friendship Room, two blocks from the Temple, to play pool or chess, watch TV, read, have a coffee and snack, or simply relax in a non-threatening environment. A welcome, and counsel if they want it, is always there.

The hookers rarely come to the center but the Sally Ann knows most of them by name, knows their haunts, knows that even an ugly girl can earn $1,000 a week. It has a special handout pamphlet for them, titled (in their own lingo) *For the Working Girl*. It says, in part:

> If you feel that you've got no problem, you enjoy the
> fast money you can make on the street and you feel that
> you have no need of God then you might as well stop
> reading this now.
> If, however, you've got some problems that you can't
> seem to sort out, or you want to quit the streets, or
> you need a friend or you just want to find out what
> real love is, then this pamphlet is for you. Being a
> hooker does not remove you out of God's love. . . .

One October night the midnight patrol plucks a sixty-one-year-old woman from the Strip. She is white-haired, cold, and alone. Whatever family she ever had is gone. She is one of Toronto's 5,000 "bag ladies," prowling streets and alleys with all her worldly goods in a single shopping bag. She does the rounds of local hostels, moving on when her welcome runs out, sleeping between times in whatever nooks the fates present to her.

The Army takes her to its Evangeline Residence, which cares for women in need. Some are long-term residents emerging from psychiatric treatment, able to hold daytime jobs but not yet able to live effectively on their own. Some are emergency cases—runaway daughters, battered wives, elderly transients like the bag lady.

To all of them, the residence means shelter and love. At night there is someone to say "good night," and mean it. At the front door, Major Constance Green, a dark sturdy woman with twenty-one years' service, greets them with "Did you have a good day?" Later, the memory softening her eyes, she explains, "I remember how important it was to me, as a kid in Brantford, to hear those words when I came home from school."

As a transient the bag lady is qualified to stay fifteen days, the limit of Ontario's financial assistance to the Army for such cases. But she is sick, frail, and at long last tired of her gypsy life. She likes her clean bed and good meals.

The Army keeps her on at its own expense. One day the chaplain takes her out to buy clothes and, to her delight, have lunch in a restaurant. Another time they take her to the doctor in a taxi—a rare treat. Finally they get her into a senior citizens' home. "We'll keep in touch with her," the major promises. "She'll probably come back here for visits." Because, at last, the bag lady has a family—maybe for the first time in her adult life.

11

The Extended Family

For fifteen Christmases he has stood outside the Hudson Bay store in downtown Calgary, manning a Salvation Army Christmas kettle. He has the Salvationist's cheerful face and sometimes wears an Army hat with his business suit. Nothing too unusual about that—until someone, slipping a bill into the kettle says, "Happy Chanukah, Rabbi!"

Rabbi?

He is Rabbi Lewis N. Ginsburg of Calgary's Shaarey Tzedec synagogue, an admirer of the Sally Ann since childhood.

"I would see its devotees staffing the kettles in my home in Minneapolis," he says. "My parents explained to me the significance of the effort, and a seed of admiration was planted. Now I appreciate the Army's depth of faith and its human concern. When one raps at their door seeking help their first question isn't 'What is your faith?' Rather, it is 'What is your need?' "

One year, to open the Red Shield campaign, the rabbi conducted the Canadian Staff Band in front of Calgary City Hall. Since he does not read music, "the fact that we finished at the same time was due to their prayers and mine." Later he was made an honorary Lieutenant-Colonel.

The rabbi—with Alberta author and former Lieutenant-Governor Grant MacEwan and Judge Gerald Sinclair of the citizenship court, who've also helped out on the kettles—is part of the Army's extended family. Thousands of non-Salvationist friends across Canada more than double the Army's actual numbers and immeasurably strengthen its work.

"Family" means everything to Salvationists. From the perceived threat to family came its policies on premarital chastity, marital fidelity, marriage enrichment, counseling, divorce, homosexuality. Within the officer ranks "family" also means a unique international brotherhood.

"That family spirit has been developed through a hundred years," says Major Stuart Booth of Quebec City. "I can't explain it. It is just *there*."

"If tomorrow I landed in a German city and an Army officer was there, I could count on being accepted and cared for," says Commissioner Arthur Pitcher. "It is a tremendous worldwide fellowship."

Pitcher recalls an officers' conference in England after World War II. Josef Korbel, a Czech not long out of prison camp showed up in Salvation Army tunic and a pair of brown trousers—the only ones he had. By the time Pitcher went to his room to offer his own spare pants, the Czech already had four other pair given him.

Australian-born officer Iain Trainor, now of Halifax, visited Sri Lanka as a child with his Salvationist father. "We got off a boat and went to Sunday morning services. There was one other European

Christmas with the band and the kettle. The civilian's skirt and the Army woman's late-model hat indicate that this was sometime in the 1970s.

face in the congregation. An officer came up and in broken English asked 'Salvationists?' 'Yes.' 'Play instruments?' 'Yes.' So we ended up playing in the Colombo Citadel band as if we had always been there. We were instantly brothers."

There are associate members of the brotherhood. Since 1966 the Advisory Council of Salvation Army Laymen (ACSAL)—soldiers and adherents—has offered advice to the Army hierarchy on everything from evangelism to uniform-wearing. At one time such advice would have fallen into a bottomless pit.

"The lay Salvationist, to be blunt, was and still is required to 'march, sing, pray and collect money' but never to question, challenge or participate in any decision of his officer or head-quarters," wrote R. Gordon Moyles in *The Blood and Fire in Canada.*

Today a few officers still regard ACSAL as they would a cobra under their beds but, says ACSAL's territorial chairman, Joseph Sears, that's rare.

"Hardly a week goes by now when I don't hear from department heads, asking for input on certain things, and I have a direct route to the commissioner if I need it," says Sears, a Toronto insurance executive. "I'd like to see us—laymen and officers—become a lot more vocal. I think we should be out there challenging governments on everything they do that affects the moral fiber of this country. You don't have to take political sides to say 'You're wrong.' "

Beyond the Salvationists themselves is another army of Canadians, each with a soft heart for the Sally Ann. Each story is a little different but the theme is unchanging. Many, of course, are war veterans. After World War II ex-serviceman Paul Zimmerman, who hadn't completed Grade 10 before joining the Army, was back at school and supporting his wife and two children on a DVA allowance.

"In the middle of this pressure course—I was working eighteen hours a day, trying to do all my high school in ten months—my wife had a serious appendicitis attack with jaundice. I remembered the Salvation Army. They sent a homemaker who took over while I went to school. There's no way I'd ever have passed my courses otherwise, so if it weren't for the Army I'd probably never have amounted to very much."

Zimmerman, former president of *Reader's Digest* (Canada), is now president of Torstar, part of the Toronto *Star* publishing empire, and is helping raise money for a new Grace Hospital in Metro.

Just before Christmas 1941 a twenty-one-year-old seaman from Saskatchewan, Max Macdonald, was invalided off his ship into Halifax with a badly injured spine. He was paralyzed from the waist down (doctors said he might never walk again), depressed and alone.

A Sally Ann soldier visited him regularly with candy, magazines, and friendship. The medics were wrong and he eventually walked out on convalescent leave but with no place to stay and no money: the navy had mislaid his records. A Salvation Army hostel near the waterfront took him in without question.

"I'll pay you back," he promised.

"Don't worry about it," the Army said. Macdonald did pay, and never forgot.

"I thought they would ask me to pray, but they were simply *there* when I needed them." Macdonald is now executive vice-president of the Regina *Leader Post*. When he was asked to serve on the local Salvation Army advisory board he quickly agreed.

With thirty-four regional advisory boards plus a national body, the Army is plugged into the *crème de la crème* of Canadian corporate society. Regina had the country's first board in 1936 and its roster of early 1984 shows how Army advisors represent key professions in a community. They included: Lieutenant-Governor Fred W. Johnson; Dr. John Archer, a leading historian and founding president of the University of Regina; Senator James Balfour; Hon. Justice R. N. Hall; G. Kenneth Little and George W. Holtby, chartered accountants; and R. A. Milliken, D. K. MacPherson, and J. A. Jameson, lawyers.

There was also Orris Keehr, western area director of London Life; George C. Solomon, reputed to be one of the wealthiest men in Saskatchewan; William Patton, owner of automobile dealerships; Morrie Sims, regional manager of Montreal Trust; Dr. Norman Church, an optometrist; J. Milton Fair, chief executive officer of the Saskatchewan Wheat Pool, and publisher Macdonald. Several influential retired men rounded out the board.

Boards are not chosen strictly for influence or wealth. Candidates must be of good moral and ethical standing in the community. The Army prefers a church affiliation but not its own. Regina's Archer is Anglican; Vern French, chairman of the St. John's, Newfoundland, board, is Catholic; Simon L. Gaum of the Halifax board is Jewish. Every board is advisory *only*, but as one officer says, "we'd be crazy to not take their advice most of the time."

"If we were contemplating a new building we wouldn't move without submitting plans and costs to the advisory board," says Major Ron Bowles in Regina. "A realtor member could tell us if the land was a good buy or not. A chartered accountant could advise us on budgeting, and so on."

"The Army is very astute to involve members of the community," says Saint John board chairman Tom Simms, owner of a brush company, one of the city's oldest family firms. Like most people Simms admired the Army from a distance but being on the inside deepens his commitment.

"It's providing a measure of stability in a very turbulent society. We're not a Third World country but we have desperate needs. The Army, with the police, is meeting them head-on. The rest of society, most of it, doesn't or can't get involved. The Army's work represents true Christianity."

If *Who's Who in Canada* married *Debrett's Illustrated Guide to the Canadian Establishment*, their progeny would be an Army advisory board. In Quebec: G. Drummond Birks and H. Arnold Steinberg, whose names are household words, Claude Taylor, chairman of Air Canada, and James C. Thackray, chairman of Bell Canada, are or have been on boards. In Toronto, John Craig Eaton of *the* Eatons. In Saint John, Jean Irving, daughter of industrialist and media baron K. C. Irving. In Vancouver, Alan Eyre, whose Chev-Olds dealership is one of the largest in North America.

Manitoba Lieutenant-Governor Pearl McGonigal, a former board chairman, is an ardent friend of the Army. ("They preach a good sermon, not only with their lips but their actions.") Robert Thompson, former leader of the Social Credit Party in Canada, is on the House of Concord advisory board in Langley, BC. James W. Kerr, chief executive officer of TransCanada Pipelines was awarded the Army's Order of Distinguished Auxiliary Service, limited to some two hundred friends of the Sally Ann worldwide.

Although the Army scrupulously avoids partisan politics many board members are or have been civic or provincial politicians, usually dating back before their election to office. Among them: Hon. Roland Thornhill, minister of development in the Nova Scotia government; Mayor Leslie Way of Saint John, NB; Hon. Nancy Clark-Teed, New Brunswick's minister of social services; Mayor Frank Ney of Nanaimo. Elected officials can usually advise the Army on policies or procedures without compromising their office.

The "family" list goes on and on. Brian Mulroney, prior to becoming Progressive Conservative leader, headed up the Army's Ministries Enrichment Program in Quebec. John Turner served on advisory boards before returning to lead the Liberal party. Newfoundland industrialist W. J. "Billy" Lundrigan furnished the General's office in London, England.

Something about the Sally Ann reaches deep inside us all. Piano virtuoso Glenn Gould left half his estate to the Army. In British Columbia, Alex and Viola Tymos, watching a TV program on the Army, decided to donate a big tractor-trailer left over from the prosperous freight company Alex owned before he retired. Today it's hauling used clothing and appliances for Men's Social Services in Vancouver.

In Regina Mae Weston, whose baker father was one of *the*

Westons, worked thirty-eight years for lawyer George Thorne. The lawyer left an estate of several hundred thousand dollars to the Sally Ann. Miss Weston, in her early nineties, administers it without pay because she too "always had a soft spot in my heart for the Army."

As a zone leader for the Army's Red Shield team in Saint John, Emma May Weisseneder ("I might have been a Salvationist if I hadn't been a Baptist") oversees about thirty other canvassers encompassing one thousand households. Mrs. Weisseneder, a psychiatric nurse by profession, does many kinds of volunteer work.

"People's attitudes are completely different toward the Army," she says. "They give out of a sense of duty to other charities. They give to the Army from the heart. And not once have I ever been told to 'come back later.' "

Theoretically there is no limit to the Army family because new friends keep popping up with memories of some distant act of kindness. Fifteen years ago Army officer David Hammond picked up a student, broke and hitch-hiking home on a Newfoundland road. Hammond staked him to a five-dollar bus ticket and forgot about it.

In the fall of 1983 Hammond, now a major and principal of the St. John's training college, was named in a newspaper story. The phone rang.

"I've been looking for you for years!" cried the boy of long ago. "Is there anything I can do for the Army?" In fact, there was. He's a consultant to the federal government and helped the Army apply for funding to help build its new training college.

The point is—and this is *why* the Army's extended family knows no limits—Salvationists don't do good deeds with a payback in mind. One afternoon in Whitby, Ontario, soldier Ken Clarke and his wife Anna-Marie overheard a local corps officer tell a pair of hitch-hikers, "I'm sorry, we don't have rooms here. All I can suggest is that if you can get to Toronto our hostel there will help you."

As the Clarkes drove home, Ken was uncommonly quiet.

"You're thinking about those two, aren't you?" said Anna-Marie.

"Well, yes. They're pretty young, it's getting late, some weirdo could pick them up and who knows what might happen."

"I suppose you're thinking we should take them home?"

"Would you mind?"

She didn't, of course. Although the Clarkes have a big house, they already had a college boy staying with them, along with their own three children. Anna-Marie went home to organize beds. Ken found the pair on Highway 401 and brought them back.

The boy, a Roman Catholic, folded his clothes neatly beside his bed and said his prayers. The girl, when loaned a nightgown, said it was the first she'd ever had. Her memory of childhood was of her mother going to work each morning and leaving her sitting in her high chair all day with a jar of baby food. "Why did you take us in?" she asked with tears in her eyes.

In the morning the Clarkes put them on a bus to Toronto, and alerted Army social services to expect them. Whether they ever see the pair again doesn't matter. "I did what I felt in my conscience I had to do," Ken Clarke explains. "Or I couldn't have slept that night. You see?"

12

In the Pubs

It is yet another measure of the Salvationist's social conscience that hundreds of them go out every Friday or Saturday night into places they personally deplore, places that are physically repugnant to many of them: the pubs. Now, fortifying themselves for the ordeal, four uniformed soldiers stand for a moment of prayer in Toronto's downtown temple. Then, bundles of the *War Cry* and small red collection boxes in hand, they hit the streets.

The two elderly women, one in old-fashioned bonnet, march off to some peaceable bars. Alan Drury and his sidekick Edward Udoh begin in a singles hangout. For two hours they trudge from bar to bar, table to table, through cigarette and marijuana smoke, the sour smell of beer, the jingle and beep of video games.

Most people greet them kindly with a quarter or two. A few regulars seem glad to see them. A well-dressed man showing off for his pals baits Alan with wisecracks: "I've been waiting for you to come around to my place with a Care parcel" (Alan: "Best we can do is send you the band!") and "Y'know, the Old Testament is a *dirty* book!" and "What if I was boss of a remote little village, very good to the people, gave them food—wouldn't *I* be God?"

A World War II veteran—there's nearly always one—tells Edward, "You fellas do good work." A hostile drunk snarls at Alan, "I don't believe in God, you're wasting your time in that funny looking uniform." Alan gently explains what he does and why, without getting into heavy theology.

Another drinker snaps, "You people are just out for the money!"

"It's not true!" says Alan, genuinely hurt. "Every cent we collect is used right here in the inner city for people who need it." But the man turns away, bitter and unconvinced.

Later Drury, ever the optimist, says, "Maybe another time I'll find him in a better mood and we'll be able to share." Marching cheerfully on to the next pub he remembers happier incidents, as when two mean-looking bikers rasped, "You! C'mere!" Drury expected the worst, but they only wanted to give money, gruffly remembering how the Army had once helped their families.

If you know anything about the Sally Ann, you know they have been "pub booming" for generations. It is one of their most visible and least understood acts. What other religious organizations would venture into drinking joints? What other would *want* to?

"Booming" is old English slang meaning to sell or "push" something, in this case the *War Cry*, yet the Army is not out to make money. Collections from an average Friday or Saturday night would barely pay for that week's edition. The *War Cry* and collection box are merely an *entrée*. The army is gathering souls.

It is the hardest kind of ministry for many. Pub booming is part of every cadet's training and in a student seminar one September morning, Major David Hammond, principal of the St. John's college, made some basic points.

"The pub population is growing perhaps five times the rate that the churches are growing," he said. "The Salvation Army has a unique opportunity to witness in the pubs. If we don't go in, no one else will."

Most pubs welcome the Army uniform, he told them. Pub booming is meeting people and "the more you do it, the more you'll be able to do it. Our presence in the pub is a witness to Jesus Christ before a single word is spoken."

But knowing how difficult this ministry can be for young people, he added, "Our greatest enemy is fear."

The flood of questions bore him out. Some cadets had already tasted pub duty and one boy confessed, to roars of laughter, "If I'd had a medical before I went out they'd have pronounced me dead!"

Most were from non-drinking Salvationist backgrounds. A few had never set foot in a bar. A few others were reformed drinkers, worrying about what that old environment might do to them.

A former alcoholic told how a drunk had abused him on his first pub ministry. He felt rage surging up inside from his old quarrelsome drinking days, swallowed it with a mighty effort, quietly said "God bless you," and walked away. Now, he told the major, he was fighting the fear of what might happen next time.

"I haven't had a drink since July fourth 1970," a bearded older student told the class. "I never liked beer but I liked my rum. Now I wonder: if I'm in a bar and someone offers me a Bacardi . . .?"

"People don't often do that, except in jest," said Hammond. "Our uniform is respected."

Well, how do you break the ice in these places, the new students wanted to know? What do you say?

"Simple things," Hammond told them. "Talk about sports or a topic from the headlines. Or 'Would you like to have a *War Cry*? Would you like to help the Army?' But remember, we're not in it for the money."

The women students were less worried about breaking the ice than falling in over their heads. Some had been chased in bars.

"Some of the guys tried to get my name and phone number," said one. The class discussed the pros and cons. Leaving a contact number for someone who might need help is a key part of the ministry. But since it appeared that some bar-flies desire Army women more than the Army, the consensus was: if you're a single female, leave only the corps number, not your home number.

"They didn't see me as an officer," one girl said bluntly. "They saw me as a woman, and they *wanted me!*" She got a big but sympathetic laugh. It takes guts for a young Salvationist and most of all a woman to go booming. But nobody ever promised them the holy war would be easy.

Another Friday night, this time in Whitehorse. Lieutenant Jim Morris and soldier Brian Hewitt are touring the bars. Morris, the corps officer, is short and jolly with reddish hair. Hewitt, a telephone technician, is tall with white hair, a firm grip and a strong noble face—the kind you have seen on a thousand Sally Ann posters.

Hewitt and his wife are ex-Anglicans who turned away from their church because of its preoccupation with such worldly things as real estate and politics.

"We tried a couple of others, came to the Army in 1980, and we're very happy."

Now he and Morris move from bar to bar with friendly greetings but no hard sell.

"I feel we are invading their territory, in a sense," Hewitt says. "So we're courteous, we don't push it. Whether they give money or not I always say 'Thank you, God bless you, have a nice weekend.' "

Hewitt dislikes collecting money, and pubs disgust both of them. They go home reeking of booze and cigarettes and have to air their uniforms. Hewitt drank little in pre-Army days and Morris has never tasted liquor.

"In training college I said, 'I hate pubs, I'll do anything but don't ask me to go into a pub,' " Morris remembers. "So who was the first guy they assigned to do pubs? Me! The first time I went a guy swore at me. I headed for the door. But then another man came up and said, 'Wait a minute. I was in World War II and a Sally Ann girl one time asked if I wanted a coffee and doughnut. The next thing, I looked around and she was blown to pieces. I'll never forget the Army.' "

After that Morris never balked at pubs. Now he accepts them philosophically: there is always the chance of doing somebody a good turn. Such as the time he helped a girl get into the Army unwed mothers' home in Vancouver. Months later she came back to say, "I just want to thank you. The Army made a woman out of me." Or the time another young woman told him after small talk in a bar, "I'm living in sin." Morris did not fall over in shock, as perhaps she expected, nor moralize nor make *any* fuss. Six months later he performed a wedding for the girl and her man, and today their children are Army church members.

Yet again, the phone woke him up at home one icy winter night. It was a middle-aged man he'd met in the pubs. The man lived alone, was in trouble with his boss because of his drinking, and was terrified of losing his job.

"I'm going to kill myself!" he shouted.

Morris thrust the phone at his wife. She kept the caller on the line while he phoned the police. They broke down a door and saved the man as he was about to hang himself. He took alcoholism treatment and now, says Morris, "We're friends for life."

It can take months for a pub ministry relationship to mature. It happens to Brian Hewitt this very night.

For months he has said only "Hello, how are you" to a certain man in his early thirties. Tonight the man tugs at Hewitt's sleeve: "I've got to talk to you."

They step outside. Suddenly this casual acquaintance bares his soul. He has lost his job. His creditors are after him. His marriage is falling apart.

"I've hit rock-bottom," he says.

"You're young, you can start over," Hewitt says encouragingly.

"There's no place else to go but up," the man says gloomily.

"Come over to my house on Sunday night, have a coffee with my wife and me, and we'll talk," urges Hewitt. The man accepts. It's a start. Hewitt and Morris exchange tired but happy smiles.

"There's hardly a night after pub ministry that I don't feel good about something," says Lieutenant Morris, the man who hates pubs.

Every officer has a favorite pub story. For Lieutenant-Colonel Albert Browning in Newfoundland, it's the World War II veteran who waved him down as he toured a bar with his collection box one night long ago.

"Evening, Captain," he said. (To the good-old-boys of street and pub, an Army officer, regardless of rank, is always "Captain"—unless they want a favor, in which case he becomes "Colonel.") "I was just thinking. Many's the time in the war the Army gave me a doughnut and a cup of coffee."

He paused with a grin to set up the punch line.

"And Captain, I've been payin' for it every Saturday night since!"

13

The Shooting War

Whenever a Salvation Army officer walks into a Canadian Legion hall or any other veterans' club in the land, a great tide of affection wells up around him. It is so genuine, so pervasive, that some Army officers seriously wonder what they'll do for an encore when the vets, most of whom are getting a little long in the tooth, are gone. The veterans and their kin are charter members of the extended family. Many young Canadians who never saw a war give to the Red Shield because the Sally Ann was good to Dad.

To World War I and II veterans the words "Sally Ann" are like a benediction. World War I *gave* that nickname to the angels who served coffee and doughnuts behind the terrible trenches. World War II wrote it into the vocabulary of an entire generation, because the Army's mercy to the troops inevitably touched their families back home.

The Army sent a few officers overseas in the first war but their role was primarily as support for the British. In World War II Canadian Salvationists mounted a massive effort, beginning in 1938 when they read the danger signs in Europe. When war came the Sally Ann was ready.

Between 1939 and 1946, 414 Army officers and supervisors (some of them civilians) and thousands of other volunteers served the Canadian troops, many of whom were Salvationists too. In those seven years the Army gave out more than 270 million free packets of writing paper in Canada and abroad, nearly 5 million magazines and newspapers, and 38 million hot beverages from their mobile canteens. It served 56 million meals and teas overseas, entertained 45

Here's where the name "Sally Ann" began: with World War I Army girls (not Canadians) like these, setting off from Paris to bring coffee and doughnuts, smiles and prayer, to the Allied troops in the terrible front-line trenches.

million men and women at free movies and concerts, pressed 615,000 pieces of clothing. But as always, statistics show none of the humanity, which is the real story.

The Army had two main jobs: contributing chaplains to the military pool for non-denominational services to all troops, and being part of an auxiliary services organization with the YMCA, the Knights of Columbus, and the Canadian Legion. Its symbol was the Red Shield, familiar from World War I.

What was different about the Sally Ann? Other service organizations did similar work. The Army's facilities were not as lavish as some. Yet nearly every veteran agrees that the Army was special. Perhaps it was their unflagging goodness; their willingness to do any kind of reasonable favor.

"Nothing was too much trouble for them," agrees retired General Clarence Wiseman, who was senior representative of Red Shield Services overseas. "They brought their faith and dedication and their sense of compassion into war services."

Virtually everywhere you went in the armed forces, the Army was there. In *Red Shield in Action*, the Army's history of its war work, author Scott Young describes a typical Red Shield Center:

It had one room where a man could be quiet, and read or think or pray, and any man who has known the washing in crowds, eating in crowds, training in crowds and sleeping in crowds that was the permanent lot of servicemen will remember how valuable that quiet room could be. It sometimes served as a chapel. . . . Another room was full of games—darts, table hockey and tennis, checkers, chess. Another was the library. Another, dominated by a great sign which said "Keep in Touch with the Folks at Home," was the writing room. Millions of words, written on millions of sheets of paper, posted in millions of envelopes, sprayed from these huts into tens of thousands of Canadian homes, a tenuous cord connecting uprooted men with their families. . . .

Home seemed real when you were in the writing room. During three years in the RCAF in Canada and overseas, I wrote a letter home every week, at least half of them on that blessed Sally Ann stationery.

In the larger centers, ladies of the Red Shield Women's Auxiliary were ready to darn a sock, sew on a button, press a pair of pants, or even do a rush bit of shopping for a man or woman who couldn't get away from camp. Red Shield Hostels across Canada gave you a clean

Troops of a Canadian armoured division stoke up on tea, coffee, and sandwiches from a mobile canteen in England, 1941.

These airmen get a welcome mug of tea from the Army's mobile canteen at an air base in Britain.

bed and probably a meal or two for less than a dollar a night. Army hostess houses gave soldiers and wives a meeting place in their itinerant partings and reunions.

Royal Air Force trainee Terry Williams even found a wife in the Sally Ann. He went into the Saint John, NB, hostel for a meal and a pretty young volunteer said, "Would you like to read the *War Cry?*"

"Will you read it to me?" said Williams archly. One thing led to another and they married in December 1943. Williams made Canada his home after the war, is president of his own knitwear company in Kitchener, president of the local Salvation Army advisory board (although he belongs to the United Church), and recently celebrated his fortieth wedding anniversary.

"The Salvation Army—I wish there were a hundred million of them!" he cries.

No request was too outlandish for the Army supervisors in charge of the centers. *Red Shield in Action* chronicles the average sixteen-hour day of one such man on a Canadian base. His morning was filled with meetings and with planning a track and field meet, a film showing and a table tennis tournament. Then a Mennonite boy in an active fighting unit wanted help in getting transferred to the stretcher-bearers. The supervisor fixed it up with the military.

A telegram came from a soldier's wife out west: she hadn't heard from her man in months. The Sally Ann supervisor found him right on camp and jogged his conscience. Another soldier wanted a money order cashed; a second had girl trouble; a third wanted leave to go home and help on the farm.

The supervisor dropped in on a Salvation Army bandsman, seriously ill in the base hospital. Now it was evening, the canteen was in full swing, and he kept an eye on it and on the nightly movie. He helped count the cash and lock up. He got to bed at midnight.

This pace was the norm. Overseas the Sally Ann stayed close to the troops. When the Canadians came back bloodied and battered from the catastrophe called Dieppe, four Army mobile canteens were waiting on the English shore with coffee, tea, cocoa, doughnuts, and biscuits. For most of the beaten men, it was the first food in twenty-four hours.

Time and again the Sally Ann solved little personal crises. A distraught soldier hadn't heard from home. Was his wife sick—or running around with another man? Cables and telegrams leaped the Atlantic to the nearest corps, an officer on the spot rooted out the problem, and the word was back overseas sometimes in a day or two. For its own Salvationists in fighting units the Army in Canada sent a letter every month from the commissioner, with a footnote from the local corps, keeping them up to date on life at home.

The Red Shield sign hung out on whatever shelter was available: a former fish and chips store, an English country home or a metal Nissen hut. During the Allied invasion of Italy, the Sally Ann set up shop in everything from an art gallery to a tent.

As the Canadian Army fought its way up Italy, God's ingenious Army was right on its heels. "Scrounging" was a high art during the war and Army supervisors mastered it. The fight to recapture Ortona from the Nazis was one of the most vicious of the Italian campaign. The Adriatic port fell two days after Christmas 1943. A month later a newcomer asked a soldier where he could find the Sally Ann.

"They run the whole town, sir," the soldier said. "You can't miss it!"

You certainly couldn't. The Army named its digs the "Monastery Inn," a refurbished ruin fitted with clean beds, a theater, barber shop, tailor, and all the other everyday wonders of a Red Shield Center. The staff was uniformed in white from liberated Italian table linen, with touches of gold braid from the epaulets of captured Italian officers.

In early February the Sally Ann issued a straight-faced formal invitation to "the gala opening of Ortona-on-sea, an Oasis for Front Line Canadians of 2 C.I.B." It acknowledged "Lumber by Scrounger and Sons, Bunks by Seaforth Pioneers Ltd., Alterations and Heating by Loyal Edmonton Pioneers Inc., Speedy Transport by Patricia Ltd., Sanitary Arrangements Approved by Field Hygiene Inc., Water from the Certified Springs of Brigade Water Works. . . ." (The Seaforths, Princess Patricias, and Loyal Edmontons were Canadian regiments on the scene.)

When D-Day came on 6 June 1944, the Red Shield supervisors were as close behind as the Allied brass permitted. The first Salvation Army man landed on 9 June, as fighting raged all around, and on 11 June showed what was probably the first movie in any part of liberated Europe.

"I know of one instance when the commanding officer stopped his men behind the lines from going up to our mobile canteen," says General Wiseman. "It was too dangerous—our canteen was too close to the front!"

Sometimes the Army functioned from a slit trench, and showed films on a screen stretched at the back of a truck with a canopy hiding its light from marauding aircraft. At least once the "theater" was a tarpaulin spread over two long lanes of military trucks. Another night the supervisor persuaded regular army engineers to sweep a field with mine detectors so he could safely assemble a crowd for the movie.

When the Allied advance reached Arnhem where the Germans had wiped out an earlier British paratroop attack, the Sally Ann outdid itself. Its man took over a ruined hangar with no roof or front wall. He bulldozed the rubble away, made a roof from bits of beams and tin sheeting, built a plywood stage from ruined gliders left from the abortive parachute attack, used ammunition boxes for seats and made two oil drums into stoves. Result: a movie house for three hundred men.

From the records of the supervisors themselves came this account of a winter with the Third Canadian Infantry Division in Europe:

> Always keeping in mind the boys who were doing the dirty jobs at the front, they were naturally given the greater portion of chocolate and cigarettes and magazines. . . . We found the best distribution was to take the supplies to the front and break them down by companies. . . . During these trips to the lines, we were able to do small favours for the boys. On inquiring whether they had sent a letter home to Mom recently, if the answer was in the negative, we would get their home addresses and drop their families a line when we got back. . . .
>
> As the weeks went by, the winter came upon us, and the boys [Nijmegen area] were taking a lot of punishment. It was hard to

keep warm and something had to be done. A large house was taken over and turned into a unit hotel or rest center. Arrangements were made with the unit commander in operating this establishment for twenty-four hour rests. Beds, blankets, sheets, dishes, cutlery and furniture were picked up from unknown places. . . . Imagine yourself spending days and weeks in the middle of a clump of trees during the winter, always half frozen, then coming to this setup. . . . You arrive at 9 A.M. to be greeted by a cup of steaming tea and biscuits. After getting the chill out of your bones you are taken upstairs and shown your bedroom—a real bed with sheets—the first you have had a chance to sleep in for six months. Then you explore still further and see a sign on one of the doors: BARBER SHOP—SHAVE AND HAIRCUT.

"Gee, isn't it wonderful to be shaved again," one lad remarks. Now downstairs again where the Supervisor says there is a truck laid on to take you for a real shower . . . then back again feeling wonderful and just in time for lunch—yes, at a table, with plates, cups and saucers, knives and forks, and a real white table-cloth. And what meals—steak, beautiful fresh apple pie with whipped cream—"Have I gone nuts? Is this a dream?" What rooms, but before you step in a sign says, BOOTS OFF MEN—WE ARE SAVING THE RUG. So off they come, and you sink into the soft springs of a sofa, while the radio soothes your tired mind and you doze off to sleep.

Just before supper the Supervisor reminds you that there is a dance on in the town—but who wants to dance. "Not me, I'm staying home. Yes, it's just like home." And yet only two or three miles from the front line. To end the evening a movie is shown in the spacious living room as you relax right on the chesterfield, and by 10 P.M. you are ready to hit the hay.

The Sally Ann stayed in Europe until December 1946. By then the troops were home. One soldier's wartime letter, eloquent in its simplicity, summed up the Army effort best: "The Salvation Army has caught up with us," he wrote to his mother, "and it's the best thing next to home. They do wonderful work."

14

God's
Corporation

Behind that wonderful work is organization. On the one hand the Army is a church. On the other it is big business. With total assets of approximately $133 million, it would easily place in the *Financial Post* "500" annual rating of the nation's top companies. Naturally it is not so rated, because the Salvation Army is a registered charitable and non-profit organization.

Nevertheless, it must be run like a business and it has many of the corporate trappings. Its organization chart fans down from the commissioner through twenty-three departments to 405 corps and outposts. It has gone into computers with its own full-time officer expert, who is also qualified to preach a sermon and perform weddings and funerals. It owns nearly twelve hundred properties in Canada and Bermuda. Its departments include a literary and publishing wing, a special efforts department that arranges conferences, congresses, and concerts, and Supplies and Purchasing (known to Army wags as SAP) which is like a small department store.

Ken Clarke, the Salvationist soldier who ran the multi-million-dollar Ministries Enrichment Program to raise capital funds, sometimes described the Army to businessmen in terms they understood: "We have 700 business offices in Canada, several thousand employees and about 200,000 volunteers." The last, says Clarke, are not necessarily soldiers or adherents (some may be); they are company vice-presidents, women who collect for the Red Shield, people who volunteer for Army crisis lines.

"Put that way, we are *not* a minority denomination of around 130,000 people," Clarke told prospective donors. "The Salvation

Army network—not just those who claim it as their religion but those who solidly support it and say 'I love that organization'—is pretty powerful in Canada."

Those supporters share a common sentiment: in financial terms, they give to the Army even if they give to no other organization because "you can trust the Sally Ann."

"That kind of remark came to me from the guy on the street right through to the prime minister himself," Clarke says. "People respect the Army for the way it is handling its funds." And the Army, acutely aware of this trust, strenuously guards its financial probity.

Where does the Army get its money, how much and where does it go? For a start, it does what it can to be self-supporting, through tithing. Every Salvationist is encouraged to give ten percent of his or her income to the corps; every corps gives ten percent to divisional headquarters; each of the fifteen Canadian divisions tithes ten percent to national headquarters.

Government and municipal grants help out. However, the major sources of income are the Red Shield campaign (over $15 million in 1983), legacies (about $10 million in a recent year), and investment earnings (ranging around $12-$14 million per year in recent times, depending on interest rates and the stock market). The Army has close to $100 million in shares, government and corporate bonds, and short-term deposits. Investment management companies handle the bulk of that portfolio, not only to get the most mileage from the Army's dollar but to be sure it is invested in reliable and *acceptable* securities. Once a junior in a trust company, investing for the Army employees' pension fund, bought some Seagram's stock. His boss quickly corrected the error, for error it was by Army standards. The Sally Ann never invests in liquor or tobacco companies.

Yet, paradoxically, the Army will accept cash donations from a distiller, brewer or even tobacco company if there are no strings attached and if the Army's name is not publicly associated with the gift. Some might call this pragmatism; others might call it hypocrisy.

"I suppose it sounds inconsistent," admits an Army spokesman. "But we don't ask governments how they make the money they give us. We don't accept money only from people who agree with our beliefs. We will gladly accept a donation, which might help an alcoholic, from a firm that *makes* them alcoholics."

The Army's investment advisory committee—outsiders who guide its hand—includes senior experts from the Canadian Imperial Bank of Commerce, Imperial Oil, and Confederation Life. A retired bank manager sits on the committee and also helps implement investments.

"I'm very impressed with the caliber of the people the Army is using here," says financial secretary Colonel Charles Sheppard, sixty-four, a Fellow of the Australian Society of Accountants, who came to his Canadian post three years ago. "It's rather exciting."

The size of the investment portfolio does not mean the Army is sitting on a gold mine, while tapping the public for donations every year. Many of the millions are held on deposit for corps around Canada. Toronto headquarters banks for them, and pays interest on, amounts in excess of their short-term local requirements. The Army's own banker is the Canadian Imperial Bank of Commerce, which provides many services without charge.

Other investment millions are funds left to the Army in trust, the capital sums of which can be used only how and when the donor specified. The Army actively invites legacies (and in 1982 received $10.7 million) but they often come as an agreeable surprise from someone done a kindness by the Sally Ann years before.

The annual Red Shield campaign is a big and perennially successful fund-raiser. The Army has dropped out of all but eighteen United Way campaigns in Canada.

"We're not anti-United Way," says Lieutenant-Colonel Frederick Halliwell, who's in charge of the Red Shield drive. "But most United Ways are by nature local or parochial in their interests. We're national and international. We don't accept that a local organization should dictate how a national organization dispenses its services."

In some cities the Army and the United Way have resolved their differences, but if any United Way funds come from lotteries the Army automatically bows out. It also drops out if a United Way campaign repeatedly fails to meet its objective. The Sally Ann likes to budget realistically and it knows the Red Shield will raise the needed money. The 1984 campaign aimed for $15.45 million and seemed sure to go over the top, as had all forty-three drives before it.

Red Shield succeeds because the Army sets reasonable targets and can justify its need for every penny. People respond because it *is* the Army and because they trust it to use the money wisely. The campaign is run by volunteers; the Army hires no highly-paid professional fund-raisers. Expenses—media time, campaign supplies, postage, phone calls, receipts and the rest—run around twelve percent of the money collected. According to a federal government guideline, charitable organizations should direct at least eighty cents on the dollar to the purposes for which they collect. The Army puts about eighty-eight cents of every Red Shield dollar directly to work.

In one recent year roughly eighty-seven percent of the Army's total expenditure went into its multitude of social services and to its corps in the field. The rest was spent on missionary and overseas services, training colleges and other education, property and maintenance expenses, administration and public relations. The last, says Lieutenant-Colonel Halliwell, "is not an internal horn-blowing department but our official fund-raising arm."

So, most money received from the public goes to help the man on the street. The Ministries Enrichment Program (MEP), which ran from early 1980 to early 1984, was a different case. Ken Clarke's assignment was to raise $10 million ("but they'd be happier with $12 or $13 million") from corporations, foundations, and governments. Objective: education.

"At one time the Army got too bureaucratic," says Lieutenant-Colonel Edwin Brown, principal of the Toronto training college. "Now we're moving with the times and sometimes ahead of them. A few years ago we were losing good people to jobs in the civilian world. Less so today. We don't feel like second-class citizens any more."

That resurgence is reflected in college enrollment. In the early 1980s, the Army had more candidates than its colleges could handle. The increasing ratio of married students with families called for more on-campus living space.

The MEP set out to remedy that by expanding the Toronto college, building a new one in St. John's, setting up a scholarship program, and building in Winnipeg the first Salvation Army Bible College in the world. International Headquarters, with massive British understatement, called it "a very ambitious program." Translation: the Canadians were out of their skulls.

Yet by late 1983 Clarke could say "I'm sitting on $9 million now and I'm not finished yet!" The college expansions were underway. The Catherine Booth Bible College was into its second year in a converted motor hotel on the banks of the Assiniboine (with a forty-acre site near the University of Manitoba marked for the future campus). Depending on their length of stay its students receive a certificate of Biblical Studies, a diploma in Biblical studies and leadership training, or BAs with majors in Biblical, theological and Christian ministries. Most are Salvationists and about one-third are prime prospects for officer training.

For Ken Clarke and the Army, the triumph of the MEP was not only finding the money but the kind of response. Clarke, slim, middle-aged and hard-driving—a heart attack laid him low in the middle of the campaign—grew up in the decent Salvationist tradition. His father often said, "If you can't say something good about someone, don't say anything."

Clarke was running a prosperous insurance business when his high ethics caught the Army's eye: as the training college's guest-counselor on personal money management he deliberately did not try to sell the students insurance. The Army pressed him into volunteer labor on small fund-raising efforts. To former Commissioner Waldron he shaped up as a natural for the MEP.

"I've never raised money like *this* before!" Clarke protested.

"Well, the Lord will help you," the Commissioner said, with the Army's characteristic sweet reason. "Let's pray about it."

Clarke put his insurance business on hold, at some personal financial penalty, and plunged into the MEP. It was the beginning of the recession. He hoped for large corporate donations—$40-75,000 from large companies; $15-30,000 from smaller ones. "But a company that two years before would have considered $15,000 as coffee money was now saying, 'Don't know if we can afford it.'"

Fortunately, Clarke has the Salvationist's faith in achieving the impossible. "It was my conviction from day one that if God really wanted us to do this, it would happen. That didn't mean we could sit back and wait. We had to work."

He did. Even companies that couldn't donate sent apologetic letters. Foundations gave $1.5 million, three times what the Army expected. A federal cabinet minister in expressing his government's support, said, "We try to help the people who need it but you're the ones who catch all those who fall through the net."

Every provincial government helped out. Here again, the Army's pragmatism emerged. British Columbia offered $340,000 from the proceeds of a lottery. The Army politely declined. Then Gerald Hobbs, the now-retired chairman of Cominco International and a great friend of the Sally Ann, went to bat. The province agreeably came up with the same donation from non-lottery sources.

Even small villages throughout Canada responded to the appeal to give ten cents per capita. By late 1983 the Army was still getting cheques of, say, $75 from communities of 750.

"The Army doesn't need splashy campaigns," Clarke says. "What's important is that every officer and soldier continue to do what the founder set out to do. The spinoff effect of that is many times more potent than any advertising campaign in the world."

Sometimes Sally Ann ethics frustrate even a staunch Salvationist. Clarke would come up with a sure-fire promotional idea but the Army hierarchy, after pondering it, would turn it down. Mustn't offend the public with gimmicks, they said.

"It was nice to be able to go to donors and say the Army really *is* to be trusted," he sums up. "They are not out to gouge every dollar out of the public."

Army corps and departments must turn in a weekly financial report to their superiors, not in suspicion of petty theft but to stress accountability. Auditors from the Army finance department are on the road at work all year. A soldier who diddles funds will be demoted, if not let out, and a Salvationist says, "I simply cannot imagine an Army *officer* doing such a thing." In fact, the first Commissioner of Canada was ultimately dismissed from the Army over a land deal. When he died, the *War Cry* stiffly referred to him only as "a friend of the Army."

An officer lunching on business invariably goes to a decent but low-priced Mom-and-Pop restaurant; chic places with wine stewards and inflated menus are out. Clarke, traveling across Canada for the Army, says he ate hamburgers more often than steak.

"Stewardship is ingrained in us and impressed on us from the top down," sums up Lieutenant-Colonel Albert Browning in Newfoundland.

The Army's publishing wing is a curious blend of Salvationist ethic and plain old-fashioned business. Its Triumph Press in Oakville, Ontario, pours out as many as thirty books a year, by or about Salvationists, plus magazines: the *Crest* and the *Young Soldier* for young people, the *Canadian Home Leaguer* for women, *En Avant* in French and the *War Cry*, perhaps the best-known religious periodical in the world.

The Canadian *War Cry* is not warlike. Its copy is approved by the top brass. Consequently—unlike, say, The United Church *Observer*—it creates no waves, no controversy, no issues unpopular with the Army hierarchy. It is a comfortable house organ with a weekly circulation of 76,000 and a special Christmas edition of 500,000.

It goes largely into pubs, hospitals and nursing homes—distributed free (donations gratefully received) by officers, soldiers, and the vast League of Mercy. It is packed with spiritual articles by Salvationists, news of soldier and officer comings and goings, a "promoted to Glory" column, a crossword puzzle devised by a retired brigadier, and recipes so popular that in 1982 the Army published a book of them.

Readers grumble if the recipe page is dropped but the missing persons section is mandatory reading. Its little one-paragraph chunks, sometimes with picture, are heartbreaking pleas for news of a runaway daughter or son, a lost father, mother, brother, sister.

Their appearance in the *War Cry* is actually the last resort, when the Army's Missing Persons Bureau has exhausted all other avenues of search. Sometimes it turns up one of the four hundred or so "lost" persons whom the Canadian Army finds, out of the approximately 1,000 queries it receives per year. (Worldwide, the Army fields around 20,000 queries annually and tracks down about 8,000 people.)

Hee Lam Leung with the Army's "Word Wagon" on Yonge Street in Toronto—a way of reaching out to the street people.

The proprietor of a dry-cleaning shop in Oakville once opened the *War Cry* to see one of his customers listed as missing. A woman sitting on a park bench in London, Ontario, picked up a discarded *War Cry* to learn her missing son was seeking her. She'd given him up as a baby to foster parents. Through the Army they were reunited.

The Army doesn't charge for its services (although grateful users often donate) and it doesn't do genealogical searches, trace under-age children or run down husbands who haven't paid their alimony. Mostly it looks for people gone missing by accident or design; now, because of a death in the family, a legacy or just plain loneliness, somebody needs them.

Such was the case of Bill Cheshire of Saskatoon in the summer of 1983. He was ill, hadn't seen his sister Alice in sixty-two years, hadn't *heard* from her since 1933 and wondered if she was still alive somewhere back home in England. His housekeeper phoned the Sally Ann's Captain Harry Zimmerman who relayed the query to England.

The Army soon found the sister, but after all those years she wasn't sure she wanted a reunion. (Sometimes "lost" people prefer to stay lost, and the Army can only report this back to the seeker.) Was her brother looking for financial help? Zimmerman reported that Cheshire, a retired farmer, was comfortably off. In June the sister flew out to a happy reunion.

Two years earlier Mrs. Rosa Webber of Trenton, Ontario, spotted the name "Norman Brookout" in a newspaper: the son she assumed was dead. He had drifted away thirty years before to seek his fortune, and been reported drowned. She had remarried, so he had lost track of *her* through the name-change. The Army found him in Toronto, they were reunited on Valentine's Day, and Brookout later brought his children to meet the Army's sleuth, Major Edna Tuck.

"This is the lady who helped us find grandmother," he beamed. It was the best reward a Missing Persons officer could ever hope for.

Supplies and Purchasing, the Army's private store, does over $2 million worth of business a year. It has retail outlets in St. John's, Toronto, and Winnipeg but mail order is its strength. Every year its catalogue, compiled by computer, goes to all corps, with seasonal flyers along the way just like Sears. That way any Salvationist in, say, remote Prince Edward Island or British Columbia can sit at home and order an Army crest or brooch or a coffee mug bearing the face of General William Booth.

"We're run much like any other business," says Major Ron Goodyear, SAP's second-in-command, "except we don't exist to make a profit. We buy at wholesale and put on just enough markup to pay the staff."

A BBb four-valve silver brass horn with a nineteen-inch bell costs $4220 from SAP but would run about $7,000 at normal retail, Goodyear says. Musical instruments are big sellers: cornets, from $215 for a Bb lacquered to $930 for a similar instrument in bright silver; snare drums and bass drums; silver bass trombones at $2025. Army flags are hot items because every corps needs five or six for its various groups, plus a four-by-eight-footer for outdoors. In a Sally Ann store, Salvationists or any member of the public can buy records made by the Canadian Staff Band, Bibles, various other Christian Books, and an infinite array of Army memorabilia. There are souvenir spoons, medallions, sets of china, mugs, place mats, table napkins, tote bags, briefcases, all bearing some kind of Army crest, or Home League emblem, or a picture of one or both of the founding Booths. The Toronto store's January 1984 clearance offered rather dismal statuettes of William and Catherine marked down to $35.95 a pair.

Year around Salvationists can buy good white shirts for twenty dollars (half price to officers), blouses, socks, pantyhose, ties of Midnight Blue with or without crest, and hats for both sexes. Seven Toronto tailors go full tilt year around, cutting and stitching uniforms in basic navy blue serge of summer and winter weight, or washable all-season polyester and wool. They will even make tiny modifications in the interests of fashion. For instance, jackets can now have a vent in the back (such frippery was once forbidden) and men's cuffs can range from eighteen to twenty inches wide (but no wider, please).

Finally—quite apart from SAP—is the store that everyone knows, the thrift store, better known as the give-it-to-the-Sally-Ann store. In and out of the Army's thrift stores pours an endless tide of old clothes, old furniture, old refrigerators, old everything. Some is given free to down and outers, or victims of fires and other disasters. Every year the Army's store in Saskatoon ships five or six truckloads of clothes to Indian reservations in the area and every spring the same store plays host to busloads of Cree Indian children on a school excursion. The Army gives them free soft drinks and doughnuts and rock-bottom prices on whatever they want for their pin-money—usually clothes, toys, and games.

To the not-so-needy—including more and more suburban bargain hunters—the Army puts a fair price on its salvaged goods.

"We don't believe in totally giving things away," says Captain Ed Pearce in Saint John, NB. "It touches people's pride. They like to shop, but buy cheap."

That includes nearly everybody. Russian sailors who come ashore at St. John's, Newfoundland, make a beeline for the Sally Ann thrift store to stock up on blue jeans which may or may not show up on the black market back home. Shrewd young shoppers in Montreal look for semi-antiques in that city's thirteen thrift stores—old gramophones, clocks, wash basins and jugs. One week a sharp bargain hunter scored a good piano for $600.

In Montreal all goods are initially funneled into the Men's Rehabilitation and Industrial Center on Notre Dame Avenue. It gets about 300,000 calls per year from homes in greater Montreal. Lately, garage sales have been cutting in on the Army's take but, says an officer, "If we ask, we get. The people of Montreal have big hearts."

The flow of donations keeps fourteen trucks on the go. Books, luggage, tires, typewriters, radios, TVs pour into a sorting room where the good, bad and useless are winnowed out. The Army draws the line at such things as filthy mattresses, but as one officer says, "It's got to be in a bad way for us not to take it in. If we can't fix it, we sell it for scrap." About 1500 tons of useless clothing are baled and sold for rags in a year.

Thrift store proceeds help pay for the Army's alcoholism program. In some cities both functions are under one roof: the alcoholics working in thrift store backrooms, repairing toasters, reupholstering furniture, fixing radios and TVs and toys, getting themselves back together and helping repay the Army at the same time.

"We're recycling goods *and* people," the Army man says.

Which is the best kind of business for *any* corporation.

15
The
Outstretched Hand

The outstretched hand, clasping the hand of a fellow-human in need, is a familiar Army symbol. In reality, that other hand is often extended palm-up.

To governments gleefully spending taxpayers' money, or journalists looking for a cause to fill the Saturday feature page, there is no such thing as an undeserving "poor" person. Yet while no one denies that millions of Canadians in recent times, and some all the time, are in need, many devote more energy to ripping off the system than trying to care for themselves. The Army's continuing dilemma is: does this person *really* need my help? And how much help is enough?

On New Year's Day 1984, Captain Gordon Bobbitt picked up his phone to hear a litany of misery.

"I'm an invalid," the male voice said. "Had several strokes. The wife has a bad heart.... We live in this townhouse with a lot of steps.... Meals-on-Wheels won't come today 'cause it's a holiday.... I fell down last night...."

Bobbitt, family services officer for Toronto, left his home and family at once. He found an elderly man and woman in the townhouse. Money wasn't the problem: they wanted someone to wait on them. Bobbitt cooked them a lunch of scrambled eggs.

Checking up later, he discovered they were well known to local agencies as chronic complainers. They had alcohol and prescription-drug problems. Public Health and Home Care had provided services, but nothing society did for them was ever good enough.

A few weeks earlier Bobbitt twice loaned twenty dollars from his own pocket to help a seemingly honest young man get by until his first payday on a new job. On payday the man vanished from work and went on a monumental drinking binge.

"I hope people like that are the minority," Bobbitt says. "Otherwise my job would be pretty frustrating."

Probably they *are* the minority but the job is frustrating all the same. The Army, being the Army, is viewed as a soft touch by some, and it tends to give people the benefit of the doubt again and again.

"Once a man touched me for ten dollars to get his truck going," recalls Major Travis Wagner in Saskatoon, "At the time I was only earning sixteen dollars a week myself but he was just out of jail. He wrote an IOU, we prayed together, he was so grateful—and I never saw him again.

"There's a definite welfare mentality out there. One guy even told one of our officers, 'If it weren't for us, people like you wouldn't have a job!' "

Still, Wagner adds, "I'd rather be taken than miss one who really needs me."

But even the Salvationist's famed patience wears thin. Most officers develop a rule of thumb and a gut instinct for chicanery. They learn to recognize many of the permanent transients who use a city's services until their welcome runs out, then move to another, floating back and forth across the country working the system.

Bobbitt usually grants a first request for furniture, clothing or a food voucher without a drastic check-up. A repeater gets a more thorough screening. On a third visit the captain says, "Okay, what other resources in the community are you using? I'd like to contact your social worker."

If it goes beyond that, he meets with other local agencies to find out how much the overall system is being used, or abused, and how they can jointly apportion their services to give the person a fair shake without duplication.

The Army never turns its back on people in real need, not only the unemployed and permanently down-and-out but the victims of disaster. From the Halifax Explosion of 1917 to the Springhill Mine cave-in, to the Mississauga train disaster and a million lesser emergencies, the Army has always rushed to the scene with food and equipment for rescuers and rescued and, later, funds to help get them going again in life.

In May 1983, a fire raced through the forest around Houston in northwestern British Columbia, burning out more than 60,000 acres of spruce and pine and the homes of six families. Lieutenants Ken and Ellen Whatman of the Army corps at Hazelton, ninety miles down the Yellowhead Highway, immediately went to work. They set up a clothing depot and donations poured in. Hazelton's mayor loaned them a truck. The Whatmans got clothing racks and hangers from local stores and drove to Houston.

By noon the next day they had opened an emergency depot with clothing, dishes, and bedding. One family although not burned out had been evacuated on one truck while, in the confusion, their worldly goods vanished on another. A small boy came in with stitches on his nose and chin: his dog, panicking in an effort to save her pups from the fire, had attacked him; then he was run over by a horse. "You could see the terror still in his eyes," Ellen Whatman remembers. Ken went out and bought him some toys.

The surrounding communities raised $25,000 and asked the Army to distribute it to the victims (one mining company gave *only* on that condition). Each family received $4300. "We look at our loss and we say how poor we are," said one couple, who had lost the home they spent eight years building. "Then we look at all the friends who helped and we realize we are much richer."

Another fire victim phoned her father in the United States.

"You were right," she said. "You told me, if I ever needed the Sally Ann, they'd be here."

"Well, sure," her father said.

For those whose welfare cheques run short Lieutenant Wendy Johnstone, family services officer in Saint John, NB, has an emergency routine.

"They get a food voucher at intervals and if the need is really great we might give a few canned goods in the interim. That way we harbor our resources."

As do all Army family services officers, she requires identification. But if they have none? This *is* the army of mercy. . . .

A man without identification pleaded that he was unemployed and had five children. What could she do? She gave him a larger-than-usual food voucher. He came back in a month; a trifle uneasy, she gave him another. He came in a third time, drunk and with a woman friend, pressing his luck. The story slipped out: he'd bought meat with the food voucher and sold it for beer money. Johnstone refused this third request—and he went away in a rage.

"I was taken that time," she admits. "It's hard. Because of people like him we have to make rules that sometimes hurt those who don't abuse the system. The hardest part is when they bring in their children." Sometimes that's a ploy too.

In dealing with suspected con artists, the officer must try to stifle his or her private frustration. Everything in the Army life and ethic shuns profligacy. Cadets in training are flatly forbidden to borrow or incur any other debt. An officer's salary precludes riotous spending.

Yet in the field they must be kind and helpful to people who can't or won't manage the money they earn or get from the state.

"People tell me 'I can't manage on that,'" says Captain Iain Trainor in Halifax. "And I say to them '*I* do.'"

"I try and try to teach them about budgets, about setting something aside per week and not touching the next week's allowance," says Wendy Johnstone. "But they spend it all at once. All they think about is food for that day."

Both she and Bobbitt see people repeatedly squander their limited funds on expensive prepackaged food. They buy at the

Christmas dinner, courtesy of the Sally Ann.

corner convenience store instead of walking a few blocks to a supermarket where prices are invariably lower. They know their food is running low on Thursday but wait until Friday night to tell the Army they've run out. They spend ten dollars on a cab to the laundromat.

"It's not just bad money management, it's bad management of their *lives*," says Bobbitt. "But that cab ride, that box of ridiculously high-priced cookies, that extra case of beer, are sometimes psychological boosts. They all want the good life, like the people they see on TV."

Bobbitt thinks the Army could concentrate less on welfare cases and more on low income workers who in some ways are worse off.

"At Christmas we could give those people a nice turkey and some gifts for the children. Welfare cases automatically get a Christmas bonus from social services anyway. So many people concentrate on the welfare people at Christmas that they have an abundance."

Another forgotten group in Canadian society, says Bobbitt, is the woman age forty-five to sixty who has maybe worked in a department store or restaurant all her life, has been shuffled into part-time employment and is a long way from her pension.

"We see them gradually go downhill—from a comfortable apartment in a respectable area, to a basement apartment in a less desirable district, to a bachelor roomette in a rooming house, to one room downtown. They *need* our help."

There *are* rewards. At eight o'clock one spring morning a forty-four-year-old man walks into the Army welfare office in Calgary. He is jobless, penniless—and in tears. In twenty-two years he has never been out of work before.

"If it weren't to feed my son I wouldn't be here begging," he sobs. "I'd have driven off a cliff." He and his fifteen year old have been sleeping in the car, the man's last possession.

A few months before, he had come to Alberta to a $40,000-a-year-job. Then the company changed hands and his job went with it. Rather than disrupt his son, who was getting good marks in school, he stayed in Calgary and sold his furniture to buy food. When his lease expired they moved into the car.

Captain Ed Ostrom, anti-suicide officer doubling on the welfare desk this day, presses a cash loan on the man, who first tries to give his car as collateral, then insists on writing a promissory note. Next, Ostrom makes several fast phone calls.

The man returns after lunch, dazed with gratitude.

"The last four hours have been amazing!" he stammers. Thanks to the Army he has an apartment, a part-time job and an interview for a full-time job. Now he can hold out until his son finishes school and, if necessary, return to his former job in British Columbia.

"I can't believe it!" he keeps repeating.

"It's the work of the Lord," says Ostrom.

16

"Pilgrims Just A-Passin' Through"

When the Lord, with a little nudge from Toronto Headquarters, sent Ken and Ellen Whatman and Dave and Gloria Woodland to the Gitksan Indian tribe of northwestern British Columbia, they were braced for something different. They simply didn't know *how* different.

There *was* a clue in the cautionary word from Toronto—"We consider this to be a homeland mission"—meaning they'd be missionaries in their own country. Afterward Lieutenant Ken Whatman called it "the most unusual ministry of my life." And Lieutenant Gloria Woodland says carefully, "It has certainly been a learning experience."

Take the funerals, for instance. At first they seemed almost pagan. Then the young Army couples realized that the Gitksan (pronounced "kuhsan") have managed to mingle the best of their old ways with white man's culture.

"They have a lot to teach us about getting rid of grief," says Whatman.

The Gitksan (literally: "people of the Skeena") are industrious and handsome with strong dark faces. They live in a good green land of mountain and forest, with the Skeena River hurrying through its midst to the Pacific and their villages with the musical names—Kispiox, Kitwanga, Kitsegukla—chiming along its banks. Many of the Gitksan are Salvationists. The Army has been serving them since the turn of the century and officers are now stationed in Port Simpson, Canyon City, Kitsegukla, Glen Vowell and Hazelton, as well as the cities of Prince Rupert, Terrace and Prince George.

A funeral in, say, Hazelton, a town on the Gitanmaax reserve, or

Glen Vowell, an all-Indian all-Salvationist village eight miles north of Hazelton, can last for days. Typically, the deceased's body comes home from the nearest funeral parlor, perhaps Smithers, fifty miles away, in a cortege of forty or fifty cars. The Army officer is expected to join the procession, or at least greet it on arrival.

The next night is a smoke feast—pipes for smoking and perhaps a light lunch—while the chiefs decide on the niceties of the funeral ceremonies. A night later people gather from all the surrounding villages for a memorial service. Here are all the high chiefs of the Gitksan clans—Frog, Wolf and Fireweed—and every chief counselor from every village.

It is a time for words of comfort and challenge. Wally Dane, the graying and dignified elder of the tribe, as well as bandmaster in the Hazelton Army corps, often serves as master of ceremonies.

"We're pilgrims, just a-passin' through," he likes to say, and the mourners murmur their amens. It's true, they assure themselves; this life is just a way-station on the human spirit's journey. If the deceased died of alcohol, an elder may warn, "Be careful that you do not end up this way." If he was a Christian, voices will call "Let us walk in his way."

These leisurely and heartfelt messages, delivered by each village in turn, can run for hours. Ken Whatman's longest funeral lasted from 7:00 P.M. until 6:00 A.M. Naturally, he stayed: it would be bad form for the officer to leave early. When Wally Dane has the say, he tries to wind up the testimonials by midnight.

"I'm leaving a note when I die to say the memorial has to be over by 11:00 P.M.," he says, with a glint of a smile.

Finally: the funeral. At all the gatherings to this point there has been an outpouring of wailing and anguish. "I found it very difficult at first," says Ellen Whatman. "Everything is designed to draw out the family's emotion. I thought it cruel—but it leads to healing."

When the casket is lowered into the earth, and the family has sprinkled flower petals or a handful of dirt over it, the grief suddenly turns off. A chief announces the time of that evening's feast. Friends by the hundreds show up, each with bowl, cup, and utensils. Soup is dished up in vast quantities, perhaps with bread and fruit.

A huge bowl comes out; hundreds, maybe thousands of dollars go into it, to pay for funeral expenses and feast. Anything left over may go to particular friends of the deceased (along with some of his or her personal effects as a memento). Anything left after *that* is divvied up among those at the feast. And the Gitksan go home, their minds at peace. The departed pilgrim has been properly sent on his journey.

In a way the Woodlands and Whatmans are also pilgrims just a-passin' through. They were not strangers to Army ways when they came to the Skeena. Ken Whatman, son of Salvationists, had made up his mind at fourteen to become an officer. Ellen, a sturdy articulate young woman, also dedicated her life as a teenager. They had served in Edmonton and Dawson Creek before orders came in December 1982, to be in Hazelton on 6 January.

December was the month their two kids had pneumonia and Ellen cracked two ribs in an auto accident. *Well, nobody ever said the holy war would be easy.* On Boxing Day they packed up their lives, as all good soldiers must, and headed for the new village. After that it seemed like nothing would ever be hard again.

Dave and Gloria Woodland were already at Glen Vowell but it was their first posting from training college so they had no edge on the Whatmans. For Dave, a lean intense young man with thinning hair, it was a startling switch from his pre-Army life as manager of a Dominion store in Winnipeg. For Gloria, daughter of officers, it was a form of déjà vu: her mother's first posting, a generation before, had been to Glen Vowell.

She knew what officership was like from "watching Mom and Dad—the long hours, tears, the heartaches. I wanted a home of my own and I wanted to be settled—I'd never lived anywhere longer than four years!"

One night she opened her Bible to Matthew 10:38—"And he that taketh not his cross and followeth after me is not worthy of me." She wanted to be worthy. In tears, she felt her dilemma was over. "God chose me and ordained me."

Despite their spiritual commitment, neither she nor the others were quite prepared for Gitksan culture shock. When Gloria was pregnant with her second child she happened to go to a funeral. Word filtered back: the Gitksan gently disapproved. Going to the scene of death was bad for the unborn child. When the baby was overdue, an elderly Gitksan woman urged her to try the sure remedy for a tardy birth: make her *husband* sit in a tub of ice water. It being March, Dave Woodland declined but the baby arrived in good health regardless.

Out visiting their flock, the Whatmans and Woodlands think nothing of helping weed the garden or pull in salmon from the river. When they leave, the shy but dignified Gitksan press a little food gift into their hands. Salmon fresh from the Skeena is a staple diet and both couples have been served the ultimate delicacy, the fishhead, which one is expected to eat brains and all. They've learned other subtleties of behavior: for example, when a Gitksan says casually that "Mary is in hospital" it means the Army officer had better get over there and visit her.

A splendid old bell calls the Gitksan in Glen Vowell to Sunday services. The Army church there is nearly eighty years old and extraordinarily beautiful: ornate towers, walls lined with glowing cedar, wooden pews built by the local people, a chandelier of light bulbs set in coal oil lamps and a stained glass window behind the altar. Services are long and heartfelt with vigorous handclapping, songs and prayers in both English and Gitksan, and fervent testimony around the mercy seat.

The Gitksan have their problems: incest, suicide, drugs and, particularly, alcohol. As elsewhere in Canada, the Army does what it can; there is no panacea for unemployment and despair, particularly among the young. But as in Newfoundland's outports the people here have relatively little use for welfare.

"In Dawson I handled more welfare in one week than I do here in six months," says Ken Whatman.

When the Salvation Army reached British Columbia's lower mainland in 1887 the word soon raced north to the native villages. They too wanted the drums, the music, and the bright red-blue-yellow flag. The north was already rich in Methodists and when some natives broke away as Salvationists, the two groups came to blows. To keep the peace, the Indian agent sent a surveyor named Glen Vowell downriver to map out a new village.

One wintry day in 1898 the breakaway Salvationists, smarting from their latest clash with the Methodists, marched down the ice with torn flag and broken flagpole singing a revival rouser, "We Are Out on the Ocean Sailing." They climbed a steep bank, camped under a spruce tree on Glen Vowell's site and built a communal log house.

When Army headquarters heard of them it sent an ensign (a rank now non-existent) to work with them. When their new church was finished, a devout eighteen-year-old native, James Wood, raced on foot through the whole area to invite neighboring villages to the dedication, stripping off his moccasins to splash barefoot through icy streams. He lived to ninety-seven, tending his trapline most of those years. "I opened the door of my heart to the Army and I never let it out," he said near the end.

Glen Vowell became a kind of Salvation Army capital. Travelers of feeble faith would cache their booze and tobacco on a back trail, grumbling, "We're going to the holy city."

The Army took care of its people. It brought a sawmill from England so they'd have work and for seventy years ran a school system, until the government took over. During those years an Army officer traveled hundreds of miles upriver every autumn with a winter's supplies, and taught the children until spring. The government paid him, so he donated his Army salary to the community.

The Army still pours thousands of dollars per year into the region. One example: a $200,000 new church and community services center for Hazelton, donated by Salvation Army supporters all over Canada. It is built on native land, over which the Army has no control, but the risk was deemed worthwhile to keep up the Christian work. For the Gitksan the Salvation Army—like the river, the mountains, and the trees—is a basic fact and mainstay of life.

Given the awful road, tourism will be a long time getting into Canyon City. Which is lucky for Canyon City. It is too pleasant a village in too glorious a British Columbia setting to be desecrated by souvenir booths and quick-food stands. Even the seventy-mile drive north from Terrace, over a wretched trail of gravel and exposed rocks, with one's headlights blazing in daylight to warn off swaying mammoth logging trucks that lay down impenetrable screens of dust—even *that* is a pleasure, on those occasional moments when you can see left, right, or forward.

The Coast Mountains soar in the west. A young bear frolics into the bush. Clear streams gurgle down rocky slopes. Sometimes the road hugs a sheer cliff with a rushing river alongside. At one point it curls through a weird contorted wasteland of volcanic rock, left over from eruptions thousands of years ago.

And at the end of the trail, a swinging footbridge dangles high over the Nass River. The Nass meanders down from the mountains to the Pacific, at the toe of Alaska. You lurch across the footbridge like a drunken sailor, pretending to be nonchalant because the locals on the opposite bank are watching with avid interest. And here is Canyon City—a busy happy Salvation Army Brigadoon, tucked between the river and a small green mountain.

The Army is church to some 180 Nishga Indians. "It's sort of what keeps us together," says young Collier Azak who, as elected chief councilor of the Nishga Tribal Council, is comparable to a mayor. Azak is a shining example of local boy who made good. He studied three years at the University of British Columbia, took two years of forestry at the BC Institute of Technology, worked several years for BC Timber in charge of its entire Nass River operation, then came home to Canyon City. He's chairman of the logging board; Canyon City has a sawmill, owned by the Indians and employing fifteen people. They also own trucks, backhoes, forklifts, and caterpillar tractors.

"It's always been that way," Azak says. "No help from the outside. Blood, sweat and tears of the people. Our heritage with our old folks is quite strong, and part of their wisdom is Salvation Army Christianity."

There are Army officers in Canyon City but the village is so steeped in Salvationism, they seem to blend into the background. Retired Auxiliary Captain Bill Young was waiting at the end of the swinging bridge when I bounced and swayed into Canyon City. He is unique in the entire Army world: a black man from Saint John, NB, who is Mr. Salvation to a village of Nishga Indians. The people call him "Captain," or *Yet* which means "grandfather."

He is sixty-eight, big and blunt with grizzled hair and a growing belly, and he tells his story with a Salvationist's typical pride and candor. He came to the Army relatively late in life. "I drank for thirty years, gambled for thirty years, smoked for thirty years. I got to be an alcoholic and I knew I needed some help."

The fact that his wife of that time was a bootlegger was no great incentive to quit. In Vancouver a Salvation Army officer befriended him. "He used to come to the house. I waited for him to give me a little sermon. All he said was 'It's hurting you more than it's hurting me.' "

Young was jailed for drunken driving.

"What can I do for you?" asked his Army friend.

"Nothing!" And Young stubbornly went to jail for ten days. When he got out the Army man was waiting, with Bill's two-year-old daughter in his arms.

"I thanked God our family was still together. I said 'I think I'll go to church.' My friends said, 'You flipped your wig?' " Young went on a Harbour Light program, stuck it out a week without a drink ("to me that was a miracle") and eventually lost the desire to drink *and* gamble.

From then on Bill Young couldn't get enough of the Sally Ann. He became a soldier in 1961, went to church every night, led a prayer meeting on Sundays, and later worked for the Army in Prince George and Terrace. When there was no officer in Terrace Young ran the Sunday school.

When the Army asked him to go to Canyon City in 1977 because it had no officer ("I was asked, not *ordered,* you understand," Young stresses; to a proud man that's important), he and his new wife Amanda did. From then until 1982 when officers were reassigned, the Youngs held the Army together in Canyon City.

Salvation arrived there in 1925. As in Glen Vowell, it was the product of earlier strife. William Moore, a Nishga in another town, was captain of the Church Army, an evangelical wing of the Church of England. Moore was so diligent that the bishop gave him a lifelong appointment. This caused so much jealousy among his peers that Moore went away and joined the Salvation Army.

Canyon City was at odds with *its* Anglicans. The people wanted help in building a church; the bishop said there weren't enough of them to *rate* a church. They turned their backs on the bishop in a snit and asked Moore to bring in the Army. The white frame church that he and others built in 1927—and would have been Anglican if the bishop hadn't been so high-handed—has a splendid stained glass window. As Moore's son Chester says with a little grin, concluding the story, "That is a very *Anglican* window."

Chester, a strong grave dark-haired man, is local logging superintendent. He also supervised the building of a $1.3 million gymnasium in the village. "This village has spirit," he says. "The difference is, we belong to the Salvation Army and they help the people a lot. They create a freedom for people to do things for themselves."

The only spirit missing is the bottled kind, thanks to Bill Young's personal crusade. He leads the way around the village, pointing out certain houses or people like trophies, shaking his head ruefully at the few remaining backsliders: "That's a drinker . . . that one's not . . . that over there's not . . . that one used to be, but not now."

At one time, after the New Year's Eve midnight service there was a dance which, because of its boozy ambience, was known as the "alcohol dance." With Young chipping away at the sinners, the drinking dwindled. Then a couple of years ago someone smuggled in a few jugs. Young went from door to door throughout the village. The next New Year's Eve dance was dry as the Gobi Desert.

"It took a lot of work and counseling but bit by bit they were won to the Lord," Young says proudly. He tells of their first uniformed Salvationist, later in charge of youth work ("She was a drinker"), of a corps sergeant major ("He and his family got off the sauce").

The Youngs still help hold the community together. Amanda writes and photocopies a small community news sheet. Bill, as social development worker, does drug and alcohol counseling. When a young man doesn't make it in to work on a Monday morning Young goes to check on his hangover quotient. "They know I used to drink. And I know what they're going through. One young guy could never afford a truck. I told him 'I know how you throw away money. I used to throw away a car payment on a weekend.' Six months later he said, 'Captain, I want to show you something, across the bridge.' It was his new truck!"

There are new houses going up. The children look clean and happy. "Our halls don't allow smoking or dancing or drinking in them," says Collier Azak. "We honor that. I strongly endorse the Salvation Army."

After Lieutenant Joan Shayler had been four months at the all-Indian village of Kitsegukla, she ran into the man who'd sent her there.

"You know, everybody at Toronto headquarters thought the commissioner and I were crazy to send you to Kitsegukla," then-Field Secretary, Colonel Ed Read told her. "Sending a single girl on her first appointment to a native village, where we hadn't had an officer in years!"

And, he might have added, where drinking was rampant, where a schoolteacher had been raped and where the RCMP had warned Shayler on arrival, "Don't go out at night and don't open your door to strangers."

"So what are you going to tell them when you go back?" she asked.

"Boy, I've got a *lot* to tell them!"

He could report that this stocky woman with the honey-colored hair, big smile and the physical overdrive that seems to power Salvationists twenty-four hours a day, had Kitsegukla eating out of her hand. In retrospect, Joan Shayler was perhaps the *only* right one for that job at the time.

Shayler grew up in an alcoholic home and ran with a tough street gang in Vancouver, where she came to love the Army's open-air bands. Naturally, she couldn't admit this to her friends so "I put on a big tough act."

One night, to get out of a pouring rain, she went into an Army youth meeting. "For the first time in my life I saw young people who had something to live for, something worthwhile. It attracted me, made me realize life was more than what was going on around me."

Around these Army people, comfortable childhood memories came flooding back of her grandmother taking her to Sunday school. She made her commitment to God that night. For nearly twenty years she worked at civilian jobs in Kelowna, Vancouver, and the Northwest Territories. In Fort Smith she landed a federal government job as a counselor, because she was an active Salvationist, despite having no formal training for the job.

"A lot of that was preparation. The Lord was preparing me. I learned a new love for people. My Mom always said I was a queer child because I would befriend the outcast and the native children in our schools."

That went back to early childhood: until she was seven she lived with her grandmother who taught in Ontario's James Bay region. Often she was the only white child in a village.

By now she knew she wanted to be an Army officer—but could she? She had not finished high school, was already past the standard age limit of thirty-five, and there was no Army corps in Fort Smith to help her with pre-admission studies. But she boned up on the Army with tapes sent by friends in the east and caught up on her schooling by correspondence course. The local Anglican minister gave her a character reference. And at international headquarters the General—Arnold Brown, a Canadian with a voluminous memory—remembered her favorably and okayed her application.

The hardest part of training was Toronto culture shock. "I couldn't get on the subway for months. All those people swarming around. I was very glad to come back to a place like this."

In her final year she heard of the forthcoming opening in Kitsegukla, a village of about 650, southwest of Hazelton. For years it had been unstaffed; then the Army sent in a woman officer who left after six months. Shayler asked Commissioner Waldron for the post. He smiled thoughtfully and said, "Well, you never know. . . ."

Two months before graduation Waldron took her aside.

"Are you serious about wanting Kitsegukla?"

"I feel that's where the Lord can use me the most."

When the appointment was announced on commissioning day she was one of the few in Massey Hall who weren't shocked. The shock extended to Kitsegukla. The Gitksan are very male-oriented, and shy even among strangers of their own tribe. "They just didn't know how to approach me or what to say."

By Christmas she was breaking down the barriers. There had been no activities for young people so she started a Friday and Saturday night games-and-coffee club at the church.

"What we have now isn't much but at least they're not giving their money to the bootlegger." Now to the amazement of the kids, even such leading elders as Gideon Johnson come to play checkers with them. "*Yet* is over there!" they cry to Joan. "He doesn't *act* eighty years old!"

Now, too, young married couples can get a reliable baby sitter from the church club—the kids simply take a friend and a game along—for a badly-needed night out by themselves. Several young couples swear by the Sally Ann girl simply because she *married* them. They had been divorced, were told by other clergy that they could not marry again, and so were living common-law. Finally a pair who had lived together for eleven years and had three children asked if she'd tie the knot.

"When I said 'yes' everybody in the five villages was shocked! I married them on Christmas Day. Since then I've done three other weddings of• the same type." Such weddings require Army permission from on high, but it comes quickly because Joan Shayler is clearly doing good work for the Lord.

Her position with the Gitksan is solid now: this officer-woman performs miracle marriages. Within two years she lifted the soldier enrollment from three to nineteen; had 149 adherents, thirty-nine junior soldiers, fifteen corps cadets, two youth groups totalling fifty kids, a Sunday school of sixty and a singing company of thirty-five young people. Alcohol-related crime has dropped dramatically.

Joan Shayler, ever the pioneer, knows where she wants to go next: the Northwest Territories. But maybe first she should talk to Lewis Babe.

17

Hard Times
in the
Midnight Sun

Captain Lewis Babe is short and graying, with the benign and bespectacled gaze of a retired schoolmaster. His voice is so soft you must sometimes lean close to hear. This gentle demeanor masks a core of steel, as many an artful alcoholic has learned. Nobody puts anything over on the quiet captain. As a reformed drunk himself, he handles problem drinkers with understanding but no nonsense. There are no elaborate hard-luck stories he hasn't heard or, in the bad old days, invented.

"I know all their little games," he smiles gently.

Babe is also a born handyman. He was therefore an admirable choice for the Army's first corps in Yellowknife in 1981. Drunkenness in this corner of the Northwest Territories was, as one Army historian put it, "as rife as during the days of the Klondike." And the corps, supposedly ready for Babe and his family when they arrived in August, had to be totally renovated.

"We know this is a difficult appointment," said then-Commissioner John Waldron, a brisk business-like American, much admired by his troops. "If you have any problems that no one else can handle, you have a direct line to me, day or night." Waldron and the Babes had no idea how difficult it would be.

Their proposed home, church and Harbour Light—a two-storey frame box supposedly redesigned from a former mining office, with two small apartments upstairs—was unusable. The Babes set to work painting, sawing, hammering, and turning it inside out.

They made the dining room into a dormitory and the recreation room into a chapel. Babe replaced lighting fixtures and reinsulated walls and ceilings after the pipes froze up. "In this appointment you gotta be electrician, plumber, and everything else," he says, not seeming to mind.

He, his wife Joanne, and their three children were supposed to shoehorn themselves into one of the upstairs apartments. Instead, Waldron instantly okayed a bungalow that Babe bought for the Army at a reasonable price in a pleasant part of town. Army families should not be made to feel second-class, the commissioner said.

The corps building was ready in December but the Babes went home on Christmas Eve with long faces. There hadn't been enough time or money to lay on a Christmas dinner for their alcoholics, as in every other Harbour Light in Canada. Then a florist's deliveryman knocked at their door with a poinsettia and card from "John and Helen Waldron," wishing them cheer on a lonely night far from home. The Sally Ann family had reached out to them, even up here.

Winter was a shock. "It's usually twenty degrees colder here than they say it is on national TV, eh?" Babe points out. Temperatures of minus forty to fifty (plus wind chill) were common. Manning the Army Christmas kettle was an ordeal; every five minutes the canvassers had to go indoors to thaw out.

The Babes' boots and purses cracked; vinyl is good enough in southern Ontario but for the north they needed leather. Joanne froze her knees in a three-quarter-length parka. Two new Arctic parkas cost nearly $700 even with a discount. Luckily, Joanne had just received a small inheritance, because officers' stipends, even with a northern allowance, aren't up to those prices.

Luckily, too, Lewis Babe had seen hard times before. He'd served three years in the peacetime RCAF as a mechanic, gone back to civilian life as a service station proprietor, and fallen into the bottle. To that point his only contact with the Army was attending its church as a kid in his hometown, Orangeville, Ontario, not through any particular commitment (his parents were Methodists) but because "it was the next street over."

He ended up in the Army's Harbour Light in Toronto, made the treatment stick the first time around, stuck with Salvationism too, and was commissioned in 1972. Latterly he was assistant director of the Toronto Harbour Light and administrator of Hope Acres, the long-term alcoholism treatment center outside Toronto.

When the Army sounded him out about Yellowknife, a year before the corps was founded, Babe tried to contain his enthusiasm: "Well . . . if you have nobody else. . . ." When it became a serious proposal he took the stoic Army stance: "Wherever the Lord wants us, we'll go."

The Lord did not warn them about culture shock. Yellowknife, perched amid rocks and bush beside Great Slave Lake, is a city of wild extremes. Its brand-new Northern Arts and Culture Centre is as elegant as anything of its kind anywhere in Canada. In the original "old town," basically a charming site, expensive ultramodern homes cling to the side of a rocky hill looking down on the lake, but they also overlook an array of wretched shacks called "Squaw Valley."

In mid-winter, daylight blinks on and off like the wink of an eye. Even with television and indoor plumbing the nights are long and the outside world is far away. Edmonton, the nearest major city, is about two hundred dollars away by air and one thousand miles by road.

And then there's the cost of living. Utilities for the Army building run $1,000 a month and heating the Babes' house costs $500 a month in winter. One summer day, Babe ticked off some typical food prices—bread at $2.15 a loaf, margarine at $3.99 a pound, potatoes the same—noting that they go higher in winter, when the waterways freeze and everything must be flown in.

In their first spring they bought $200 worth of bedding plants ("Would have cost us about $40 down south"), planted a garden after 24 May, which is deemed the safe planting date in southern Ontario, and sat back to let the extra-long sunny summer days perform their magic. They lost everything in a June snow.

For Salvationists, the seamy side of Yellowknife was hardest to bear. To a segment of the local people, alcohol is the antidote for boredom, self-pity, unemployment and long winter nights. In summer a few dedicated drinkers hang out with a bottle around the downtown post office steps.

"Broken bottles around," Babe sighs. "They'd go to the washroom right out in the open. One time my wife and young daughter were going up a street and a couple of 'em were having intercourse right on the bench up here. My little girl says, 'Mommy, what are they doing?' What do you say to her?"

Some of them ended up in his Harbour Light program. Many are natives but the captain does not buy the theory that Indians are psysiologically prone to alcoholism. Welfare and the white society are ruining them, he says.

"The whole problem is, they've taken these fellas out of the woods and they are very confused people. All they know is hunting and trapping. In here, there's no work, no nothing, so there's not much to do but drink all day long."

Yet there's much they could teach the white culture. A sense of family, for instance.

"These folks here, they look after the old folks. They're not shipped out to nursing homes, and that. The old folks can't go on a hunt, but the meat is brought back to the village and divvied up and everybody gets his quota."

As he warms to his subject, Babe pours a stiff black coffee. For many Army officers, especially those who have licked a drinking problem, coffee is a constant companion.

"Most of these lads still put the whole family on a big sled pulled by dogs or a skidoo, follow the caribou, sleep on the ice, bring the meat back to the village. Sometimes I can't get them under the sheets here at all. They just lie on top with a blanket. For some, even the beds are too soft; if you don't watch out they're sleeping on the floor."

His Harbour Light program is a typical round of devotions, discussion groups, good food, and classes. Since many of his clients have little or no education, Babe gears his lectures to a Grade 2 level. What they lack in formal education they make up in native wisdom.

"They can survive off the land. They know when it's gonna rain or snow. They have a knowledge of living that most whites don't. One lad here—he's in his sixties, from the Dogrib tribe—he's lost an eye through booze, his legs are all crippled up because of booze, he's spent a lot of time in jail, and that. He said in class one day, 'Captain, there's no hope for me. I got no education and I don't believe God would want a man with no education.' "

Babe assured him that a PhD is no ticket to the kingdom of Heaven.

His admiration and compassion do not cloud the captain's vision. No one gets into the Harbour Light stinking drunk. Anyone who falls off the wagon during the program is immediately ousted. It's the only way to earn respect.

"But I know what they're going through." For a second his eyes go bleak with memories of a time when happiness for Lewis Babe meant four bottles of wine a day.

"The alcoholic becomes a con artist. He'll cheat, he'll do anything for a drink. You gotta watch them. We've got a situation here, three or four second-hand stores that buy used clothing, eh? So I gotta keep everything under lock and key or they'll grab clothes or anything else when they get thirsty, and go sell 'em, eh?"

Babe chuckles in grudging admiration at their ingenuity.

"I had one lad here who took a coat and a pair of pants up to Second Hand Rose to panhandle them. Rose said, 'You can't sell them here, I just took them down to the Salvation Army!' They still had her tags on them. Little games like that, they'll be up to."

There've been successes, but a reformed drunk always treads the knife-edge between wet and dry. "A couple of lads were right down to the Lysol. Now they're out and have jobs. Sad part is, some can't find a job. And they get discouraged awfully easily. So, in a small community like this, they find a buddy with a bottle. You don't need money to drink, as long as you don't get cut off from the street community. You can always find a buddy."

The Harbour Light is only one of Babe's daily chores. Some thirty-five adults—many of them Newfoundlanders come north to seek their fortunes—attend Sunday services. Sunday School classes are overflowing. Babe attends police court regularly ("These lads are always up to something") and he and Joanne do family counseling.

"There's a lot of what we call . . . well, shack-ups, eh? People living out of wedlock. White folks living with Indian girls. A lot of breakups. Or we get married couples come to Yellowknife and the wife can't take the life. It's a tough situation."

The community is getting full value from its little Sally Ann corps. Everyone plays in the band. Frank, the cook, who came with Babe from Hope Acres, also runs a soup line. When Frank went on holiday, Joanne cooked all the meals along with her regular stints: corps bookkeeping, Sunday School, Home League, and doing all the laundry once a week.

"So what do you two do in your spare time?"

"Well, it was reaching the point where our health was liable to break down," Babe says. "When Frank was on holiday my wife and I were coming in here at eight in the morning and not leaving till midnight lots of times. And I'm looking to the future too. I'm not always going to be here." (Is there a hint of relief in his voice?) "That's why I'm hiring another counselor. When we move on, the next officers will have somebody already here with northern experience."

Whoever came next would have a hard act to follow.

In June 1898, six men and two women trudged out of Skagway, Alaska, laden with fifty-pound packs and two Peterborough canoes. The women were swathed from head to ankles in hooded fur-trimmed coats. The men, likewise swaddled and furred, were topped off with rakish cowboy hats. Like thousands of others that year, they were about to claw their way over the terrible Chilkoot Pass—part of it on their hands and knees—bound for the Klondike and one of the great adventures of the nineteenth century. They would not be panning for gold. They were Salvationists, prospecting for souls in the Yukon.

The Chilkoot wriggled thirty miles uphill through a narrow gorge. Its last four miles rose through a gully of ice and snow at an angle of forty-five degrees. Pierre Berton, Canada's chronicler of the Klondike, writes that "there were only two places where a climber could properly rest. The first lay beneath a huge over-hanging boulder which was known as the Stone House. The second was a flat

Off on the Trail of '98—the Canadian Army's Klondike Brigade. Here, the eight (plus the editor of the War Cry) *pose before leaving Toronto.*

ledge only a few city blocks square at the very base of the final ascent, known as The Scales, because everything was reweighed here and the packers' rate increased to a dollar a pound." Even dogs had to be carried on men's backs. At the Divide, where a Union Jack and a Mounties' patrol marked Canadian territory, the snow-blown slit through the pass was only a hundred yards wide.

At the summit, one Salvationist recalled later, "It was blowing a frightful hurricane and we could scarcely see ten feet in front of us."

Until then their Klondike mission had been rather a lark. Territorial Commissioner Evangeline Booth herself, with the family flair for showbiz, had dreamed up the Klondike mission and led it from Toronto to Skagway. There, according to some accounts, she met the notorious Jefferson Randolph "Soapy" Smith, gangster, con-man, and boss of Skagway.

Smith and his gang infiltrated every level of Skagway society and ruled both town and trail to the gold fields. It's said that he tossed a gift of gold onto the Army drum at one open-air meeting and, after a series of spirited exchanges with Evangeline Booth, was saved. That would indeed have been a miracle because, as fellow Salvationist Ensign Rebecca Ellery wrote in her diary, Evangeline spent only one night in Skagway before heading home to Toronto. In any case, if Smith was converted, he had little time to rejoice in salvation. A local vigilante shot him, six weeks later.

For the intrepid eight who stayed on, getting through the Chilkoot was only a beginning. Going down the slope on the opposite side, they sometimes sank to their thighs in soft snow. They finally dragged their boats to water on sleds fitted with sails.

Through a chain of lakes and into the swift Yukon River, they fought their way through rapids that had already wrecked hundreds of boats and rafts. So dangerous were these that the Mounted Police made women and children disembark and walk around, and insisted that experienced boatmen pilot all craft through. This created a thriving trade for rivermen: one of them charged twenty dollars per boat to lead the Salvationists. Ensign Thomas McGill and another officer followed in the second canoe and Rebecca Ellery told her diary: "Oh it did look wild! . . . The boat shot over the waves like a duck. We thought our two boys were going down; their boat turned completely around and went over the rapids backwards."

Later she described a typical day on the water: "I don't think there was any point where we could see a mile ahead. It was one turn after another and around nearly every turn there were rocks in the river." Rebecca sat in the bow of the lead canoe to sound the alarm. Along the way they helped rescue a man clinging to a rock; his ruined boat was gone and one of his companions had drowned. When they reached Dawson City on 25 June after three weeks and 480 miles Ensign McGill, the expedition's second-in-command, wrote, "That was the heaviest job I ever had in my life."

Dawson was crammed with humanity. "Just like in Fenelon Falls on the 12th of July," writes Rebecca Ellery (who came from that Ontario town). "People stand around with nothing to do. This is no place to be if one gets homesick, for no one can go back the way we have come." The prospectors were eager for any entertainment, even religion, and they were generous. The first Army collection in a saloon netted sixty dollars in gold dust.

The Salvationists paddled upriver, cut logs for their barracks, and tied them into a raft, with the notion of floating them across to

In Dawson they cut logs, floated them across the river, and built this shelter for the lost souls who'd come to seek their fortune (and, more often, found despair).

Dawson. The river was too swift so they towed individual logs in countless canoe trips. "We were young and very strong," McGill wrote succinctly.

Then, in the historic Army manner, they offered Christianity and a helping hand to Dawson's thousands. Few had struck it rich and *kept* their gold. The rest never had it or quickly squandered it. Soon the Army's shelter was brimming with lost souls, broke or so close to it that they were ashamed to go home.

A lawyer helped cook Christmas dinner for the shelter. "A great singer is mushing dogs," Ellery wrote. She and Nurse Emma Aiken ministered to typhoid and scurvy victims. With butter at $1 a pound and eggs $2.50 a dozen (sky-high prices in 1898) the Army had to scrabble for funds, but three weeks after their arrival they had collected $600.

In three years it was all over. The gold petered out. The Klondike died. Dawson dwindled from thousands to a few hundred. The Army closed its doors in 1912. But not for ever.

The Trail of '84 leads right past Lieutenant Jim Morris's office window. His blood-and-fire emblem looks down on Fourth Avenue, Whitehorse, the in-town leg of the Alaska Highway. All year traffic streams up and down the highway—trucks, campers, dusty cars with dusty plates from every province and state; old couples having a retirement fling; young couples seeking a new thrill or a new job in the Yukon.

Whitehorse snuggles among low hills with a gentle blue swell of mountains in the distance. It has the clean open look of a city that's going places. Which is why the Army came back to the Yukon in the mid-1970s. But on this late summer day the Yukon, like much of Canada, is riddled with unemployment. Many highway travelers, having started out short of cash and common sense, are broke by the time they hit Whitehorse. The blood-and-fire draws them like a magnet. Since there is no Army hostel, and hotel rooms cost sixty dollars and up, Morris says "It's cheaper to give them a tankful of gas than put them up for the night."

But he can give them a hot meal. He, his wife Emma, and their civilian staff dish up as many as 670 meals a month: soup, plenty of bread and nourishing stew. Local merchants donate bread, canned goods (one Christmas the local Kiwanis gave two and a half tons) and the occasional windfall. One night a local group canceled a banquet but forgot to tell the Klondike Inn, which was catering the event.

"Want a complete dinner?" the KI manager asked Morris. "It's yours!" That night the soup line gang thought they'd died and gone to Heaven, as they bellied up to salads, baked potatoes, and prime rib of beef.

The land of the midnight sun seems like a world away from Newfoundland where Jim and Emma were born, where he taught school at age sixteen, and from whence, as teenagers, they set out for Montreal with one suitcase each. After sixteen years there, during which Jim became an assistant manager for Air Canada, they heeded the call. Morris, now in his early forties, is one of the Army's older lieutenants.

"But I don't regret all the civilian years," he beams, with a salesman's ebullience. "Business administration, public relations—it all helped prepare me for this."

"This" means everything. The Morrises run a Home League, handle a dozen suicide calls per year, hold Sunday services for congregations of forty to fifty, counsel couples with crumbling marriages. Soon after they arrived, four local mines closed. In the following year the Army gave out 220 food hampers to needy families (compared with 15 the year before) and 1200 pieces of clothing a month.

In a place temporarily grounded by the economy but so full of promise, the Army was trying to keep Whitehorse's young people, its hope for the future, out of trouble.

"In the winter we get four hours of daylight," Morris says. "If you're not into skiing or hockey, it can be pretty depressing. So we have a Saturday night coffee house, for kids thirteen and up."

It's in the Sally Ann basement and still has the fancy light fixtures and a built-in bar (now a *coffee* bar) from its previous incarnation as a restaurant. The local Lions donated a TV, Rotary gave $500, and grateful parents bring their teenagers here—as many as seventy per Saturday night, from all church backgrounds and no church background—to keep them off the streets.

And who better to run the place than a product of the Floundering Generation? Bill Giesler, thirty-one, bearded and in sandals, explains that he came to Whitehorse with his parents in 1969.

"I never got into any *serious* trouble. I was pretty much a loner. If I didn't like a situation, I left it." The loner in him still eyes you a trifle warily, as though he does not entirely trust anyone over thirty-two.

By his late twenties Giesler was looking for "a place where you could go and sit down and nobody stared at you" and for something to do besides drink or smoke dope. "I was into dope once, but I escaped from it."

He had no particular religious faith when he drifted to the Army coffee house in the winter of 1981. He stood by the door a long time, listened to the hymns and upbeat gospel music, and went away. He was not going to be trapped into religion.

It drew him back in a couple of weeks. He began attending, cautiously but regularly. Captain Bob Wilson, the first Army officer in Whitehorse, a big hearty one-time motor-oil salesman from the Ottawa Valley, coaxed Giesler to participate. One night he said, "I'd like you to run this place."

"I felt like a door had opened," Giesler remembers. Now he gives every weekend to the Army: on Sunday he drives the Sunday School bus; on Saturday he spends hours getting the coffee house ready with juice, soft drinks and coffee, "righteous rock" music and Christian films.

The place is open from 7:00 P.M. to midnight. Smoking and alcohol are not permitted but, Giesler says, "we try not to be wishy-washy about it. I just say 'if you have to smoke dope, go away from the building.'" The coffee house is so successful they're planning a junior version for nine-to-twelve-year-olds. And it's a Godsend for at least one young adult.

"I like to think God led me here," Bill Giesler says.

18

One Day
at a Time

He is tall, thin and fifty-nine, a civilian worker at the Toronto Harbour Light on Jarvis Street, and like Bill Giesler in Whitehorse, he feels God showed him the way here. You would never know he has been an alcoholic, except for a certain tightness around the eyes, a frayed expression, the indefinable look of all these men who have been through hell.

"How long have you been back here now?" Captain Bert Lewis asks.

"One year and ten months, Captain." He has it memorized almost to the day. Earlier than that, he graduated from the alcoholism program, went to Montreal, felt himself slipping back into the bottle, and reached out again for help. The Harbour Light took him back, of course. Just being here was the moral support he needed to stay dry. Now he's a supervisor.

"You're doing real well," the captain says. "Maybe I shouldn't tell you this, but I wrote your wife in Ottawa the other day to see if she'd have you back."

The man lights up and crosses his fingers.

"Wish she would. I pray she would."

He knows, as the captain knows, that he will never be cured. Alcoholism, which the Army calls the twentieth century's most epidemic disease, has no "cure." (A latter-day contention, that some drunks *can* be cured and allowed to drink again, is still highly controversial and refuted by many experts in the field.)

"It's sort of like a cold—it can always come back," says Captain Lewis Babe in Yellowknife. Even after the best of treatment, you simply aim to stay dry one day at a time.

There are an estimated 605,300 alcoholics in Canada, and many kinds of treatment. No one program is best. "I went to Alcoholics Anonymous and it didn't work for me," adds Lewis Babe, "but many a guy has made it in AA. Our program doesn't work for everybody."

A spokesman for the Addiction Research Foundation of Ontario agrees: "Different strokes for different folks." Some organizations keep an alcoholic waiting days or weeks to get treatment, he adds, and cater mostly to the middle- or upper-classes. The Army acts quickly, if it has space, and doesn't care about a drunk's bank balance. Consequently, it's a boon to problem drinkers at lower economic levels.

"I used to regard the Army's program as run by untrained people but, increasingly, it is being staffed by trained professionals," concludes the ARFO man. "It's still not as professional as our institute, but my bias is, none of these organizations has that striking a batting average."

In fact, much depends on whether a man or woman has a support system on the outside. For those Toronto Harbour Light graduates who have some outside help there's a seventy percent success rate. Those without such support have only half that chance of success.

Across Canada the Army's Harbour Lights for men and Homesteads for women treat 6,500 people per year. Many go there as a last resort because, ironically, they shy away from one of the Army's strengths: spiritual faith.

"Many want to be cured but not preached at," says an officer. "It's particularly true of middle- or upper-class people who perhaps pride themselves on atheism or agnosticism."

The Army doesn't just preach at them, but a cornerstone of its treatment is a ten-step sub-program, beginning with: "Recognize that you are helpless without God" and "Believe that God through Jesus Christ can deliver you from the curse of evil." It is the only alcoholism program in Canada with such strong spiritual orientation.

The ever-practical Army does not base treatment only on religion. A typical Harbour Light program requires the drunk to dry out in a detox unit before beginning treatment. Next comes a three-week regimen of classes, counseling, plain nourishing food, plenty of rest, and a little recreation. If the man can then function without booze but needs a bed while job-hunting, the Army usually provides it. If he still can't make it on the streets, but is trying, he can go to one of the long-term rural treatment areas—Hope Acres near Toronto or Miracle Valley east of Vancouver, for up to six months of light work and a stern attack on his drinking habit.

An Army officer in a Harbour Light comforts and counsels a man at the chapel mercy seat.

"Anybody can get you physically dry in a week with food, rest, and therapeutic use of vitamins," says Toronto's Captain Lewis. "But you may simply be a 'dry drunk.' Contentment might not come for six or eight months. Even then a forgotten police charge, a wife filing for divorce, any such problem from the past, can plunge a man back into the booze."

Last comes stability, Lewis says, and then a reformed alcoholic can usually cope with most of life's problems.

Canada's first Harbour Light was started in Vancouver in 1953, by Major David Hammond (whose son and namesake is now principal of the Newfoundland training college) and was expanded by one of the Army's most vivid personalities.

Major "Banjo Bill" Leslie was a youthful drinker who found the Army at nineteen. After becoming an officer he made down-and-outers his mission. With his banjo and rich baritone voice, he toured small towns with a sound truck that bellowed: "Come to the Salvation Army hall tonight! Hear Banjo Bill and his Rock and Roll Band! We are founded on the Rock Jesus Christ and when the Roll is called up yonder we'll be there!"

In his years as administrator of the Vancouver Harbour Light, Banjo Bill made magic with his ebullient personality and a lot of help from his friends. One Christmas, skid row was agog: the major had promised every man a turkey dinner. He had no money for turkeys and no pans to roast them in but these were mere bothersome details. The word raced through Vancouver—Banjo Bill needed help. A technical school loaned pans, the public pitched in money, and Bill and his staff served two thousand turkey dinners on Christmas day.

Leslie dreamed of a country retreat where alcoholics could get well, far from city temptations. He found a perfect wooded tract, fifty-eight miles from Vancouver; bought it on a shoestring (somehow neglecting to tell Toronto headquarters of his plans); coaxed all kinds of materials from donors, and built the place, with the aid of tradesmen graduates from skid row and the Harbour Light. Miracle Valley, as Banjo Bill's farm for drunks was called, was nicely under way before Army headquarters gave its official sanction.

On his wall hung his favorite text:

> Some wish to live within the sound
> of church and chapel bell.
> I want to run a rescue shop within a
> yard of hell.

Bill Leslie, ever the individualist, subsequently left the Army but he set a pattern for much of the Harbour Light work today.

They come from every conceivable walk of life: doctors, lawyers, ex-cops, business executives, and sad old men who've known nothing but skid rows all their lives. Strange corrosive chemical mixtures are churning in their guts. Those who can't afford wine or whiskey take to Lysol, direct from a spray can or as a liquid cut with water. Some melt shoe polish and extract alcohol from the liquid.

Feisty Brigadier Tom Smith of the Vancouver Harbour Light says eighty percent of his clients are hooked on dual addictions: alcohol and soft drugs—such as Valium and Seconal mixed with jug wine. Which reminds the Brigadier that marijuana, in his opinion, is *not* as innocuous as some would say.

"I think it's a most hideous thing—any mind-altering drug is devastating—and putting it under the Food Act is folly."

The Brigadier (a rank now being phased out) has peppery gray hair and a temper to match. In the Army since 1941 and near retirement when we met, he doesn't care whose toes he steps on. He is not overly fond of governments.

"We have government agencies that reject some of these people because they don't fit in, because they are so-called 'outcasts,'" he snaps. "In fact, they just don't fit the tailored suit of the system.

Governments shouldn't reject anyone. It's *our* money they're spending!"

Like all Harbour Light administrators he wins a few and loses a few. The brigadier mentions his favorite success stories. A doctor from up the coast who "drank himself to zero," lost his home, family and practice, graduated from Miracle Valley, and is now successfully back at work. A printer from Ottawa, "very clever boy, lost everything, drank his way across Canada. Now he has a good job and stands to be vice-president of his company." A sailor from Newfoundland, "you couldn't even trust him with a shirt hanging on the line; then the Lord got a hold of him." He dried out, married, retrained, and now works as a male nurse.

In Toronto Captain Lewis tells similar tales. But the majority are not professional men and women. Many are social misfits, chronic losers. "We know they are on welfare, or Old Age assistance or DVA," says Lewis. "And we know they are going to drink their money away. So why do we bother? Well, we are keeping them alive. We know we are going to be able to reach some of them."

Most of the bigger Harbour Lights have a soup line which, usually, the users can only reach by going through the chapel for a prayer service. Now and then, one will kneel at the mercy seat and make a show of accepting the Lord.

"They think they're pleasing us by doing it," says Lewis. "But we know that a lot of them aren't serious—we call it 'taking a dive.' " The Army doesn't require them to be converted; it just feels a little brush with God can't hurt.

As a port city with a pleasant climate, Vancouver gets an abnormal number of transients and its Harbour Light runs the biggest feeding line in Canada. At noon one warm June day, more than two hundred men and women have shuffled in from tacky boardinghouses, dusty highways, or a night in Stanley Park or under the Granville Street Bridge.

In the chapel Ken Murphy, civilian head of the detox unit and boss of today's soup line, leads an earnest prayer but a short one, allowing that it is a hot day. Then, strangely silent, the crowd files patiently into the kitchen. Every soup line is manned by men who are on the Harbour Light program. It's deliberate therapy to demonstrate how they may end up if they don't shake the booze.

Today they are dishing up good thick stew, plenty of bread and some sticky buns. The men and women quietly fill their trays, eat at stand-up tables in total self-absorption, scoop up extra bread to carry away, and swiftly vanish.

Murphy, short and balding, watches them—his brothers and sisters, a mirror on himself. His eyes are kind, and deep with remembered pain. He came nine years ago as a patient. Once he skipped out, raging at himself and the world, and was caught speeding at eighty m.p.h. through the Fraser Valley. He's dry now but he lost his home, his family, "everything. You never think of all the things you're losing, when you're drunk."

As the soup line inches past—young, old, clean, stinking—the regulars lean over to touch Murphy's arm or call his name.

"How you doing?" he says to one. The man is middle-aged, good-looking, clear-eyed, clean plaid shirt. He shrugs.

"Not much. But I'm not drinking."

Murphy smiles and nods encouragingly. It's a start.

19

A Divine Melody

One Sunday afternoon early in this century, perhaps 1920, when he gave concerts in Montreal and Toronto, the Italian tenor, Enrico Caruso, was resting on the front porch of a hotel in Cobourg, Ontario. Suddenly across the street a Salvation Army group struck up with drum, tambourine and song. The greatest tenor of his time, and possibly any time, rose impulsively from his chair and said, "Do you mind if I sing with you?"

Then he sang "Lead, Kindly Light" and "Abide With Me" in the voice that had enthralled every opera house in the world. What a concert it must have been!

And yet, how natural. Who can resist a Sally Ann band? Its sound is not always refined nor its tunes complex but its music surrounds you and beckons you to follow, as it marches stoutly onward like the Army itself. In Newfoundland I tape recorded a Sunday morning service in the outport of Arnold's Cove. Weeks later, replaying it on a dreary Toronto workday, there was an irresistible urge to roar out the songs again with that congregation.

Sooner or later in every temple, citadel or hall they sing "the Founder's song," number 167 in the songbooks. (Once it was number 1 and when a revised songbook shuffled it out of first place, Newfoundland Salvationists were thoroughly miffed.) In his book, *O Boundless Salvation,* former Canadian Commissioner John Waldron tells how William Booth wrote the words in 1893, as part of a planned series of evangelistic meetings.

Early one morning Commissioner Theodore Kitching, the General's aide, found the old man sleepless and agitated.

"Kitching, I have been praying all night," he said. "I have been agonizing for these great meetings. God has helped me put it down in words which express my feelings."

From the clutter of notes Kitching deciphered the song:

> O boundless salvation! deep ocean of love,
> O fulness of mercy, Christ brought from above,
> The whole world redeeming, so rich and so free,
> Now flowing for all men, come, roll over me!

Through seven verses it spells out the *raison d'être* of the Salvation Army and the founder. It is the Army national anthem, a grand thundering old tune, sung so lustily that it never fails to send shivers up the spine.

Waldron tells how an Army band visiting Rome in 1967 was invited to play in the Vatican. They sang and played "O Boundless Salvation" for Pope John XXIII. After World War II a British Salvationist in the occupation forces found a German in the tattered uniform of an Army Corps Sergeant Major playing a violin in the rubble of his devastated city. The tune was "O Boundless Salvation." The local corps had been obliterated, the German explained. Even street names and numbers were gone. He did not know how to find the city's surviving Salvationists, if any.

An outpouring of song at the centennial congress.

"But I stand here every day in the hope that, recognizing that melody, they will come."

"I can help," the Englishman said, and he sang the Founder's song as the German played. Day after day they returned, and gradually people trickled out of the ruins, rallied by the song to pick up the pieces of their lives.

Music is a cornerstone of Salvationism. Music and the love of God are the threads that bind the Army together. Hundreds of officers would not *be* officers today had they not been lured to a deeper commitment by some band in some never-to-be-forgotten small town. Years ago in Yorkton, Saskatchewan, a United Church girl was enchanted by a street corner band and followed it curiously to the Army hall. Today Lieutenant-Colonel Gladys McGregor, assistant to the Commissioner, is one of the two highest-ranking single women in the Canadian Army.

The early Salvationists made up in volume what they lacked in talent. One way to their listeners' hearts was through the pop tunes of the day, which the Salvationists artfully fitted with their own gospel words. Favorites such as "The Girl I Left Behind Me," "Oh, Dear, What Can The Matter Be," "Just Before the Battle, Mother," and "The Wearin' of the Green." Only a Salvationist of that rollicking era could get away with singing "For He's A Jolly Good Saviour" (to the tune of "He's a Jolly Good Fellow").

The music, like the Army itself, became less bizarre but lost none of its vigor. By World War I Canada had songster (choir) brigades in most major cities and a thoroughly professional forty-man Territorial Staff Band. In May 1914 that band, with a shipload of other Salvationists sailed for an international congress in England—and into the greatest tragedy in the Canadian Army's history.

There were 167 Salvationists, including Commissioner David M. Rees and his wife, aboard the S.S. *Empress of Ireland* when the boat slipped out of Quebec City on a Thursday afternoon. The staff band played "God be with you till we meet again" as the crowd waved farewell from the dock. On board that night the mood was cheerful and full of song, as it always is with Salvationists.

By 11:30 P.M. most were in bed, as a thick fog crept over the St. Lawrence River. The ship stopped at Rimouski to take overseas mail, and hurried on. Around 1:30 A.M. its captain spotted a Norwegian collier, the *Storstad*, about two miles distant. Then the fog blotted everything out. At 2:00 A.M. the *Storstad* suddenly loomed from the night, tore into the *Empress* and left a gaping hole in her side.

To the awakening passengers it felt like a minor bump, but the

Empress heeled over swiftly. The lights went out. Water gushed into the passageways. The vessel went down in fourteen minutes.

Survivors flailed in the icy water. Some gave up their lifejackets to others, and drowned. Commissioner Rees stood quietly at the rail; some said he was not aware that the ship was lost. Others said that he started to sing a hymn just before she went under. He and his family were among the 133 lost, including twenty-nine members of the staff band.

A stone memorial stands now in their honor in Toronto's Mount Pleasant cemetery. An even greater memorial is the torrent of music pouring forth from nearly four hundred musical groups in today's Army. Nearly all of the corps have one or more songster groups, and three-quarters of them have a band of some sort.

"Our finest bands will match any others, anywhere," says musical director Major Robert Redhead. "And some are pretty awful!"

The important thing is that everyone has a chance to get involved and sometimes it leads far beyond the village band.

"I got my first gold medal for singing in a Kiwanis music competition when I was six years old," says soldier Ken Clarke, who now plays country-gospel music with his wife and children for Christian gatherings all over Canada and the United States. "In the Army you learn not to be shy. You never know when you may be called on to sing in church. It's part of life, especially in the smaller corps, when all kids get a chance to take part."

"Any kid with musical aspirations can, in the Army, be well on the way by age sixteen," says Major Redhead. Beginning at the local band level, and working up through an intricate training system of youth music camps, a boy or girl can learn cornet, horn, trombone, euphonium, tuba, drums and that greatest of crowd-pleasers, the timbrel or tambourine.

The timbrel is one of the oldest percussion instruments on earth and it was made to order for Booth's flamboyant troops. The founder allegedly said, "If standing on my head and beating a tambourine with my toes will win a soul for Jesus, I will do it."

Today's timbrel brigades don't stand on their heads but just about anything else goes. The tambourine has come a long way from the undisciplined bang and rattle of early times. In Australia, where the timbrel tradition is particularly strong, brigades have skillfully accompanied a Tchaikovsky symphony. In Canada the Army's eighty-page timbrel manual, with forty pages of drills, arrows, loops, numbers and diagrams, looks like the play-book for the BC Lions.

A timbrel is a tiny drum with a skin head stretched taut over a circular wooden frame and trimmed with "jingles"—shiny brass or nickel discs strung around the rim. To this the Army adds decorative ribbons in red, blue and gold. Timbrels come in eight, nine and twelve-inch sizes, cost from $7.50 to $31.50 (for a high quality double-jingle double-roll model from England), and come in bass or treble tones, according to the arrangement of the jingles.

The trained timbrellist does not just whack the head and holler "Hallelujah!" There's an art to holding it, with thumb and little finger around the rim and middle fingers gripping the inside. By quickly running a thumb dipped in rosin paste around the edge of the head, she gets an effect called the "roll." The "run" or "trill" is a sharp wrist action that vibrates the jingles. Your accomplished timbrellist can also do the "shake" (hands, not body), the "swing-slash" and several other choreographic tricks with the heel of the hand, the elbow and the hip.

"Put yourself into it," says the timbrel manual, and the senior

Major Redhead and band in recording session; it could just as well be a rehearsal.

brigades do, shifting body as well as hands and arms, swinging through intricate routines like a precision drill team. One timbrel brigade put *so* much hip into the act (to compound matters, one of the group was an attractive divorcee) that some of the elders complained. Thereafter, the timbrels praised God with a little less body-english.

The elders could be forgiven. Army music is, above all, a form of spiritual praise.

"Our music is an expression of service and commitment to God," says Major Redhead who is, of course, an ordained minister; earlier in his career he preached from the very platform in East London where William Booth once stood. "It helps bring our people into a deeper awareness of God."

Every member of every formal band must be a soldier, with all the purity of lifestyle that this entails. Bandsmen are commissioned, in effect becoming lay officers, and must sign a bond promising to honor the orders and regulations of the Salvation Army. Even the instruments are formally dedicated with prayer to the glory of God. The bandmaster can insist that each member be on hand for practices and performances, and backsliders can be dismissed. Here, as in other aspects of the Army, discipline pays off with quality.

Workshops, once or twice a year in each of the fifteen divisions, help train aspirants in vocal music. Every year the two hundred best sixteen-to-twenty-five-year-olds meet at the National School of

The Canadian Staff Band, conductor Major Robert Redhead seated in front (glasses).

Salvationists take to the stage: a scene from Chains of Gold, *an original musical written by Major and Mrs. Robert Redhead for the Army in 1982.*

Music to hone their skills and to let the Army's musical leaders spot talent.

Like farm team players in professional sport, some instrumentalists in the small bands work up to the big league: the Canadian Staff Band. Its thirty-four players are the cream of the crop. In their scarlet dress tunics they perform seven weekends a year across Canada and make a major tour—to England, say, or Australia—every second year. They also cut one or two records a year, which sell from 4,000 to 11,000 copies.

Many corps have, along with the traditional band, a good jazz pianist or a little gospel combo. "Gospel rock" emerged during the sixties and seventies. "Follow The Son"—a group of young Salvationists in Listowel, Ontario, with guitars, keyboard, flute and drums—produced a sweet mellow sound that, apart from its gospel content, could pass for any quartet on the pop music charts. The Earlscourt Citadel Band in Metro Toronto has appeared in concert with the Elmer Iseler Singers, and its own Earlscourt Songsters, renowned for their a-capella singing, have produced excellent recordings. The massed voices of the Salvation Army Festival Choir on record or in such concert settings as Toronto's Roy Thomson Hall, could hold their own with anything—the Mormon Tabernacle Choir, for instance—on the continent.

The Canadian Army even produces musicals, with music and lyrics by Major Redhead and his wife Gwenyth. Their first, *Chains of Gold* performed in 1982, the Army's centennial year, included a discreet Sally Ann kickline.

But the core of Army music will always be the band. If you are lucky there is a time of year when you can hear an Army band outside your door. Each Christmas season, on my street as on others, a little Army band from the training college bursts into carols. The pure brassy notes soar in the cold air, and you open the door to enjoy their sound even before a pink-cheeked girl reaches your doorstep with her collection box. You thrust in money gladly, before she asks.

"Thank you, God bless you!" She smiles.

And somehow, because the Army has said it and sung it, you think He will.

"If we ever lose the philosophy of the band we will lose something very fundamental to the Army," says Redhead. As society moved into the suburbs the Army moved its music to the shopping malls. Redhead wishes there were more downtown streetcorner bands, reaching out to the "unchurched" people as the Salvationists did long ago.

Still, the music reaches out in the most unlikely corners of the world. John Waldron tells of a Salvationist on a business trip to Russia who found a functioning church—a sight almost as rare as a live capitalist. It was Baptist and to his astonishment the congregation began to sing in Russian the tune of the Founder's song.

"What are the words?" he asked a man near him.

"Something about salvation," said the other, struggling with the translation. "The size, dimensions of salvation . . . it is boundless. . . ."

Then the visitor remembered that George Scott Railton, who once brought Salvationism to Halifax, had founded the Army in Russia long ago and that it survived until Communism drove it out. Yet even now in Russia there is a musical remnant of the Army and General Booth.

20

L'Armée
du Salut

Nearly a century after hostile mobs bedevilled those first Salvationists in Quebec City, l'Armée du Salut is back as a church. Fittingly, as though the founder himself had come back to haunt those hecklers of long ago, it is led by a great-grandson of General William Booth.

Major Stuart Booth is tall, straight-backed and bald, with the forceful family nose. He looks out steadfastly from behind spectacles, full of humor but with such British understatement that anyone weaned on TV sitcoms, with laughtracks telling them when to bray, would find Booth a very dry stick.

What is it like, bearing this legendary name, being one of the "royal family" of the Sally Ann?

"Sometimes I feel unworthy of carrying such a name," Booth says seriously. "You learn to live with it. I will say that since we've arrived in Quebec City, people who discover I'm a descendant of the founder make quite a point of it. Perhaps we are pushed a bit more into the limelight because of it."

He pauses, studies his listener for humor-level and adds with an almost imperceptible grin, "And at such times I cash in on it. After all, why not?"

Booth is entitled to use all the leverage he can find. Although the persecution of the 1880s is only a dim memory, Quebec province in the 1980s—when the Army returned to open its corps—is a trying place for Anglophone Salvationists.

The province has approximately 1,450 Salvationists to 5.6 million Roman Catholics, a ratio of 4,000 to one. On this particular autumn day, total Army membership in Quebec City is *nine*—seven officers, one of Booth's daughters, and a British Columbia Salvationist studying French at Laval University. Sunday services, with an additional two or three men from the local hostel, rarely draw more than a dozen souls.

The hostel, which has remained in Quebec City since the Army's beginnings, can accommodate sixty men but has only fifteen. Anglophone transients used to cross the St. Lawrence River from the TransCanada Highway for a stay in Quebec City. Now they don't bother. Unless they speak French there's no chance of a job.

For the Army, as for any other institution that does its primary business in English, Quebec's stringent language laws (as they existed in 1984) pose enormous difficulties and adjustments. Throughout the province, unilingual Army personnel have been replaced with bilingual. Some of the former who have held jobs up to thirty years were, says Booth, about to "find themselves out on their ear because they can't speak French."

The mail must be written in French, addressed in French, received in French.

"When I write my divisional commander, who is English-Canadian, I must write to him in French. When he replies he must ask some person of his staff to do so for him. You say to yourself, it can't possibly be happening. But it is. It's here to stay so we've jolly well got to get on with it."

Booth himself is so fluent that when he came to Quebec City a newspaper reported, to his enormous embarrassment, that he spoke better French than the mayor. It's the legacy of his rich bicultural life.

He was born in England, son of Wycliffe Booth (who for nine years was commissioner for Canada) and grandson of Bramwell, the founder's faithful son. As a baby Stuart was dedicated to the Army in highly unconventional fashion. His grandfather, then the Army's second General, conducted the ceremony—but the *wrong* one. "He apparently got mixed up and made me a *soldier* on the spot."

Despite this instant elevation to the ranks, and even though he was a Booth, his conversion to Salvationism was not necessarily a sure thing. "There had to be a personal and private commitment. But by the time I was six I felt the need for Christ in my life." This time they properly made him a Junior Soldier.

His parents were posted to France, then Switzerland, so young Booth grew up a continental European, with all the accompanying *savoir faire*. After his father was called home in World War II to administer the Army's canteens for Allied troops, Stuart was called up into the regular British Army. He served four and a half years, ending in Burma with the British West African Frontier Force.

Somewhere in the jungle he realized he wanted to be a different kind of soldier for life. After the war he graduated from training college and met his future wife, Charlotte, daughter of a noted French psychiatrist. She was a member of the Reform Church, changed to the Army, and they were married as soon as she completed officer training.

By the early 1980s, with more than thirty years of service, Booth could have expected some cushy headquarters post. He had seen Canada only twice. He tells of one visit here in his elegant modulated English, facts and dates all neatly in order, with little flashes of self-deprecating humor. Sometimes he pauses to search out the right word because, after so many years in France, his native language has almost become his second language.

"When they opened the new wing [named after his father] at Toronto training college a few years ago they asked my mother to come dedicate it. She was then eighty-five and said she couldn't make the journey alone, although she moved around better and quicker than I could. So it was rather a farce; I accompanied her to look after tickets but she was telling me when to get on the plane."

On that visit, Booth glimpsed something of the Quebec problem. In 1981 General Arnold Brown asked if he would be willing to go to Canada.

"Yes, General, but it won't be Quebec, will it?" said Booth.

It was. He was being offered one of the toughest jobs in Canada, despite the grand title: "coordinator of Salvation Army services, a very big title for a job that was unknown."

Like all good Booths he moved swiftly to the attack. Soon after his arrival the Canadian Staff Band played a scheduled engagement in Quebec City, giving Booth a chance to meet four hundred local people, including the lieutenant governor and all the consuls. Within a year he was: a Knight of the Order of Malta, St. John of Jerusalem (a Catholic group); president of the local Mission to Lepers Society; and a member of the Bible Society Committee, the Boy Scouts Committee, an Anglophone ministers fraternal organization and an ecumenical group that includes Catholics.

As well as administrator, Booth is public relations officer, Missing Persons officer and runs the Red Shield campaign. In 1983 the Army reached its Quebec City Red Shield target ($105,000) in the first nine months.

"That's nothing compared to the million dollars it is costing the Army to be here," Booth points out. "But we wouldn't have brought in five more officers in the past three years if the Army hadn't thought it worthwhile."

So he and his tiny band soldier on in what sometimes seems foreign territory to Salvationists.

"Anne and I have started to streetwalk," says Captain Joy Rennick, with a mischievous glint. She is a sparkling woman in her thirties with curly auburn hair. Her streetwalking is, of course, *not* the oldest profession. With Anne Maurais from the 1983 Heralds of Hope graduating class, corps officer Rennick takes the Army message out to Quebec City people. "The needs are tremendous. The pimps, prostitutes, druggies—they're all here."

So on Friday nights the two Sally Ann girls bravely set up a speaker system on the streets, play the guitar, sing songs and welcome questions and conversation from everyone. A few onlookers derisively throw bottle caps or money. ("They have to pick up their money afterward; *I* certainly won't," Joy says indignantly.) Most are polite, even if they don't accept the Army gospel.

"They won't openly disagree; they don't like to offend," she says. "So some stand and listen from a great distance. And that's fine. We don't push it." Like the Little Prince, says Rennick, the Army simply seeks and offers friendship.

Joy Rennick has no illusions about the difficulty of her task. The daughter of Army officers in Noranda, Quebec, she remembers her father and his followers being plucked from their street-corner Bible meeting by the police, although they were quickly released. As do so many Army children, she shied away at first from the idea of "wearing black and white [slang for the uniform] and taking orders all my life." For six years after high school she traveled and worked for an investment company and a stock broker.

But the holy upbringing nearly always bobs back to the surface of a Salvationist's life. Her parents, she remembers affectionately, were equally dedicated to Christ in their personal and public lives. "They lived what they preached. I was exposed to God as a living vital Person who was intimately acquainted and involved with human beings, and to whom we would be giving an account on 'the other side.'"

After her taste of civilian life, it "occurred to me that if I lived to be ninety-nine and one-half years of age, I did not want to look back and realize my life had been a disappointment." She became an officer in 1968 and came to Quebec City in 1980.

Rennick is a thoroughly modern Army woman with a mind of her own. While studying French at Laval, she insisted on wearing a cardigan over her Army blouse and skirt, instead of the regulation uniform. She knew she could blend in and study most effectively in that electric environment as just another civilian.

Similarly, at the corps evening coffeehouse she sometimes wears slacks. Even in these enlightened times it is a trifle unorthodox style of dress for duty, but it sets the street people at ease. Every street-wise officer adapts to the local situation which, in Quebec City where the Army is not well-known, is vastly different from, say, Toronto or Regina.

Is Rennick a women's libber? "If you mean, do I burn my bra, no!" But she thinks the Army has some distance to go in achieving equal opportunity for women. Why, for example, are there almost no women in really senior positions?

Part of her ministry, with Anne Maurais, is to go door to door among the homes of children who've attended Army summer camp. It's an effort to make Salvationism better known and to offer a hand to any who need it. The people greet her kindly. Some know of the Army from its thrift store. Some are baffled. ("Are you Jehovah's Witnesses?" asked one.) All are Catholic (or lapsed Catholics) and sometimes Rennick asks herself in the Army vernacular: *What are you, Joy, a sheep stealer?* But she is not out to raid the Catholic Church.

"My job is not to build the Salvation Army here," Joy Rennick says. "My job is to preach the word of Jesus Christ. It's the Lord's job to build the Army here. It's my job to represent it. If God wants a Salvation Army corps here, there will be one."

In this respect the Almighty is getting full support from Toronto headquarters.

"We have a supreme desire to be of help and of blessing to Quebec as we do everywhere," says Commissioner Arthur Pitcher. "For generations we grew up as a largely Anglo-Saxon organization in Canada. We did not produce many French-Canadian officers who could go back and relate to their people."

Pitcher plans to reverse that trend. He has promised that if Quebec produces Salvation Army candidates the Army will train them in Quebec *in their own language.*

"We're developing more programs and creating more literature in French Canada," Pitcher says. "We're there and we're going to *stay.*"

21

Behind Bars

"Anybody want to see the Sally Ann?" the duty officer hollers.

Eight o'clock on a sunny Wednesday morning, but the sun never shines down here in the bowels of Toronto's Old City Hall. In the holding cells beneath the courtrooms, last night's haul of miscreants, red-eyed and disheveled in jeans and T-shirts, awaits this morning's judgment. A fairly typical docket: theft, obstruction of police, break-and-enter, carrying a concealed weapon, assault with bodily harm, a pair of brothers charged with wounding. Whatever rage, bravado, or desperation brought them all here has melted away now. They are subdued, or scared.

"Anybody want to see the Sally Ann?"

A few file out to the bars where Major John Wood, prison chaplain, short, pink-cheeked and smiling, waits for their requests. Will he phone a wife, mother, girl friend? Ask her to call a lawyer. Can she come to court? Ask her to bring money. Can you find out what happened to my friend? Went to hospital last night with a gunshot wound.

Wood promises to do it all, and stands the first twelve supplicants to a paper cup of coffee (all that his budget permits). Upstairs in the tiny office he shares with two other chaplains, he makes the phone calls, finds out that the gunshot case is recuperating, and by 10:00 A.M. is on hand in courtroom number twenty-three.

In court one man is discharged but has no place to sleep; Wood will get him into an Army hostel. Another's case is pushed forward on the court calendar so fast that his mother, looking on, doesn't

Every weekday morning Major John Wood goes into the cells to offer help to the night's crop of miscreants (Toronto).

understand. Wood tiptoes over to explain. A third man charged with shouting and swearing at a streetcar driver is discharged. Wood gives him a streetcar ticket to get home, hoping he doesn't mouth off at *another* driver.

Across Canada, some hundred other Army officers and four hundred lay workers are working in other prisons and courtrooms to ease the lot of men and women in, just out of, or going to jail. John Wood has been doing it for more than a third of his thirty-four years in the Army. Sometimes the interminable diet of despair preys on him.

"If I wasn't a Christian I'd find it pretty hard, day after day," he admits. "But behind those bars are human beings. And they know I'm genuine. They can read a phony a mile away."

He was born a Presbyterian on a Prince Edward Island farm, took a night course in electrical engineering, and was working on the

Halifax waterfront when he met a Sally Ann girl who turned him on to the Army and its evangelism: "I feel it's how Christ would function if he were here on earth."

His prison ministry is as old as the Army itself.

"I believe I am in the proud position of being at the head of the only religious body which has always had some of its members in jail for conscience sake," William Booth once said. "Our people, thank God, have never learned to regard a prisoner as a mere convict. He is ever a human being to them, who is to be cared for and looked after as a mother looks after her ailing child."

In Canada the Army's role was summed up admirably by the parole commissioner for Ontario in 1918: "The idea that prison makes men better is a fallacy. The law can punish but it seldom reforms. As a rule, the contaminating influences of prison life tend to make men worse, and discharged prisoners will do things they would have scorned to do before they were imprisoned.

"Thus there is great need for some moral and spiritual force within the prison walls to counteract and overcome this evil influence. That force is supplied by the Salvation Army. The religious services they conduct and the personal and kindly contact of the Army officers with the men are of inestimable value."

Today that contact takes many forms. In British Columbia, at the request of the provincial government, Army officers visit the accused before trial to inform them of court procedures and help them contact legal aid lawyers. In Ontario the Army has (subject to government funding assistance) operated a bail verification program, supervising people who cannot provide bail or be released under their own recognisance. It keeps those people out of jail and reduces prison costs.

In Ontario and Nova Scotia the Army has eleven community resource centers for men serving the last few months of their sentences. They work in the community by day and live in the center under Army supervision by night. These are not necessarily hardened criminals—one man worked at his job of land developer, while working off his sentence. Another who'd been jailed on an impaired driving charge drove to work and back every day in his Mercedes.

The Army, through its network of contacts, helps inmates get jobs upon release from prison. It has looked into the revolutionary (to some) concept of "restitution and reconciliation"—surely the ultimate in practical Christianity—wherein offender and victim are brought together by a mediator to work out a program of reconciliation. But in early 1984 the judicial system was still not unanimously supporting the idea.

Finally, the Army's typically humane Victim/Witness Assistance

(VWAP) program lends aid and comfort to those people whom criminal justice tends to forget.

So far the VWAP is offered in five Ontario cities in conjunction with the provincial government. To encourage more people to testify in court, Army volunteers help witnesses find their way through the judicial labyrinth right into the courtroom if necessary.

Others help the victims of crimes after the police have done all they can. Of some $3 billion spent annually on the criminal justice system in Canada a mere $15 million, or .5 percent, is spent on victims. So, as in the Toronto suburb of Rexdale, the Army corps helps those that society forgets—as many as four hundred in a typical year.

Civilian supervisor Marilyn Field, mother of two teenage boys, handpicks volunteers from the corps: some forty housewives, executives, or husband and wife teams of all ages. She looks for "a very caring kind of person who can listen and can work hard." She also has interpreters in Punjabi, Italian, Polish and Greek, as needed.

They clean up and patch up after burglaries; sit with weeping survivors after fatal accidents; help battered wives find baby formula, diapers, temporary lodging, and legal aid; find shelter for teenagers kicked out of unhappy homes. They'll go out in the middle of the night on thirty minutes' notice, if necessary. Once they arranged a funeral.

When a teenage girl ran amok in her mother's apartment—"She literally tore it apart" says a Sally Ann worker—four VWAP volunteers led by Mrs. Field were on the scene the same day. First they cleared a space in the rubble and poured coffee for the stunned mother (a single parent). Then they spent four hours cleaning up. As they left, one volunteer gave the mother a bright checked tablecloth as a cheering gift. Later they arranged counseling for parent and daughter.

"We're just ordinary people helping ordinary people," says Marilyn Field.

To get into Her Majesty's Penitentiary in St. John's—assuming you do not arrive in a paddywagon as a guest of the province—you buzz the first locked door in the grim blank wall. Guards in blue and gray uniforms patrol overhead. You sign in at a guardhouse, go through another locked gate, through a heavy main door, and face another clutch of guards.

"We won't take anything out," Auxiliary Captain Herb Goodridge promises. It's an in-joke; visitors are forbidden to carry anything in or out but if one man doesn't have to be searched it's this Sally Ann officer. He shines with integrity. He stands well over six feet, a grave man with crisp gray hair and eyes that can be kind or commanding under his peaked hat. Even his smile is contained and serious.

One of the guards grins back. "All you'd take out of here is a heavy burden," he says in his lilting Newfie accent.

The guards are not the potbellied goons or southern-sheriff sadists of the late-late show. They do their best in a trying job, often seeing the same culprits come back time after time.

"The druggies'll go out and make a few thousand dollars and get caught again," a young guard says. "So they come back and serve their time with no great discomfort."

The guards know, too, that drugs are being smuggled in but they can't stop it. "You can search them when they come in, but if they've swallowed the stuff in some waterproof package they just pass it out through the bowels in a day or so. You can't police the bowels of every prisoner."

So Herb Goodridge doesn't forget the guards on these five-days-a-week visits. "I talk to them, have a coffee, keep up a friendly relationship. It's a hard job, mentally, and they put a lot of effort into rehabilitation."

His main mission is to offer the prisoners whatever hope or counsel they need and will accept. Sometimes he feels overwhelmed by the steady torrent of men in and out of court and prison.

"But you keep pushing on, hoping, praying that a smile, a warm handshake will do something."

Goodridge is relatively new to prison work, and to the Army. He was born in St. John's to a United Church family. His earliest connection with the Sally Ann as a kid was to throw rocks downhill at its temple. But during twenty-five years in the Canadian regular army, the last six in Europe, he learned that the Army was "a real lifesaver." Less than a month after he retired in 1981 he traded one uniform for the other. He was too old to qualify for officer training but under a new arrangement for auxiliary officers, he can become a regular in a few years.

He has learned the art of dealing with prisoners: for example, not to become intimidated by their cynicism. "You must not apologize for who you are and what you stand for, but must not offend either. You don't preach to them." He knows he must never promise favors he can't deliver. "Prisoners have a saying: 'He's playing a head game,' meaning he says one thing but means another. If you break a promise to one of them, the word gets around."

Above all, he has learned not to be conned by the cons. They invariably test a new Sally Ann officer, most often with a request for transfer into the Harbour Light. If the request seems genuine he passes it on with his recommendation to a penitentiary board. The maximum sentence at this prison is two years less one day; the men must serve at least one-third of it.

"From day one they're trying to figure how to shorten their time, and they'll go for any program that might do it," Goodridge says wryly. "When I first got here, they came in droves. I thought we'd have to build a new Harbour Light!" He's had disappointments—men who skipped out after being granted the favor—but he tries not to hold it against the next one.

This prison is about as good or bad as any other. The men—some in khaki, some in slacks and T-shirts—do not look as immaculate as the prisoners in TV shows, but *nothing* in prison looks much like TV. There's a new modern wing housing hard cases such as murderers, and protective custody cases such as sex offenders (who sometimes stand to be beaten or even killed by the others). Each floor on the wing has a large central recreation area with a television, overlooked by guards inside a glassed control room with a console that opens and closes doors or switches lights at the touch of a switch.

The older wing has traditional cells in long rows looking out on a corridor. Some cons like it best because they can fetch their own food from the kitchen and, consequently, pick out what they like.

This day, as every day, Herb Goodridge will counsel those who made appointments on his earlier visits. He takes them, one by one, in a tiny room with bilious green walls, one plain table, two plain chairs, a standup ashtray and a single overhead light bulb. The door has a single pane of glass so the guards can see in, and help if needed.

He holds the interviews to fifteen minutes, continuing the next day if necessary. "You have to dig to get at the truth. They test you, to see if you're a soft touch. Oh, they'll con you! It's almost a game." Goodridge, who spent two years of his regular army life as a military policeman, is not easily conned. "I don't baby them. If I feel a guy's lying to me, I'll confront him and we'll have a little spat. You're trying to establish trust, so the word'll get around: 'Yeah, Captain Goodridge'll do it for you but you gotta level with him.' "

The requests and hard-luck stories are as old as prison itself. A wife or girlfriend is sick back home. Anything you can do, Captain? Can I get into the Harbour Light? Can you get me a ride home after I get out? On all but the simplest of requests, Goodridge says, "I'll look into it and get back to you" or "It doesn't look good but we'll try." For men who've lost everything—job, home, a marriage, hope—it's something to cling to, but not unrealistically.

If a man asks for spiritual counsel, Goodridge first offers to put him in touch with a minister or priest of his own faith. Otherwise, he'll maybe ease into a discussion of God and the Bible.

"I want them to know there are people who care, and that things *can* be turned around if they'll make an effort themselves. I have a tremendous responsibility. I must not leave a man supposing that by accepting Christ all his troubles will be over. He has opened himself to me; I have to be very careful not to make his life worse."

It is difficult for this thoroughly decent officer to curb his feelings when, inevitably, he becomes friends with a man and that man moves on. He remembers one such: "I never did much for him, just general talk." The prisoner, tough and overbearing, poured out his curses and bitterness. Goodridge listened quietly. When the man was transferred to a long-term federal prison, he sought Goodridge out, thanked him, shook his hand, turned back, and thanked him again.

"I like to believe I left a little bit of hope with him, and maybe somebody else over there will offer him a little more," says Goodridge. "You have to believe that some good will come in every case. But we're not fooling ourselves. I have to accept the fact that some guys will never change, or it will take a miracle to transform them."

For all of its moments of disillusionment, Goodridge wants to stay at this work for the rest of his Army career. He clings to hope, and tries to pass it on.

"Have a nice day," he says to a guard on the way out.

"That's hard to do, in here," the guard says.

22

Matters
of Life
and Death

There is hope enough in Grace Hospital, Halifax, to make
up for all the lost hopes and frail dreams of every prison in the land.
This is where life begins.

Every year Halifax Grace ushers more than 5,000 babies into the
world, at least one-quarter of them high-risk deliveries. That is its
specialty. It's self-appointed task is to keep these little humans alive
and healthy, having brought them here against extraordinary odds.
Halifax Grace does its job surpassingly well. Here, the "miracle" of
birth is exactly that.

It is a wonderful place to have a baby because the quality of care
is special and the level of infant mortality has been, and may still be
(statistics are forever changing) the lowest of any maternity hospital
in North America. The national average for Canada has been twelve
to fourteen deaths per 100 births; at the Halifax Grace it is 7.2 per
100.

In Grace's neo-natal (babies at risk) unit the mortality rate has
steadily declined in the last fifteen years. The most striking drop is
in the improved rate of very low birth-weight babies—tiny persons
around the one-thousand gram (two pounds, three ounces) weight
level. At Grace, the mortality rate for this category dropped from one
hundred percent in 1972 to twenty-six percent in 1982. The
hospital's smallest surviving child was a four-hundred-gram (four-
teen-ounce) morsel of humanity—so small that if the baby had died
it would have been registered as a miscarriage.

This remarkable record results from a kind of chain reaction:
because Grace *is* such a fine maternity hospital it attracts the finest
doctors and nurses.

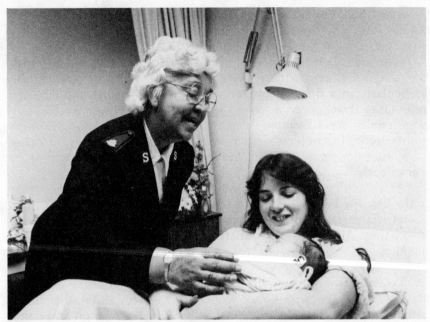

The miracle of birth at Grace Hospital, Halifax.

"Its entire function is obstetrics, so you don't have doctors and nurses who don't want to be here," says Major Eleanor Johnson, executive director and, as in virtually all ten Grace Hospitals across Canada, one of two Salvation Army officers on the premises (the other is the chaplain).

The tradition of excellent medical care goes back to the Grace's unfashionable beginnings: as a house called the Rescue Home for Fallen Women in 1906. At the time, it was the Army's outstretched hand to pregnant prostitutes who, being of no further use to their pimp or madam, had nowhere to have their babies. The Army asked local doctors to volunteer their services. So many good ones did that it became the best place in Halifax to have a baby, especially for a difficult birth. Such was the demand that one floor was set aside for "respectable" women. By 1922 the hookers were crowded out—or blended in—and Grace moved to its present site. (The original Rescue Home is now a residence for unwed mothers.)

The hospital has been pioneering ever since. In 1928, for example, its iconoclastic chief of staff, Dr. H. B. Atlee, led North America in the "early rising" concept. Until then, new mothers were kept in bed for twelve days after delivery, with little exercise. Naturally they went home weak.

"Even when I began nursing," says Eleanor Johnson, "mothers went home in an ambulance after a week or ten days. Usually they hadn't walked until then, and were told to not open the baby's blanket until they got home." Now the mother is quickly up after birth and usually home in four or five days.

Grace is called the "flagship" of thirty-seven hospitals in Nova Scotia. Doctors across the province know that it can be counted on, particularly in a difficult birth. It averages two airlifts and a dozen ambulance transports a week from all over Nova Scotia, and occasionally New Brunswick and Prince Edward Island. Mothers with potential problems—such as diabetes, which tends to cause premature delivery—may go into the high-risk unit several days or weeks early.

As a teaching hospital for Dalhousie University, Grace has access to the best medical talent, and its 5,000-plus births per year mean its obstetricians stay in practice. Grace also gives post-graduate courses in nursing. Although its graduates don't necessarily end up at the hospital, the nursing staff (one hundred in delivery and about ninety-five in the nursery) is a mother's dream.

When a patient is admitted, her nurse meets her at the door and stays with her. Because Grace works twelve-hour shifts, that nurse often sees the mother through the birth, giving medication and doing the other tasks that in other times and places several nurses did or still do. She becomes the patient's friend.

Which is how the Army likes it.

"Our nurses are not required to be Salvationists, and generally are not," says the major, whose youthful face and light young voice belie her snowy hair. "But I spend ten minutes or so with each new group of employees, talking about the Salvation Army. I indicate what our Christian standards are, and invite the new people to come to chapel if they wish."

The Army's strong sense of family is in tune with the homey feeling of the place. Grace in 1971 was one of the first maternity hospitals to treat childbirth as a family affair. Now, as do many other hospitals, it welcomes fathers in the pre-natal and labor periods. Approximately eight hundred pregnant women and their men attend classes every month. Outside the labor room there's a porch where in decent weather the mother-to-be can walk with her husband.

Some psychologists believe the infant senses this total involvement, before and after birth, and is made more secure by it. For the same reason, Grace has experimented with low lighting and gentle handling of the baby in the delivery room.

A normal delivery takes place in a colorful room with wallpaper, pictures and an easy chair. The apparatus for delivery, kept ready behind a curtain, includes a "birthing chair": unlike a flat surface with stirrups, the chair provides a more natural position for birth and gives the mother more leverage to push. Outside the delivery room there's a curtained-off area where, right after the birth, mother, father and children can be together and phone their relatives.

For several years, Grace has practiced "combined care": the infant stays with its mother from 9:00 A.M. until 9:00 or 10:00 P.M. instead of being isolated in a nursery. She feeds and changes her baby, and her nurse attends to both. There are rooms with rocking chairs and curtained-off sections, for breast feeding.

Often a mother goes home ahead of her baby, if the infant is undersized or needs intensive care. For these stay-behinds there's a cot room where volunteer "cuddlers" feed, rock, change, and cuddle the temporary orphans. (There is always a cuddlers' waiting list.) Pediatricians think it's good for infants to be stimulated with color, voices, exercises, and musical toys. When the mother returns for her baby, she can stay overnight while Grace's nurses reassure her and tune up her mothering skills.

This forward-thinking in human terms is backed up with fine technology. Grace has the newest ultra-sound equipment to examine the foetus before birth, spotting defects that may need immediate attention after delivery, and harmlessly scan the baby's head after birth for potential problems. Among premature babies, blood vessels in the skull are particularly fragile. Ultra-sound can detect hemorrhaging which, unless quickly treated, could lead to retardation.

For Major Johnson, daughter of Army officers, this place is everything she wanted in life. She trained as a nurse, with no idea of being an officer. Before training ended she knew she wanted a job with meaning. She joined a Bible study group and was assigned to prowl through Ezekiel, chapter by chapter. One day it told her, "I send you to a rebellious people, and whether they will hear or whether they will forbear, I send you and you go in my strength." She felt it was God's answer to her prayers for guidance. The Army staked her to higher education; like all administrators of Grace Hospitals, she has an MA in health administration. Best of all, she says simply, "I love my work."

Captain Lynn Byrnes and Major Thelma Richardson also spend their days with mothers-to-be, days not always full of the pure joy of the mothers in Halifax Grace. Their mothers are unmarried and some as young as twelve. Some have been kicked out of home by the mother and father. An occasional one has been impregnated by her father.

All of them find shelter, and a kind of love that makes no demands, in the major's Lindenview Residence in Winnipeg and the captain's Bethany Home in Saskatoon. Here, they begin to sort out the rest of their lives. Lindenview is a bright modern one-storey place, designed for its purpose. Bethany is a handsome old house. Their aims and results are identical.

"The main focus is hominess," says Thelma Richardson. She has been known to play hide-and-seek with new arrivals, some of them little more than babies themselves, to help make them feel at home. She is a big woman with a smile that invites, then waits to see if you will respond. The daughter of Salvationists in Hamilton, Bermuda, she graduated from Toronto training college in 1958. A classmate remembers how pleased and surprised she seemed—although she was among Christians—that her white classmates accepted a black girl without question or prejudice.

Both homes offer a chance to keep up with schooling on the premises, and there are films and lectures on childbirth and motherhood. Lindenview takes them on visits to a Grace Hospital labor room. ("They come back pretty white-looking!" says the major.) Bethany has public health lectures on nutrition, and lessons on writing a résumé and preparing for job interviews.

Both have church services for those who choose to attend. "They tend to hide from the world," says Major Richardson. "I say 'Come out to church. So you're pregnant? So are lots of others!' Once you get them to realize that *you* feel there is something good in them, *they* begin to feel it too."

How did they get into the mess they're in?

"If family relationships aren't good, the teenagers often rebel sexually," the major says. "Your peers are *all*-important at that age, and all kids are tempted to try sex. If communications are good at home, they can probably come through the teen years not too badly. Otherwise, they do what their friends do, try what they try. They have to feel important somewhere. When girls become pregnant it is mostly a close relationship they are looking for: 'At least somebody loves me.'"

Because the girls are often outcasts from their families, there is only the Sally Ann to stand by them through the birth.

"None of us likes to go through an unknown experience," says Thelma Richardson. "So, if the girls need us, we are there."

Sometimes Lynn Byrnes gets calls in the night or at dawn: "Captain, I'm in labor!"

"That's the quality time for me," she says. "I often think, if Mother and Dad were there at that time, all the hurts would be healed."

"At a time like that parents should be there," Major Richardson agrees. "I sometimes feel I cheat the parents of something nice."

Lynn Byrnes grew up in Ontario and had her heart set on being a policewoman until a girl friend talked her into joining the Salvation Army. "I told her, 'I'll go if you'll stop bugging me.' A year later I was in training for officership; she got married and never did join the Army!"

Byrnes was never more sure her decision was right than on the April night in 1982 when she shepherded a seventeen year old to the delivery room. The girl had been through enough in her short life: her mother had been shot to death three years before and a favorite grandmother had just died. That night her baby was stillborn.

Lynn Byrnes stayed with her until she slept. As she turned away a feeble voice called out, "Captain, I love you . . . I wish you were my Mom. . . ."

After a birth the Army lets the girls decide whether they keep their child, simply explaining the pros and cons, and letting them talk it out with young women who have exercised both options.

"It's a traumatic time in their lives," says Major Richardson. "Should they see it through or not? Have they the ability to be a parent? They listen to everyone else but they are the only ones who *know*—maybe. The memory of the birth will always be with them. They make the best decision they can, at the time. Sometimes it's the wrong one."

She urges each mother to look ahead to when the child is three or ten or in its teens; not to be swept away by the sight of a lovable baby. "But sometimes a girl's maternal instinct floods over everything else. You just hope it works."

One two-year veteran of motherhood says, "It's neat. I wouldn't trade it for the world!" But she's lonely and comes back to visit. Both Lindenview and Bethany have an old girls' network for informal reunions: a barbecue, an evening around the Christmas tree. The Sally Ann is their second home, the place where they discovered they were humans with some worth.

When Thelma Richardson came to Lindenview, she noticed most of the native girls were expert at cribbage. The major's strict Salvationist parents had taught her that such games were sin. She didn't know the *names* of cards, much less how to shuffle them. Now she learned, to get on the same wave-length with her girls.

And it worked. The girls always won, which made them feel good. "That's a stupid play, Major!" they'd say affectionately. But they also opened up and talked. One of the least communicative went to hospital, insisting she didn't need anyone with her. Once in labor she was scared.

"Major, will you come?"

In a flash of inspiration the major took along a deck of cards. They played crib between labor pains. After the baby came, the girl clutched the major's hand and cried triumphantly, "I did it!"

At that moment Thelma Richardson wouldn't have traded jobs with anyone on earth.

The sixth floor of Toronto Grace Hospital is decorated in warm yellows, beiges and browns, with paintings on the walls. Opposite the elevator hangs a large quilt, each of its thirty squares stitched by one of the nurses with designs of flowers, birds, butterflies, small animals, peaceful scenes, and the occasional motto—their concepts of "happiness." At the end of a corridor a canary named Stewart divides his time between singing and admiring himself in his mirror.

Rather an extraordinary hospital ward, but these are not ordinary patients. Most hospital patients expect to get well. Everyone on this floor knows that he or she is soon going to die.

This is the only palliative care unit in the Grace hospital chain (it also cares for one hundred chronically ill). Its twenty patients, ages twenty to seventy-five, have terminal cancer. Grace's palliative care team—clinical director, nurses, civilian volunteer force, social worker, occupational therapist, physiotherapist, and chaplain—is dedicated to one goal: give each patient the highest possible quality of life for his or her remaining time on earth.

"Success for us is a comfortable patient and a comfortable family—physically, psychologically and emotionally," says clinical director Dr. Margaret Scott (who is not a Salvationist). "And being run by the Salvation Army is a distinct advantage. Because of the Army's roots and goals, service and charity, you know that any reasonable request will be met."

Most people are afraid of dying. Often the "how" is more fearsome than the act itself: "Will I choke? Will I have a lot of pain?" For most, the very word "cancer" is terrifying. It is the job of Major Jessie Pilfrey, Army chaplain, to help them face these fears and fears of the beyond. Tall and gray-haired, she radiates quiet strength and serenity.

"I feel if a person is at peace with God, with himself and with his fellow man, then he is ready to die," she says. "I try to lead the patients to that state, and to realize that beyond this life there is something better for them, if they are at peace with God."

To do that she simply becomes their friend, counselor and sounding-board. Few are Salvationists. Since Toronto Grace—funded by the Ontario Ministry of Health and administered by the Army—changed from a general hospital to its present role in 1979, it has welcomed patients of the Buddhist, Islamic and Jehovah's Witness faiths, among others.

"Some come with no religion and some die with none," says Major Pilfrey. "I never press it on them nor try to make them into Salvationists. But a lot of them have roots in religion and I strive to bring them back to those roots, if they wish it."

Once a patient in her late fifties asked, "What do I have to do to join the Salvation Army?"

The major, frankly astonished, explained that she could become an adherent without the demands of soldiership.

"No, I want to be something like you."

Well, first, the major said, it was essential to have an experience of salvation.

"I've had that."

Then there'd be some heavy study and acceptance of doctrines.

"I still have some time left in my life," the woman said firmly. "I should do something worthwhile with it."

She ultimately was enrolled in the chapel, under the Army flag, and happily and courageously lived out her remaining months as a soldier.

The major's working day begins about 7:30 A.M. During that day she speaks to every patient on the palliative floor. She counsels the hospital staff if they seek it; conducts daily morning prayer, two chapel services per week with her assistant, Captain Jim Ellis, and holds funerals for those families who ask for it. Often she is called out in the middle of the night to be with a patient or family.

"It's not *all* sad," she stresses. "We celebrate birthdays and anniversaries. The aim is to make the hospital as much like home as possible."

There's a TV and video lounge, stereo music, and a roof garden where in summer patients can take the sun and in winter feel the wonder of snowflakes on their faces one more time. One patient baked chocolate brownies in the occupational therapy kitchen for her children to take in their lunches. A son brought in a fresh catch of fish for his father's lunch and cooked them in the hospital microwave. These are the sweet-sad times.

"It is very emotionally draining," Major Pilfrey admits. "But I feel God has fitted me for this, because of the sorrows I've known."

She was raised a Presbyterian but became acquainted with the Army through a school friend in Calgary, her hometown. "I liked the music and the happiness of it. The whole thing seemed to offer so much to a young person."

After a job in the Calgary senior citizens' lodge, she went into training and made the Army her life. For years, before and after her marriage she was in corps and youth work. The death of her husband at forty-four left her with the task of raising two half-grown children. She married again, to a former officer. After thirteen happy years he too died, at seventy-eight. Four years ago, with her children grown, she returned full-time to Army work, at Grace.

Her ministry is not just to the dying but to the survivors. Sometimes, after a death she gathers the family around the bedside and gives a prayer of thanks for all that the person's life has meant. And sometimes that is a comfort. Because she has walked with them in their sorrow, many families keep in touch. "Quite a lot of them come back and give you a big hug and a kiss."

"People say 'thank you' here more than in any other hospital I've known," agrees Dr. Scott.

How does even a Salvation Army officer, with all her inner strength, bear up in the face of constant death? In fact, some days she simply has to walk away, facing the fact that there is nothing more she can do. And some nights she goes to bed exhausted at 7:00 P.M. and sleeps the night through.

"You'd have to be a stone wall not to be touched by people's lives in a place like this. But you can't have it both ways. If you want the rewards you have to bear the pain. If you stand aloof, you are not able to help."

23

On Being
the General

It could never have happened to the Pope.

A tourist in the lobby of a Sheraton hotel in Buenos Aires spotted the short erect man in neat blue uniform with an "S" on each lapel.

"Bellhop!" she called imperiously. "Carry these bags!"

So General Arnold Brown, commander-in-chief of three million Salvationists in eighty-six countries of the world, did.

"We've done more menial things than that," he smiles. Brown likes to tell the story on himself, partly to remind his troops to wear full uniform (some like to go hatless, as he was that day, and some free-wheelers want to abolish the entire outfit). Partly, he likes to stress that there's no pomp or ceremony in being the General.

The tourist would certainly have known the Pope by his distinctive robes and his entourage. Still, there *are* faint similarities between the Army General and the Prince of the Roman Catholic Church. One is elected to office by a High Council of Army Commissioners; the other by the College of Cardinals. Each is the focal figure of a worldwide and highly disciplined faith.

"The General is our spiritual leader and as such we give him due honor," says Canadian Commissioner Arthur Pitcher. "But . . ." with a small grin ". . . we don't believe in his *infallibility.*"

"And we don't send up different-colored smoke when he's elected," adds an aide.

The current General, Jarl Wahlström of Finland, is the twelfth in the Army's 119 years. Two, Clarence Wiseman and Arnold Brown, are Canadians, both now retired in Toronto. Their careers are a glimpse of the path that leads to the top and what life is like, once there.

Both are trim, straight-backed, and handsome, far younger-looking than their years (Wiseman turned seventy-seven in 1984; Brown, seventy-two). Wiseman is taller, a brisk grandfather with white hair and moustache. Both are uncommonly fine speakers—Brown has a particularly deep resonant voice—with a deep love of words. Both have written books.

When Brown was small his father read to him from such classics as Shakespeare or Edgar Allan Poe every night. As a young adult he kept a Bible and a dictionary on his night table. Wiseman as a boy persuaded his officer-father to turn a storeroom in their Barrie, Ontario, citadel into a study, so the son had room for his library, everything from Horatio Alger to Emerson's *Essays*.

"Even today when I acquire a good new book it is as though it were the most precious treasure on earth," Wiseman says.

They are unassuming men, infinitely more approachable than, say, the average high churchman or head of a multinational corporation, but they share the unmistakeable air of authority that was essential to their job. It did not come easily to either. Brown speaks of his "natural reserve" and remembers the years of service before he fully gained self-confidence. Wiseman in his autobiography, *A Burning in My Bones*, tells of his teenage misery: "In fact, I 'turned off' most people. When asked to give a short Bible address in a public meeting I was thoroughly frightened. Though copious notes were carefully prepared, when I faced the congregation they fled from my mind—and I fled from the hall."

Naturally, both have strong Salvationist roots. Wiseman was born in Moreton's Harbour, Newfoundland. His father bore the distinction of having once been ticked off by the cantankerous founder himself. Booth was visiting St. John's, the meeting hall was packed, Wiseman Sr. arrived late and was the only one left standing. The sight of one upright figure offended the General's eye.

"That young man standing at the back," he roared. "If you can't sit down, lie down!"

Young Clarence was a fairly average Salvationist youth. Once he sneaked into a forbidden movie theater but was soon overwhelmed with guilt. Once his father caught him smoking dried maple leaves wrapped in newspaper, and strapped him. Although a Christian, Clarence had no intention of following his officer-father's path.

"Though I tried evasion tactics it soon became evident that my surrender to Christ inevitably would lead to officership. This was the last thing I wanted. It would foil my personal plans [to be a journalist]." But in 1927 he graduated from training college, married fellow-graduate Janet Kelly as soon as the Army law allowed, and was off on his life's work.

Only once did he falter. As a young captain in London, Ontario, he was offered fully-paid studies at an American theological college, with the guarantee of a comfortable Presbyterian church on graduation. It was the heart of the Depression. Not long before, the Wisemans had arisen one Saturday morning to no food and no money; a bag of groceries from their corps saved the day.

They discussed the job for hours. Wiseman labored over his letter of resignation all one Friday night. The next day, before mailing it, he and Janet knelt for morning prayers. He looked up and saw her weeping.

"I guess we can't do it, can we?" he said. She shook her head. He tore the letter to bits and was never tempted again.

Arnold Brown was born in England with the red-blue-and-gold coursing through his veins. His parents were officers as were six aunts and uncles. All but one were married so sometimes there were thirteen officers at family gatherings.

"As a boy," Brown says, "I thought the Salvation Army ran the world!"

The family moved to Belleville, Ontario. At sixteen Brown was an Army Sunday School superintendent. While in high school he got a secretarial job with Canadian National Railways, learned short-hand and practiced by taking down Sunday sermons.

Brown dreamed of entering the diplomatic service but at twenty he spent six months in England with his relatives and steeped

General Arnold Brown (now retired) and Mrs. Brown, taking the salute in Switzerland.

himself in the Army. One day he visited scruffy East London where it all began. An old drunk leaned against an iron railing beside a statue of William Booth.

"I was turning away when I thought I heard somebody say—it was the mind working, I suppose, and perhaps the spirit of God—'Who will carry on Booth's work?' " He went home and entered training college.

After his first corps in Bowmanville, Ontario, Brown moved to the Army editorial department for ten years, then into public relations where he developed, "This Is My Story," one of the longest-running programs on Canadian radio, and a weekly television show, "The Living Word," which is still replayed in Third World countries.

Next came two years as national youth secretary. "I thoroughly enjoyed it but at fifty-two it's a bit too late to go on skiing weekends. I offered myself on the altar of ridicule more than once to keep the friendship of the young people!"

Then international headquarters tapped him for a tough but influential job: five years as international public relations secretary in London. He set up the Army's 1965 centennial celebrations, tied to a major fund-raising program to rejuvenate the Army's facilities in England. Brown rocked the Salvationist world with the slogan "For God's sake, care!" which outraged some until they realized he was putting a Christian twist on a familiar expletive. It seized the public by the heart. In three years Brown raised more than £3 million.

One night he came home from his twenty-first trip to Birmingham—an exhausting day of little food and long conferences with aldermen, councilors, social service workers and the city treasurer, over a planned Army building. But he was elated, waving a cheque for £280,000. Then his wife reported with some distress that the family kitty was short thirty-five cents, Canadian.

"I don't understand this life," Brown said wryly. "Look at this cheque! And now you're putting me through the hopper over thirty-five cents!"

On the plus side, the job put him in touch with every level of authority up to and including Buckingham Palace, and many of England's rich, titled, and powerful. He was made a freeman of the City of London, the first Salvationist so honored since William Booth. From there it was up to the Army's number two job as chief of staff to then-General Wickberg; then home to be commissioner of Canada, following Wiseman who was on his way to the top job.

"The ten years away had broadened me," Brown says. "I knew what made the Army tick at the center. It gave me a confidence I didn't have before."

Wiseman meanwhile had soared up through the ranks with his World War II job, then various senior posts in Canada, territorial commander in East Africa, principal of the International Training College in London, and commander of Canada-Bermuda from 1967 to 1974.

In 1969 he was nominated as candidate for General but turned it down. "I just had a strange, I believe a divine sense of direction. I think it turned out to be right. There was a job to be done in Canada."

In 1974 he made his third trip to England to help elect a new General. The High Council—all territorial commanders plus all other commissioners—assembles specifically for this purpose at Sunbury Court, a handsome Georgian mansion overlooking the Thames, fourteen miles from London. Although its only legal task is the election, it can sit for weeks discussing questions and problems affecting the Army everywhere in the world. It is a total learning experience, particularly valuable to the new General—who at that point doesn't know he *will* be General.

On this occasion as all others, nominations and the election by secret ballot were the forty-man council's final act. Wiseman was one of the four nominees—a surprise to him because he was sixty-seven. (Today a General can not serve more than five years, or past age sixty-eight; at that time, the limit was seventy.) It was a nerve-wracking time.

"I don't think I've ever been more keenly aware of the Lord's presence than at that council," Wiseman remembers. "I went back to my room and stayed a long time, trying to figure out if this was really God's will."

In the end he accepted. Each nominee was submitted to a barrage of questions on every conceivable aspect of Army policy or matters likely to affect that policy. Each was subjected to private questions: for example, did he have any health problems that would stand in the way of the job? Finally each made a speech. Wiseman was elected on the second ballot.

Each council member signed a document of allegiance to him before they disbanded. He moved out into the glare of publicity and the four-storey international headquarters near St. Paul's Cathedral. In the bundles of congratulatory mail from Canada came a letter from an officer's son: "Have fun, General!"

That letter-writer, Geoff Ryan, now a twenty-one-year-old soldier, runs the Toronto Temple's drop-in center for street people, under the leadership of his parents, Majors Max and Patricia Ryan. Does every Army son dream of growing up to be General?

"Maybe, but nobody in his right mind would seek it," says

Arnold Brown. "It is a very responsible job, not honorary, not like a one-year presidency. You're expected to *be* the leader, to set the pace. You call the tune and all down the line people are waiting for you to say what's going to happen."

There are no financial inducements. Brown did not retire with wealth.

"I rent this house," he says of his bungalow in Toronto's Willowdale. "I couldn't afford to own a house like this."

As General his salary was on a par with a Canadian major's at the time—he and his wife received about one hundred dollars a week—because Army salaries are geared to the standard of living in the country of residence. A modest house and car with driver were provided, but the driver worked full-time in Army headquarters, and when Brown needed a late-night ride to the airport he often said, "This is your love-service!"

The General travels constantly but Brown never carried a camera. "I would not allow myself to be regarded as a tourist. I didn't see the sights in those countries. I stayed in a hotel, often provided on a complimentary basis, or in an officer's home or an Army hospital. I'd see leaders of government and the Army's work, and tell myself, 'I'll see the sights after I retire.' "

It is, in fact, a gruelling life. Within two months on the job Wiseman's three years in office were mapped out down to the last event. Despite their age, he and his wife kept every commitment, even though she once fractured a knee in a fall in Bermuda. "We felt there was a supernatural hand holding us through those years. And we had immense joy."

Brown agrees that it was exhilarating.

"Where would I have been if it hadn't been for the Army? Maybe still a clerk with the CNR, or editor of a small-town newspaper. Instead, I've had the opportunity to talk to royalty, heads of state, military dictators. And I've walked through the shadow lands of Calcutta, the barrios of Lisbon, the shanty towns of Rio—the nadir and the apex."

On some matters the Army worldwide defers to the General. For example, a divorced or overage officer candidate must receive special dispensation from the General's office. But a territory such as Canada-Bermuda is autonomous in most things. "It's a gracious freedom but a spiritual discipline," says Commissioner Arthur Pitcher of Canada's relationship to international headquarters.

Brown concluded that the prime role of General is as a unique focus for the Salvationist.

"As an individual I found it very hard to accept that the spotlight should be on me so much," he says. "But I came to realize that when you go into the heart of the Congo or up northern Kenya, the thousands of people who come out may only see a General once in their lives. For them, he *is* the international Army."

When he took the job Brown said he hoped the Army would never become institutionalized. Some took him to task for that. But, in early 1984 in the twilight of his career, he strongly reiterated the point, his voice deepening with conviction and passion.

"I hope it never becomes so big business, so top-heavy with administration, so computerized, so statisticized, that we forget what the real mission was," Brown said. "Because it doesn't lie in our buildings or in the computers. It's a man putting his arm around the shoulders of a guy who really needs a friend. It's providing a coat for somebody because, through bad luck or through his own stupidity, he needs a coat. It's preaching the gospel of Christ, which is the fundamental aim of the Army, a message of hope to somebody who hasn't got any hope.

"That's what we should do. And that's why I've often said the Army must live only a yard away from Hell."

His words should be etched in the heart of every young officer in the front line, because that indeed is what the Sally Ann is all about.

24
A Day
on the Front Line

At 8:10 A.M. on this January Monday in 1984, Lieutenant Henry Legge spots the eighteen-year-old boy loping along a snowy sidewalk. Legge swings his blue '78 Chrysler around for another look. Yes, it's the same kid who has been missing all weekend.

"Get in, I'll drive you home," Legge says curtly. The kid had merely goofed off to his girl friend's but his mother has been worrying herself sick—and she already has trouble enough.

Four months ago the mother, a single parent here in Mississauga just west of Toronto, phoned Legge for help. She's a Catholic but when her world caved in it was the Sally Ann she turned to. Behind her were two broken marriages and a broken back that had left her a semi-invalid. By autumn 1983 she was desperate: she didn't have enough money to buy the son a pair of sneakers for school.

Legge gave her a food voucher so she could free some welfare money for the shoes, and befriended her. She began attending a Tuesday crafts and Bible class, given by Henry's wife, Lorraine. "Return to your own church if you can," the Legges told her, "but you have a spiritual home here if you want it." At Christmas Henry took her a food hamper.

On the weekend just past, her neighbor's place was being sprayed for cockroaches so, by law, her own spotless townhouse had to be sprayed too. She had wrestled all the furniture away from the walls, with no son to help.

Legge drives on to his Erin Mills corps, not liking the teenager much. One day soon he will sit those two down together, tell the kid to stop using his mother and, if he doesn't respond, advise her to kick him out.

At 8:45 he pulls in to the white temple building in this municipality of 300,000, largely a bedroom community for Metro Toronto. Here, for six busy months, Lieutenants Henry and Lorraine Legge have served on the "front line."

If his corps and temple are the front line, Henry's office is his foxhole—his refuge and center of operations. It is warm and bright with a wallful of religious books, a chair, small settee, and table for meeting and counseling parishioners. Legge is the same brisk personable man of training college days, revelling in the running of his own show.

"I'm a bit of a time-management man," he says, pointing out a date diary, file folder with separate section for every day of January, and catch-all folders for every other month of the year which, as the month arrives, will be divided by day. Time-management is imperative. Life on the front line is a constant seige of details in a corps of two hundred soldiers and adherents (about half of whom are faithful churchgoers), a profitable day-care center with five employees and thirty-two kids, and a total budget of around $200,000.

Legge is both pastor and small businessman. It is the same in hundreds of other small corps. This is the bedrock of the Salvation Army: not constant drama or tragedy, but a steady flow of everyday humanity.

This morning's phone calls are a sample. An anti-alcoholism group wants to rent a room in the temple for Wednesday nights; it's okay if they agree not to smoke. Toronto training college phones to say it is assigning three cadets to his corps for periodic visits during their final semester.

"Start them on Wednesday," he says cheerfully. "It's my first inspection [by headquarters]. They can see the new lieutenant get picked apart!"

A woman wants Henry to perform a marriage. Well yes, he says, but the Army favors pre-marital counseling and he *insists* on it—as many as eight sessions so man and woman can compare their views on children, finances and all the other potential conflicts of marriage. She doesn't want to wait, so she'll marry elsewhere.

About forty percent of his work is administrative.

"I would never finish a sermon if I had to find the fifteen hours of research and writing it takes, all in one lump," Legge says. "I find an hour here and there. I always have it done by Friday and preferably Thursday. That way I'm ready if an emergency comes up."

After six months he has the corps humming. It has been a test. The previous officer, Captain Jim Ellis, had been in the hearts and lives of his people for three years. Would Legge measure up? Why didn't he do all the things Captain Jim did? And those new ideas of his—weren't they a bit strange, even radical?

"Some of the old hands support you, just because you're Army," Legge reflects. "Others sit back, arms folded, and wait. You come in as commanding officer, but you're the only one who *thinks* that. The people let you know after a while whether you are!"

Ellis had the "gift of mercy." He excelled on visitations, and went on to Toronto Grace Hospital as assistant chaplain. Legge says his own gift is preaching and administration, both legacies from his teaching career. "Yesterday I had a tremendous number of good comments on my sermon after church. I'm not as good at hospital visitation. I do it but I don't have the intensity of Jim Ellis. I can't pretend. I have to be myself."

Being himself, he's the model of efficiency. He tries to spend mornings in the office, on paper work and his Sunday sermon. Afternoons are for visiting the sick or parishioners' homes. His congregation, symptomatic of today's urban area, has many single mothers. He prefers to visit them by day. "It's more discreet. They're eager to talk, hungry to talk, and usually I just sit back and listen."

Legge's week nights are full. Tuesday nights he supervises junior band practice (there is no senior band) and the weekly corps bookkeeping chore. Wednesday is Rotary, a useful contact for a corps officer. One Thursday night each month is men's fellowship meeting; another is when he, Lorraine and their three small sons take hymns, prayers and the *War Cry* to a nursing home. Friday nights and Saturdays are usually family time, partly for the children's sake, partly for health. Henry's officer-father had his first heart attack at forty-seven and died of another at fifty-seven. The Legges will serve their corps and God but try to keep their home intact.

Home is a pleasant three-bedroom Army house with a recreation room finished in knotty pine. The furniture is Army Respectable. The tasteful prints on the walls, the silver and the dishwasher are the Legges' own. Lorraine, in sweater and maroon slacks, is making dinner and getting Steven, seven, David, six, and John Michael, five, ready for Beavers, lowest rung on the Boy Scout ladder. After dinner she leads three Beavers—in brown vests, blue scarves and pork-pie hats with dangling leatherette beaver-tails—to a nearby school.

Lorraine is frustrated. She and Henry have resolved that the boys shall not have absentee parents—"we avoid baby-sitters like the plague"—but it ties her down. Every second Thursday night she heads up the women's fellowship meeting for mostly working women. On Tuesday mornings her "Take A Break" meeting, a three-hour mixture of crafts and Bible study, is an outlet for her talents. She has too much ability and energy—some nights she's up until 1:00 A.M.—to settle for this. Yet for now, she must.

"It's not as they led you to believe it would be in training college," she says wistfully. "You come out full of ideals and plans, but you have only a few afternoons free. That's the frustrating part for a wife."

Initially she preached the sermon every third Sunday. "But I'm only a fair preacher, not a fabulous one, and anyway I didn't have time to research and write it."

She has a fine soprano voice and on Tuesday nights could have organized a songster practice (the corps has no songsters) but with Henry at the corps she stays home with their sons. . . .

So the disappointing fact is that Lieutenant Lorraine Legge, in what is still rather a man's Army, will not reach her full potential until her sons are older.

"Anyway," she says loyally, "Henry is the commanding officer."

So he is, and tonight at corps council his skills are much in evidence. It's an advisory group of a dozen church members, men and women, all ages and occupations. This corps has been notorious for late meetings and Sunday services. Legge is getting them back on the rails. He runs the meeting firmly but with humor.

"I'm reading a book on 430 ways to make money," he says, as they discuss the perennial subject. "Unfortunately, about 300 of them are illegal for the Army!" He reports on his and another council member's visit to the Canadian Legion and how the other, a World War II veteran, "had such a good time he says he's going to join." Since the Legion is noted for its beer drinkers, he gets a good-natured laugh in this teetotal group.

They run through a long agenda. The Temple needs repairs dating back to its previous owners. This weekend they'll hold their first business-and-dinner meeting; it being subsidized, the hotel meal will cost each person only five dollars; it's a tempting change from their usual potluck supper and forty-three people have signed up. A corps members' retreat is in the works, eighteen months ahead—a kind of forward planning that dazzles and delights them.

Everyone has a chance to speak but if they ramble Legge deftly leads them back to the point. He warmly compliments each piece of good work. The meeting ends on time, with a prayer, and council goes home in good humor with a sense of achievement.

Lieutenant Henry Legge is ready for home too. Except . . .

And this is the magic of the Salvation Army; the quality that sets it apart from anything else on earth; the melding of mercy and practicality that will keep it marching on as long as mankind exists.

Off and on today, pricking at his mind and his Salvationist conscience, has been that woman who had to move all her furniture for the cockroach spray.

"I've been thinking," he says. "I should maybe go over there and see if she needs a hand, moving her fridge and stove back to the wall."

Bibliography

Begbie, Harold. *The Life of General William Booth.* New York: MacMillan, 1920.

Berton, Pierre. *Klondike.* Toronto: McClelland & Stewart, 1972.

Booth, Catherine. *Female Ministry.* London, England: The Salvation Army, 1859.

Brown, Arnold. *What Hath God Wrought?* Toronto: The Salvation Army, 1952.

Coutts, John. *The Salvationists.* Oxford: A. R. Mowbray & Co., 1977.

de Saint Exupéry, Antoine. *The Little Prince.* New York: Harcourt, Brace & World, Inc., 1943.

Ervine, St. John. *God's Soldier: General William Booth,* Vols. 1 and 2. London, England: Heinemann, 1934.

Moyles, R. Gordon. *The Blood and Fire in Canada.* Toronto: Peter Martin Associates Limited, 1977.

Palmer, Ted. *Marching On.* Toronto and Bermuda: The Salvation Army, 1981.

Pumphrey, Ron. *Who's Who & Why in St. John's and Area.* St. John's, Newfoundland: Mimeograph Printers Ltd., 1983.

Rowe, Frederick W. *The Development of Education in Newfoundland.* Toronto: The Ryerson Press, 1964.

Salvation Army, The. *Chosen To Be A Soldier, Orders and regulations for Soldiers of the Salvation Army.* London, England: International Headquarters, 1977.

The Salvation Army Yearbooks, 1982, 1983. London, England: International Headquarters.

Sandall, Robert; Wiggins, A. R.; Coutts, Frederick. *The History of the Salvation Army,* 6 vols. London, England: Nelson and Hodder & Stoughton, 1947-73.

Vancouver City Archives. *The Founding of the Salvation Army in Vancouver.* Vancouver, 1962.

Waldron, John D. *O Boundless Salvation.* Toronto and Bermuda: The Salvation Army, 1982.
Waldron, John D. *Women in the Salvation Army.* Toronto and Bermuda: The Salvation Army, 1983.
Wiseman, Clarence D. *A Burning in My Bones.* Toronto: McGraw-Hill Ryerson, 1979.
Young, Scott. *Red Shield in Action.* Toronto: The Salvation Army, 1949.

Periodicals:

The Canadian Home Leaguer, issues of 1972-1973.
The Globe, Toronto, 25, 26, 30 November 1887.
The Globe and Mail, Toronto, 7 September 1972; 22 December 1978.
Saturday Night, Toronto, 7 April 1888.
Sentinel-Star, Cobourg, Ont., 20 February 1948.
The Star Weekly, Toronto, 26 June 1965.
Reader's Digest, Montreal, September 1971; December 1982.
The War Cry, 3 January 1885; 27 August 1887; 17 September 1887; all issues 1982-83.
The World, Toronto, 8 July 1882.

Index